This is a book about the religious life of the Greeks from the eighth century BC to the fifth century AD, looked at in the context of a variety of different cities and periods. Simon Price does not describe some abstract and self-contained system of religion or myths but examines local practices and ideas in the light of general Greek ideas, relating them, for example, to gender roles and to cultural and political life (including Attic tragedy and the trial of Socrates). He also lays emphasis on the reactions to Greek religions of ancient thinkers – Greek, Roman, Jewish and Christian. The evidence drawn on is of all kinds: literary texts, which are translated throughout; inscriptions, including an appendix of newly translated Greek inscriptions; and archaeology, which is highlighted in the numerous illustrations.

SIMON PRICE is Fellow and Tutor at Lady Margaret Hall, Oxford. He is the author of *Rituals and Power: The Roman Imperial Cult in Asia Minor* (1984). With Mary Beard and John North he co-authored *Religions of Rome* Vol. 1: *A History* and Vol. 2: *A Sourcebook* (1998).

# KEY THEMES IN ANCIENT HISTORY

EDITORS

P. A. Cartledge
*Clare College, Cambridge*

P. D. A. Garnsey
*Jesus College, Cambridge*

Key Themes in Ancient History aims to provide readable, informed and original studies of various basic topics, designed in the first instance for students and teachers of Classics and Ancient History, but also for those engaged in related disciplines. Each volume is devoted to a general theme in Greek, Roman, or where appropriate, Graeco-Roman history, or to some salient aspect or aspects of it. Besides indicating the state of current research in the relevant area, authors seek to show how the theme is significant for our own as well as ancient culture and society. By providing books for courses that are oriented around themes it is hoped to encourage and stimulate promising new developments in teaching and research in ancient history

## Other books in the series

*Death-ritual and social structure in classical antiquity*, by Ian Morris
0 521 37465 0 (hardback), 0 521 37611 4 (paperback)

*Literacy and orality in ancient Greece*, by Rosalind Thomas
0 521 37346 8 (hardback), 0 521 37742 0 (paperback)

*Slavery and society at Rome*, by Keith Bradley
0 521 37287 9 (hardback), 0 521 36887 7 (paperback)

*Law, violence, and community in classical Athens*, by David Cohen
0 521 38167 3 (hardback), 0 521 38837 6 (paperback)

*Public order in ancient Rome*, by Wilfried Nippel
0 521 38327 7 (hardback), 0 521 38748 3 (paperback)

*Friendship in the classical world*, by David Konstan
0 521 45402 6 (hardback), 0 521 45998 2 (paperback)

*Sport and society in ancient Greece*, by Mark Golden
0 521 49698 5 (hardback), 0 521 49790 6 (paperback)

*Food and society in classical antiquity*, by Peter Garnsey
0 521 64182 9 (hardback), 0 521 64588 3 (paperback)

# RELIGIONS OF THE ANCIENT GREEKS

SIMON PRICE

CAMBRIDGE
UNIVERSITY PRESS

PUBLISHED BY THE PRESS SYNDICATE OF THE UNIVERSITY OF CAMBRIDGE
The Pitt Building, Trumpington Street, Cambridge CB2 1RP, United Kingdom

CAMBRIDGE UNIVERSITY PRESS
The Edinburgh Building, Cambridge CB2 2RU, United Kingdom    http://www.cup.cam.ac.uk
40 West 20th Street, New York, NY 10011–4211, USA    http://www.cup.org
10 Stamford Road, Oakleigh, Melbourne 3166, Australia

© Cambridge University Press 1999

First published 1999

Printed in the United Kingdom at the University Press, Cambridge

Typeset in Baskerville MT 11/12½ pt in QuarkXPress® [SE]

*A catalogue record for this book is available from the British Library*

ISBN 0 521 38201 7 hardback
ISBN 0 521 38867 8 paperback

# Contents

$5.20

97/64

# Figures

# Preface

I have written the sort of book that I myself would have found useful when I started to work on this subject. Rather than treating religion as an abstract and self-contained system, I have examined the interplay between local and Panhellenic practices and ideas: the plural 'religions' of my title is designed to suggest the resulting variety, in both space and time. I have also tried to look outwards from religion to other contexts. I have tried to avoid the pigeon-holing which places Attic tragedies in 'literature', archaic statues from the Athenian Akropolis in 'art', and Socrates in 'philosophy', and I have therefore tried to draw connections between material that is too often treated separately. In writing about the archaic and classical periods I have focused on evidence from these periods. Because this book goes right down to the Roman period, I have cited Pausanias (for example) not as evidence for the classical period, but as evidence for his own day. I have also included explicit discussion in the last chapter of the reactions of Romans, Jews and Christians to Greek religions

I am most grateful to the editors of this series, Paul Cartledge and Peter Garnsey, for commissioning this book, and then helping me to bring it forth. I was lucky to be able to write the first draft in the Ward Chipman Library of the University of New Brunswick at Saint John, where the staff were indulgent of my demands on the system. Revised versions were made possible by the resources of the Ashmolean and Bodleian libraries. I have been most fortunate in my typists, Susan Waters (Tutors' Secretary of my college) and Rachel Chapman (in the Classics Faculty office), who got my text into presentable form. I am also extremely grateful to Lucia Nixon who advised throughout and commented decisively on one chapter; to Robert Parker who read the penultimate version of the whole book; to Beate Dignas who improved the book throughout and also gave valuable assistance with the appendix of epigraphic texts; and to a variety of colleagues who facilitated the acquisition of photographs.

S.R.F.P.
*Oxford*

# Abbreviations

| | |
|---|---|
| *AION* | *Annali dell'Istituto Universitario Orientale di Napoli: Sezione di Archeologia e Storia Antica* |
| *AJA* | *American Journal of Archaeology* |
| *AJPhil* | *American Journal of Philology* |
| *ANRW* | *Aufstieg und Niedergang der römischen Welt*, eds. H. Temporini and W. Haase (Berlin, 1972–) |
| *BCH* | *Bulletin de correspondance hellénique* |
| *BSA* | *British School at Athens, Annual of* |
| *CQ* | *Classical Quarterly* |
| *EPRO* | *Etudes préliminaires sur les religions orientales dans l'empire romain* (Leiden, 1961–) |
| *FGH* | *Die Fragmente der griechischen Historiker*, ed. F. Jacoby (Berlin and Leiden, 1923–58) |
| *GRBS* | *Greek, Roman and Byzantine Studies* |
| *HSCP* | *Harvard Studies in Classical Philology* |
| *HThR* | *Harvard Theological Review* |
| *IG* | *Inscriptiones Graecae* |
| *IGUR* | *Inscriptiones Graecae Urbis Romae*, ed. L. Moretti (Rome, 1968–90) |
| *JHS* | *Journal of Hellenic Studies* |
| *JRA* | *Journal of Roman Archaeology* |
| *JRS* | *Journal of Roman Studies* |
| *LIMC* | *Lexicon Iconographicum Mythologiae Classicae*, eds. J. Boardman et al. (Zurich and Munich, 1981–) |
| *LSAM* | *Lois sacrées d'Asie Mineure*, ed. F. Sokolowski (Paris, 1955) |
| *LSCG* | *Lois sacrées des cités grecques*, ed. F. Sokolowski (Paris, 1969) |
| *LSCG Supp.* | *Lois sacrées des cités grecques, Supplément*, ed. F. Sokolowski (Paris, 1962) |
| ML | R. Meiggs and D.M. Lewis, *Greek Historical Inscriptions* (Oxford, 1969, 2nd edn 1989) |

PCPhS     *Proceedings of the Cambridge Philological Society*
RE     *Paulys Real-Encyclopädie der klassischen Altertumswissenschaft,*
    eds. G. Wissowa, E. Kroll et al. (Berlin and Stuttgart,
    1893–1978)
SBL     *Society of Biblical Literature*
SEG     *Supplementum Epigraphicum Graecum* (Leiden, 1928– )
Syll.³     W. Dittenberger, *Sylloge Inscriptionum Graecarum*, 3rd edn
    (Leipzig, 1915–24)
Tod     M.N. Tod, *Greek Historical Inscriptions*, 2 vols (Oxford,
    1946–8)
ZPE     *Zeitschrift für Papyrologie und Epigraphik*

# CHAPTER I

# Introduction

In 402 BC Cyrus the Younger raised an army, including 13,000 Greek mercenaries, to depose his brother from the Persian throne. Among these mercenaries was Xenophon, whose account of his experiences, the *Anabasis*, brings Greek religions to life for us.[1] The *Anabasis* recounts the march of Cyrus' army from the west coast of Asia Minor to Assyria, where Cyrus died in battle, and the subsequent retreat of the '10,000' Greeks to a Greek settlement on the north coast of Asia Minor.

Throughout the march of the 10,000, divine guidance was sought for the actions of the group and of individuals. Before the army went into action animals were sacrificed to the gods; professional diviners (*manteis*) inspected the entrails of the animals to determine whether the gods favoured the proposed action. Divine assent was far from automatic: sometimes plans were aborted because of unfavourable sacrifices; and sometimes sacrifices were offered repeatedly in the hope of obtaining a definite response.[2]

Individuals too sought divine guidance. Uncertain about joining the expedition in the first place, Xenophon decided to consult the oracle of Apollo at Delphi. He enquired to which of the gods he should sacrifice and pray in order for his participation to be a success (3.1.5–8). Another Greek who was eager to become commander of the force sacrificed to the gods for three days, but gave up on his plans when the sacrifices did not prove favourable (6.6.36). The gods might even send guidance in dreams. After the disaster of Cyrus' death, Xenophon had a dream from Zeus the King, which he interpreted to mean that the Greeks should galvanise themselves to escape from the Persian Empire; he immediately set about persuading the Greeks to follow him (3.1.11–15).

The interpretation of such signs from the gods was of course open to dispute, and even accusations of fraud. Xenophon says that the

---

[1] Cf. Nilsson 1955–67: 1.784–91.    [2] E.g. 6.4.12–5.2. Cf. Jameson 1991.

sequence of seven unfavourable sacrifices which prevented the army from moving was initially ascribed to his own plan of keeping the army there to found a new city (6.4.15). Xenophon's defensiveness is also clear in his account of the consultation at Delphi, which served as a defence against accusation for treason. Cyrus was an enemy of Xenophon's own city of Athens, and Xenophon was exiled from his native city after the expedition.

Sacrifices were also offered to gain divine assistance. Xenophon, claiming poverty towards the end of the expedition, was told by a diviner who had inspected the entrails of a sacrifice to Apollo, that Zeus the Merciful (Meilichios) stood in Xenophon's way. Xenophon realised that he had not sacrificed to Zeus the Merciful since leaving Athens, did so the next day, and was immediately favoured by the return of the horse which he had just been forced to sell (7.8.3–6).[3] One might promise to offer something to a god if he or she helped one. When Xenophon was trying to persuade the men that they had fair prospects for leaving Assyria safely, a man sneezed and the crowd took this to be a sign from Zeus of Safety (Soter) and immediately did obeisance to him. Xenophon proposed that they vow to sacrifice in thanks to that god (and to others) as soon as they reached a friendly land (3.2.8–9). When they reached the north coast, they duly sacrificed oxen to Zeus and the other gods, and celebrated athletic games, a normal component of Greek festivals.

On one occasion the Greeks set aside in thanks a tithe for the gods Apollo and Artemis of Ephesos on the west coast of Asia Minor (Ephesos being the place where the expedition had begun). Xenophon recounted how he had dedicated as general his share of the tithe, to Apollo at Delphi, and to Artemis in a new sanctuary on his estate some three kilometres south of Olympia which he lovingly described:

Here Xenophon built an altar and a temple with the sacred money, and from that time forth he would every year take the tithe of the produce of the land in season and offer sacrifice to the goddess, all the citizens and the men and women of the neighbourhood taking part in the festival. The goddess would provide for those encamped there barley meal and loaves of bread, wine and sweetmeats and a portion of the sacrificial victims from the sacred herd as well as of the victims taken in the chase . . . Within the sacred precinct there is a meadow and hills covered with trees – suitable for raising pigs, goats, cattle and horses, so that even the beasts of burden belonging to those who attend the festival may be well

---

[3] Zeus Meilichios was worshipped widely throughout the Greek world, largely by individuals and families: Jameson, Jordan and Kotansky 1993: 81–107; Appendix no. 1; see below, p. 51 for his cult at Selinus.

fed. Around the temple itself is a grove of cultivated trees which produce fruit in season. The temple is a small scale version of the temple at Ephesos; the image of the goddess, carved from cypress wood, is like the image at Ephesos, although that one is made of gold. By the temple stands a plaque with the following inscription:

'This place is sacred to Artemis. He who owns it and enjoys its produce must offer in sacrifice a tenth each year, and from the remainder must keep the temple in good condition. If someone fails to do these things, the goddess will take care of it.'[4]

Many aspects of Xenophon's account are surprising to those reared on Jewish or Christian religious assumptions.[5] In place of one male god, in the *Anabasis* there is a multiplicity of gods, even unidentifiable gods. Gods are both male (Zeus, Apollo), and female (Artemis). There is no religious sphere separate from that of politics and warfare or private life; instead, religion is embedded in all aspects of life, public and private. There are no sacred books, religious dogma or orthodoxy, but rather common practices, competing interpretations of events and actions, and the perception of sacrifice as a strategic device open to manipulation. Generals and common soldiers, not priests, decide on religious policy. The diviners are the only usual religious professionals, and religion offered not personal salvation in the afterlife, but help here and now, escape from the Persians or personal success and prosperity. Religious festivals combined solemnity and jollity. Practice not belief is the key, and to start from questions about faith or personal piety is to impose alien values on ancient Greece.

## A PANHELLENIC SYSTEM

The religious system exemplified in the *Anabasis* was one common to all Greeks. The 10,000, drawn from numerous Greek cities, were not just an army of Greeks, they were almost a Greek polis on the move. Their practices and attitudes illustrate a religious system common to all Greeks. They were able to operate easily with a common set of rules, despite the fact that they and their diviners were drawn from numerous cities in different parts of the Greek world. Delphi functioned in the background as a Panhellenic Greek sanctuary of indisputable authority.

---

[4] 5.3.4–13. On the site of this sanctuary see *BCH* 64–5 (1940–1) 245–6; Delebecque 1955; Themelis 1968.
[5] Price 1984a: 11–16; cf. Phillips 1986: 2697–711. Gould 1985 exemplifies a thoughtful modern approach.

Everyone knew who Zeus the Saviour was and what a proper sacrifice was. Only after celebrating communal sacrifice did the army sometimes celebrate processions and athletic competitions in separate regional groups (4.5.5). Only when negotiating with non-Greeks did new rules have to be established. One non-Greek tribe wishing to establish friendly relations with the Greeks asked the Greeks to exchange pledges: 'thereupon the Macronians gave the Greeks a barbarian lance and the Greeks gave them a Greek lance, for the Macronians said that these were pledges and both sides called the gods to witness' (4.8.7). The Greeks, of course, knew that other people had their own gods and worshipped in their own ways and only with them were they uncertain over how to articulate common ground.[6]

These common practices can also be seen very nicely in the material records. The same types of dedications were made in sanctuaries all over the Greek world. For example, especially in the sixth century BC marble statues of men and women, life-size or larger, were often dedicated in sanctuaries of the gods or put up as grave markers. They have been found everywhere from Sicily to the Crimea, and from the north Aegean to Cyrene in Libya (Fig. 1.1).[7]

Common rules of course did not eliminate debate. After the battle of Delium (on the border of Attica and Boeotia) in 424 BC, the Athenians and the Boeotians exchanged heralds, each side accusing the other of transgressing Greek customary practices. The Boeotians claimed that, while it was an established custom of all Greeks for invaders to keep away from sanctuaries in the country they invaded, the Athenians had actually fortified Delium, the sanctuary of Apollo, and even dwelt in it, doing there whatever men do in a profane place, even drawing for common use the water which was untouched by themselves except for use in lustrations connected with the sacrifices. The Athenians responded that they had not and would not damage the sanctuary: according to custom the sanctuary belonged to whomever had control in a country (as the Boeotians had done on originally invading the land), and the water they had turned to only due to the constraints of war, which would meet with indulgence even from the gods.[8] Disputes of this kind show that common Greek customs provided a framework to which people of different states could refer.

Greeks pointed to the significance and value of these common prac-

---

[6] Rudhardt 1992.

[7] Cf. Snodgrass 1983 on transport of such sculpture. For their dedication, see below, p. 62.

[8] Thucydides 4.97–8. For appeal to accepted deities, 2.74.

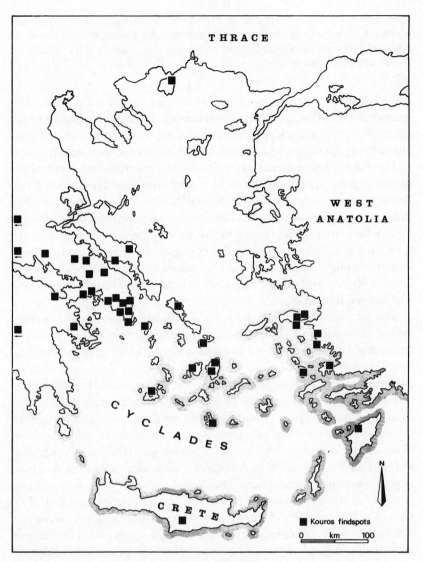

Fig. 1.1. Findspots of marble statues of men (*kouroi*).

tices in order to strengthen unity at times of crisis. According to Herodotos, this is what the Athenians did when they declined a last minute invitation to capitulate to the Persian king Xerxes in 480 BC:

> for there are many reasons why we should not do this even if we so desired, first and foremost the burning and destruction of the images and dwellings of our

gods, which we are constrained to avenge to the utmost rather than make covenants with the doer of these things, and next the sameness of all Greeks in blood and speech, and the shrines of the gods and the sacrifices that we have in common and the likeness of our way of life, to all of which it would ill become the Athenians to be false. (8.144)

Although these arguments were not decisive for some Greeks, who either went over to the Persians or remained neutral, for many the experience of shared religious customs, especially in the face of an enemy who had actually destroyed temples, was a factor that strengthened their will to resist.[9]

The Panhellenic system referred to by the Athenians was constructed in the archaic period (eighth to sixth centuries BC). The material evidence for civic sanctuaries begins around 800 BC and continues for more than a thousand years.[10] It was also in the eighth century that Olympia and Delphi emerged as sanctuaries of more than merely local interest; the games at Olympia, which probably began in the eighth century, were joined from the early sixth century by games at Delphi, the sanctuary of Zeus at Nemea and that of Poseidon at Isthmia to form the centre of a Panhellenic festival cycle.[11]

The system of different deities was also articulated in the archaic period. According to Herodotos (2.53), it was Homer and Hesiod who constructed the genealogies of the gods and gave to the gods their names, distributed their honours and skills and indicated their appearances. Before then, the Greeks did not know the origins of each of the gods, whether they were all eternal or what sort of appearance each had. Herodotos puts this view forward as a personal opinion, but it is one with much plausibility. Homer's *Iliad* and the *Odyssey* (of the late eighth or possibly seventh century) and Hesiod's *Theogony* and *Works and Days* (c. 700 BC?) did serve as classic formulations of Greek ideas about the divine to which subsequent generations responded in their own ways (below, p. 13).[12] Many of their ideas were still alive in the second century AD. The Greeks of this later period continued to believe, for example, that Athena was the daughter of Zeus and that gods might appear to individuals as they had to Homer's heroes. The latter belief is depicted (and criticised)

---

[9] For other appeals to Panhellenism see Herodotos 7.132, 8.121, 9.81; ML 27, trans. Fornara 1983: no. 59 (serpent column, below p. 60). Epitaphs: ML 24, trans. Fornara 1983: no. 21 (Corinth); ML 26, trans. Fornara 1983: no. 51 (Athens); Tod 1.20, trans. Fornara 1983: no. 60 (Megara).

[10] Some mainland sites (Isthmia, Olympia, Amyclae, and sites in the Argolid, all in the Peloponnese, and Kalapodi in central Greece) illuminate the nature of changes between the end of the Bronze Age palaces and the ninth century BC: Morgan 1996; 1997. Burkert 1992b offers a sketch of eighth-century developments.      [11] Morgan 1993; Golden 1998.

[12] West 1995 argues for a mid-seventh century date for the *Iliad*.

most vividly in the Acts of the Apostles; when Paul and Barnabas visited the town of Lystra in southern Turkey and Paul cured a crippled man, the crowd shouted in their native language 'the gods have come down to us in human form', and they called Barnabas Zeus and Paul they called Hermes because he was the spokesman.[13] This was not a mere figure of speech. The local priest of Zeus, whose temple was just outside the city, brought oxen and garlands to the gates, and he and all the people were about to offer sacrifice. The story thus offers the Christian author of Acts an opportunity to explain the nature of the true god.

This book ranges widely in time, from the archaic period down to the second and third centuries AD (and indeed beyond). The system was, I believe, fairly stable over this long time span, and, crucially, cities, though increasingly subject to the rule of kings or emperors, retained their role as providers of the principal framework within which most Greeks interpreted their existence.[14] There were of course some changes over this long period. Although Greeks may have believed that their rites were completely 'ancestral', civic practices certainly changed. New cults of the gods were introduced and new ideas about the gods were developed; and when Greek cities came under the dominance of external rulers, whether Greek or Roman, they established cults of those rulers using as a template the existing cult of the gods. For example, after Athens had fallen to the Macedonian Demetrios Poliorketes (Besieger of Cities), the Athenians welcomed him in 291/290 BC with offerings of incense, crowns and libations and sang a processional hymn comparing Demetrios, a theophoric name, and Demeter

for the greatest and dearest of the gods have come to our city: here indeed the time [of the Eleusinian mysteries] has brought together Demeter and Demetrios. She comes to celebrate the solemn mysteries of the Daughter [Persephone] but he, as is fitting for a god, is here in gladness, fair and smiling. Something august he seems, all his friends around him and he himself in their midst, his friends the stars even as he is the sun. Oh son of the most mighty god Poseidon and of Aphrodite, Hail! For other gods are either far away or have not ears, or exist not, or heed us not at all, but you we can see in very presence, not in wood and not in stone, but for real. So we pray to you, first bring peace, you most dear. For you have the power.[15]

---

[13] Acts of the Apostles 14.8–18; cf. Lane Fox 1986: 102–67.

[14] Cf. Price 1984a; Lane Fox 1986: 27–261. Parker 1996 demonstrates the lack of sharp divides in the history of Athenian cults, at least down to 250 BC. On the Hellenistic period see Gordon 1972; Stewart 1977; Chaniotis 1995 on new festivals; Mikalson 1998.

[15] Athenaios 6.252f–254a = Demochares, *FGH* 75 F 2, Duris, *FGH* 76 F 13. Habicht 1997: 92–3. Cf. Parker 1996: 256–64. Earlier honours at Athens, below, pp. 28–9; cults of emperors, below, p. 158.

Such language struck some later and perhaps some at the time as 'flattery', but we cannot dismiss it so simply. It shows not the decay of the old cults, but their continuing ability to express the relationship of a Greek city to the ruling power.

Another change is that the geographical scope of the system expands over time. While the Panhellenic games of mainland Greece were originally limited to Greeks, the definition of 'Greek' changes, as those once classified as 'barbarian' adapted Greek mythology to signal their membership of the Greek world. Already in the early fifth century BC a king of Macedon, initially refused permission to compete at the Olympic games, gained acceptance by claiming Argive descent. And c. 200 BC a man from Sidon, a Phoenician town on the coast of what is now Lebanon, was able to participate in the Panhellenic Nemean games by virtue of the place of Sidon in Greek mythology.[16]

The vitality of the system in the Roman period is illustrated most clearly in the description of Greece by Pausanias. Pausanias, who came from Lydia in Asia Minor, travelled extensively in mainland Greece in the mid-second century AD and wrote up his *Description of Greece* between c. AD 150 and 175. This work, which is often seen simply as an antiquarian guidebook, in fact depicts the religious culture of mainland Greece as central to Greek cultural identity. Pausanias is very conscious of the history of Greece: when he visited the sanctuary of Delium, he knew about the battle there nearly 600 years before. But he is not interested simply in the past. He evokes a living religious system, of festivals with their local peculiarities, and local stories about the gods in whose honour the festivals were held and who were sometimes thought to be present at the festivals. As an outsider in mainland Greece, he weaves together the local particularities in his travel narrative. Like Herodotos expressing the religious community of the Greeks in the face of Persian invasion, Pausanias articulates the Panhellenic religious system of a Greece under Roman rule.[17]

The sources for the history of Greek religions are numerous and very varied. Of the literary sources it has been said that there is hardly any

---

[16] Panhellenic games: below, p. 39. Macedon: Herodotos 5.22. Sidon: L. Moretti, *Iscrizione agonistiche greche* (Rome, 1953) no.41, trans. in Austin 1981: no.121. From the second century BC onwards Romans too were allowed into the Panhellenic games – they also could claim Greek origins (below, ch.8).

[17] Elsner 1992, who misses the significance of Pausanias' origins and focus. Cf. Calame 1995a and Alcock 1996 on Pausanias as ethnographer. Arafat 1996 and Swain 1996: 330–56 on attitudes to Roman rule.

ancient author who did not have something to say about Greek or Roman religion, because 'religion' impinged everywhere.[18] The texts include not only those by authors of the fifth and fourth centuries, like Herodotos and Xenophon, but range in date from Homer to Pausanias and beyond. The sources also include more than just literary texts. Inscriptions on stone or bronze record details of religious calendars, sacred laws and civic decrees regulating cults. Much of our evidence concerns Athens, and this is partly why Athens will feature quite largely.[19] I have tried, however, not to make the book Athenocentric, nor to write another study of Panhellenic religion, but to examine local practices and myths and their relationships to the common Greek system.

Reconstructing rituals or myths by drawing on such texts can be very problematic. Written 'sources' for Greek religion are of extremely variable quality (and date). Those wishing to reconstruct classical Athenian rituals or myths, for example, draw on allusions in Aristophanes, descriptions in Pausanias, and antiquarian details preserved anonymously in Byzantine commentaries on ancient authors.[20] I have tried to eschew the composition of a melange derived from texts spanning a millennium and more. Though I have tried to show elements of continuity in Greek religions between (say) Xenophon and Pausanias, I present the later authors as voices in their own right. I have also tried to start my arguments not from antiquarian statements of dubious date and validity, but from texts of known contexts and perspectives.

Archaeological evidence of sanctuaries or of representations of rituals is also always pertinent; this book lays especial emphasis on presenting this material evidence. Methodological issues arise when one tries to relate texts and material evidence.[21] Some of the problems can be illustrated in connection with the oracle of Apollo at Delphi. A myth, perhaps articulated in the early fifth century BC, told that four temples preceded the one built towards the end of the sixth century BC:

(i)   a laurel temple in the shape of a hut,
(ii)  a temple of wax and feathers built by bees,
(iii) a bronze temple built by the gods Hephaistos and Athena,

---

[18] Nock 1933: 272.
[19] Parker 1996 on Athens; Parker 1989 explores the differences between classical Athenian and Spartan religions. On religion in Roman Sparta see Cartledge and Spawforth 1989: 193–7; Spawforth 1992.
[20] For an exposition of the problems and inadequacies of later texts on one Athenian festival, the Anthesteria, see Hamilton 1992: 5–62.
[21] Cf. Renfrew 1985: 11–26 on problems of analysing the archaeology of a religious site.

(iv) a stone temple built by the heroes Trophonios and Agamedes, burnt
down in 548 BC.[22]

Though it might be tempting to find archaeological correlates of all four
of these temples, the temptation should be resisted. Though there might
have been an eighth-century temple at Delphi constructed out of laurel
and with an apsidal end, it is more likely that the laurel temple (i) is a
refraction of the importance of the laurel in the cult of Apollo. There
was an all-stone temple at Delphi from 675–650 BC, but temples (ii), (iii)
and (iv) are likewise mythical creations designed to express ideas about
the ideal evolution of Delphi from nature to humanity through the
divine and heroic spheres.

The point that we must not, in the first instance, interpret archaeological evidence in the light of written evidence can also be seen in another
Delphic example. A myth, perhaps originating in the Hellenistic period,
told how the site of Delphi was first discovered by a goatherd who had
lost some animals down a chasm in the rocks.[23] When he approached
the spot, he was overcome by vapours and began to prophesy. A vivid
story, which was taken at face value by some modern scholars who
asserted that this explained the workings of oracular prophecy at Delphi.
Unfortunately, the geology of Delphi is such that there can never have
been actual vapours, and there was, at most, only a symbolic chasm in
the temple itself.

Archaeological evidence and the written record each need some care
in their interpretation and should ideally be studied in isolation before
they are combined. The structures of the texts are themselves at least as
interesting as the 'factual' details in them. One cannot pile together
'facts' culled from texts without regard for contexts, in categories of
which one is unconscious and which may well be inappropriate. The historian of Greek religions needs to be alert both to modern categories
and questions, and also to those of the ancients.

---

[22] Pindar, *Eighth Paean* 58–99; Pausanias 10.5.9–13. Cf. Sourvinou-Inwood 1979.
[23] Diodorus Siculus 16.26. Cf. Price 1985.

# CHAPTER 2

# Gods, myths and festivals

According to a Christian writer of the second century, the Greeks had 365 gods.[1] For the proponent of one (Christian) god this alleged fact demonstrated the absurdity of Greek religion. Moderns too sometimes assume the nobility and superiority of one supreme god ('monotheism') as against the proliferation of little gods ('polytheism'). But the number of the Greek gods (not as great as 365) does not mean that those gods lack significance, any more than does the multiplicity of gods in the Hindu tradition.[2] In addition, proponents of monotheism (whether Jewish, Christian or Islamic) are often not ready to note the disruptive consequences of monotheistic intolerance or the extent to which alleged monotheisms contain plural elements. Within Christianity, what about the Trinity, the Blessed Virgin Mary, or the Saints? In fact the categories 'monotheism' and 'polytheism' do not promote historical under-standing. In both ethnography/anthropology and ancient history schol-ars have sometimes sought to 'rescue' polytheism by arguing for an element of monolatry or henotheism, in which the power of one god in the pantheon is proclaimed as supreme.[3] But the manoeuvre is condi-tioned by a Judaeo-Christian evaluation of monotheism. The terms 'polytheism' and 'monotheism' are best abandoned to the theologians.

## PANHELLENIC MYTHS

The principal Panhellenic Greek deities were quite limited in number, though infinitely extensible via epithets: Zeus, Hera, Athena, Apollo, Artemis, Poseidon, Aphrodite, Hermes, Hephaistos, Ares, Demeter, and

---

[1] Proclaimed by Orpheus: Theophilus, *To Autolycus* 3.2 (trans. R.M. Grant, Oxford 1970); also Lactantius, *Divine Institutes* 1.7.6–7 (trans. M.F. McDonald, *Fathers of the Church* 49, Washington DC 1964). Cf. below, p. 161.
[2] Historiographical debates: Schmidt 1987; Hinduism: Fuller 1992.
[3] Desy in Schmidt 1987; Versnel 1990a.

Dionysos.[4] These 'twelve Olympians', the number that became conventional in the fifth century BC, formed a family. Zeus, 'father of gods and men', was at its head, Hera his sister–wife, and the others his siblings or children. The family structure was important up to a point: a nephew (Apollo) or a niece (Athena) might yield to an uncle (Poseidon) in Homeric contests.[5] However, the extent of detail of family trees given in modern books and wall charts is very misleading. There was no one canonical ancient version and the Greeks were not bothered whether or not Poseidon was a first cousin of Demeter. What mattered was that they were related, that they all lived together on Mount Olympos and that there were other 'chthonic' (*chthon* = 'earth') gods who lived beneath the earth, Hades king of the underworld and his wife Persephone.

Stories about this family were told or represented in many different contexts.[6] Children heard the myths at the knees of their mothers or nurses.[7] Aristocratic men in archaic and classical Greece attending their *sumposia* (formalised drinking parties) liked to tell myths.[8] As we shall see later, myths were omnipresent in sanctuaries and festivals, both iconographically and verbally. They were also very visible in other public places: in the Athenian agora, for example, one stoa (portico) gained its name 'Painted' because it served to display four fifth-century BC paintings by the outstanding artists of the day on mythical and historical topics (cf. below, p. 22). The thousands of extant vases of the seventh to fourth centuries BC depict scenes of the gods and heroes. Some of them are influenced by now lost works in other media (paintings, tapestries, metalwork), others are fresh creations of the individual pot painter. The contexts of these pots is important. They are the product of artists, including non-Greek slaves, working in different states and should ideally not all be lumped together as 'Greek'. Many of the pots, though preserved for us because they were exported to Etruria in Italy where they were buried in chamber tombs, were designed in the first instance for the aristocratic Greek *sumposion*. Myth-telling and the pottery for the wine-drinking were complementary.[9]

The most notable tellings of Greek myths were the works of Homer

---

[4] Introduction: Guthrie 1950. For some approaches to Dionysos see McGinty 1978.
[5] Homer, *Iliad* 21.469; *Odyssey* 6.329–30, 13.341–2. Cf. Euripides, *Troades* 48–52 (Athena and Poseidon).   [6] Buxton 1994: 18–66.
[7] Plato, *Republic* 377a; Dionysios of Halikarnassos, *Thucydides* 6–7; cf. Aristophanes, *Wasps* 1174 ff.; below, p. 129.
[8] Xenophanes 1.19–23, trans. Loeb *Elegy and Iambus* 1, criticised the usual absurd tales; cf. below, p. 127, for his other criticisms of myths.
[9] Bérard 1989 explores the imagery of Athenian pottery; Carpenter 1991 systematises this material. On the imagery of the *sumposion* on pottery see Lissarrague 1990.

and Hesiod. The Homeric narratives describe interactions between the gods and the human protagonists: how Apollo attacked Patroclus in battle (*Iliad* 16.778), or how Athena gave guidance to Telemachos (*Odyssey* 1.178–323). Such interactions between gods and humans, and other Homeric stories about the gods, presuppose a degree of anthropomorphism: that the gods are like humans. Though this was a lasting legacy in Greece, sometimes criticised by later generations (below, p. 127), Homer equally emphasises that gods were also *un*like humans, in their power and their immortality.[10] When characters in Homer talk about divine interventions, they use not the names of specific deities, which the narrator uses, but indeterminate terms like a god (*theos*) or divine being (*daimon*). Hesiod's *Theogony* is a systematic treatise on the Greek pantheon, which has at its centre the establishment of the rule of Zeus and how he mastered challenges to it by other powers (Titans, Typhoeus).

The pre-eminence of Hesiodic thinking can be seen, for example, in the iconography of the massive altar of Zeus and Athena built at Pergamon in north-west Asia Minor in the second century BC. The wonderfully dramatic sculpture running 110 metres round the podium on which the altar stood celebrated the successful struggle of these and the other gods against the giants (Fig. 2.1). The casual observer could readily understand the frieze, but the attributes of the gods and the fact that all the gods and giants were also labelled would permit the more learned and leisurely viewer to appreciate the complex iconographical scheme of the monument. It deals with the battle of the Gods and the Giants, which does not appear in the *Theogony*, but Hesiod's account of a struggle of the divine order against a threat from outside was the inspiration for later accounts, which invented the battle of the Giants and then often conflated the two battles of the Titans and the Giants.[11]

Homer and Hesiod were, as we have seen, privileged texts in the articulation of the Greek pantheon, but this did not mean that their stories were definitive. Neither author claims divine revelation, though both claim that the divine omniscience of the Muses, daughters of Zeus, remedied their own ignorance.[12] Nor was either writer comprehensive. Homer's *Iliad* focuses on four days of fighting during the ten-year Trojan war, and the *Theogony* is a genealogy of the gods, not a recounting of all the exploits known to the author. Subsequent writers, therefore, could

---

[10] Griffin 1980: 144–204; Vernant 1991: 27–49; cf. also Burkert 1991.

[11] Cf. Smith 1991: 155–80. See further *LIMC* 4: 202–7; Kästner 1994.

[12] Homer, *Iliad* 2.484–93; Hesiod, *Theogony* 1–35.

Fig. 2.1. Part of the east frieze of the altar of Zeus and Athena, Pergamon (height 2.30m). In the centre Zeus is about to slay, with the thunderbolt in his right hand, a kneeling giant (Porphyrion?). To the left a captured giant watches; to the right a snake-legged giant (Typhon?), below the eagle of Zeus.

fill in the gaps left by Homer and Hesiod – such were the other, now lost, Homeric epics of the archaic period, and (especially important for mythology) the *Catalogue of Women*, a continuation of Hesiod's *Theogony* which was accepted in antiquity as being by Hesiod but which probably dates to the sixth century BC. They were also, as we shall see, at liberty to offer novel tellings of familiar tales. The tradition of telling and re-telling myths extends from the archaic period right down to the mid-fifth century AD when Nonnos composed his great epic on Dionysos.[13] Ancient scholarly handbooks of mythology were composed mainly between c. 250 BC and AD 150, but they could not cope with all the variants and conflicting versions. They fell into two types. One set of mythological studies collected myths to aid in understanding major Greek authors. For example, in the imperial period there circulated a huge collection of myths as background to Homer. The second category

---

[13] Bowersock 1990: 41–9; Hopkinson 1994.

of mythological works took particular themes, such as love stories, transformation tales or genealogies. The principal extant example is the
*Library* said to be by Apollodorus (first or second century AD), which is
organised in terms of mythical genealogies, and which has been the
foundation for many modern handbooks of Greek mythology.[14] Given
that Greek myths were not rigid, it is methodologically very important
that we respect the individual telling or representation of the myths. It
is absurd to weave together a compendium of Greek mythology from
extracts in different authors.[15]

Reflection on the standing of the stories of Homer and Hesiod is
attested already in the sixth and fifth centuries BC,[16] and the iconography of sanctuaries also demonstrates the existence of privileged stories
about the gods. Difficulties arose when historians and antiquarians
sought to construct narratives down to the present on the basis of mythical tales. Was it reasonable for a writer in the classical period to treat a
traditional tale about Theseus, the hero who united Attica, in the same
way as one about the tyrant Peisistratos in the sixth century BC? Some
writers did attempt to do just this, for example Hellanicus, writing the
first history of Attica in the 420s BC; later historians of Attica, in the
fourth century, were similarly committed to recounting a continuous
tradition from Kekrops, the first king of Athens. But others took a more
critical line to distinguish mythical from human history (below, p. 131).
Just where that line was to be drawn was a matter of arbitrary personal
judgement. Herodotos put King Minos of Crete in the mythical category unlike the sixth-century tyrant of Samos Polycrates (3.122), while
Thucydides was perfectly happy to refer to Minos' dominion of the sea
(1.4). Four hundred years later the geographer Strabo still found it necessary to assert his (personal) distinction between myth and history
(1.2.35). Some degree of rationalisation was necessary, from the classical
period onwards, if myth was to be recuperated for history.

Modern approaches to these myths have been very varied, but all distance themselves from Plato's rejection of others' myths as obnoxious
and therefore false stories and all assume that myths are ways of con-
structing meaning, whether they are Greek myths of gods and Titans,
Christian myths of the incarnation or New Age myths of Atlantis.[17]

---

[14] Henrichs 1987. For best translation and commentary of Apollodorus see Aldrich 1975 and
Simpson 1976; also Loeb and World's Classics.
[15] Morford and Lenardon 1995, a work so much used for teaching that it is now in its fifth edition;
cf. Rose 1958.    [16] Xenophanes, below, p. 127; Herodotos, above, p. 6.
[17] Cf. Calame 1991a on Greek categories 'myth' and 'ritual'.

There is no one modern method which is the key to all mythologies; different approaches seem to reveal different aspects of the subject; one needs to be eclectic, depending on the material one is considering and the objectives one has, and one needs to be alert to the dangers of imposing a modern model of myth (which arose in the eighteenth-century Enlightenment) onto the Greeks.[18]

The origins of Greek myths have interested many scholars. Though the details are largely lost to us, the origins of the Greek gods and their stories are certainly varied.[19] The Greeks were Indo-Europeans and the names of their gods go back to Indo-European prototypes. Most clearly Zeus Pater (father) is cognate with Roman Dies Pater (Jupiter) and the Indian Dyaus Pitar (the sky), regarded in the ancient Indian sacred books, the Vedas, as the father and with the earth the origin of everything. But etymology tells us very little, and priority should be given to the function of the deities.[20] In our earliest evidence the (hypothetical) Indo-European mythology does not survive in a pure form. It is already an amalgam with elements borrowed from the Near East. The close parallels between Aphrodite and the love goddess of the Near East Inanna, the main divinity of the Sumerians circa 3,000 to 2,100 BC, the Semitic Ishtar and the Phoenician Astarte, suggest that Greek ideas of Aphrodite were at least in part modelled on those deities.[21] The backbone of Hesiod's *Theogony*, the succession list, also has Near Eastern origins. In the beginning were Gaia (Earth), and Ouranos (Heaven), but Ouranos used to prevent his children being born until Gaia incited his son Kronos to castrate him. Kronos in turn swallowed his own children for fear of being overthrown by one of them until Rhea gave birth secretly to Zeus on Crete and gave Kronos a stone to devour in his place. When Zeus had grown up he forced his father to disgorge the children whom he had swallowed and, with their and other people's aid, he overthrew Kronos and his Titans.[22] Although the story is fully assimilated to a Greek context, some of its elements can be understood much better with reference to Near Eastern deities. Knowing for example that Zeus' name is cognate with the ancient Indian word for 'sky' makes more comprehensible his relation to Ouranos, 'Heaven'. In fact, earlier versions of the succession story exist in various Near Eastern languages, including

[18] Edmunds 1990, Bruit Zaidman and Schmitt Pantel 1992: 143–214, and Graf 1993a: chs. 1–2 between them survey the main current approaches. Buxton 1994 argues for eclecticism. See also Dowden 1992 and Calame 1996: 5–55. Vernant 1980: 186–242 remains a good introduction.
[19] See Mondi 1990.  [20] Dumézil 1968–73: 1.11.
[21] Friedrich 1978; Burkert 1987b; see further Burkert 1992a: 88–127. For a cult of Phoenician Aphrodite, see below, pp. 76–7.  [22] Detienne and Vernant 1978: 57–130.

the Akkadian epic of creation, sometimes known from its first two words as Enuma Elish, dating probably to the second millennium BC, and certainly recited at the new year festival in Babylon.[23] The stories contain close parallels to Hesiod's succession of gods, including also castration, swallowing and a stone.

The origins of myths have also been sought in their relationship to rituals. Myths of sacrifice or specific local myths are indeed sometimes said to be derived from actual ritual procedures.[24] In one modern formulation of this old theory sacrificial rituals themselves are then traced back to the palaeolithic period by means of parallels from modern hunter–gatherer societies; parallels with animal behaviour then suggest that the need for such rituals is located at a very deep level.[25] Much of this is wishful thinking based on a peculiar selection of Greek data and an inadmissible retrojection of the practice of contemporary 'primitives'.

A variation of this search for meaning through origins lays great emphasis on 'initiation' as a category for understanding both myth and rituals.[26] Initiation rituals or 'rites de passage' are held to underlie many if not all myths, for example, that of the Athenian *arrhephoroi*.[27] As a matter of fact classical Greece had very few initiation rituals and so the theory hypothesised that, while rituals had been lost or transformed, myths continued to be told in the classical and later periods. Compulsive detection of initiation rituals can be rather arbitrary and in the end casts little light on Greece of historic periods.

The search for origins cannot be the end of an enquiry into myths or rituals. In fact, the borrowing of a myth from the Near East does not entail that the myth had no meaning for the Greeks. Aphrodite is a composite figure whose Greek configurations are different from the originals, and Hesiod's succession myths make good Greek sense in emphasising the struggles lying behind the present sovereignty of the world. Zeus' first wife Metis ('Cunning Intelligence') was to have given birth first to Athena and then to a son who would overthrow Zeus. Zeus therefore swallowed Metis, gave birth himself to Athena (through his head), and prevented the birth of the son. Zeus' rule was not to be challenged.[28] That is, study of origins has to lead to a synchronic study of contemporary meanings.

[23] Trans. Dalley 1989: 233–77.    [24] Versnel 1990b.
[25] Burkert 1983, supported by Versnel 1990b. Cf. below, pp. 35–6, on sacrifice.
[26] Versnel 1990b: 44–59.    [27] Burkert 1983: 150–4; below, pp. 91–5, on *arrhephoroi*.
[28] Hesiod, *Theogony* 886–900; cf. Aeschylus, *Agamemnon* 168–75.

The most influential contemporary studies of the synchronic meanings of myths, originating in France, have shown how Greek myths are ways of thinking about issues fundamental to society. They have explored the structures of thought and particular tellings of myths as structures that are common to many or all of the surviving versions. Analyses have been made both of texts and of images. The foundations of civilisation and its defence against disorder preoccupy both Hesiod and the kings of Pergamon. This reading of the story is fairly unproblematic, except that, in Hesiod, the Titans are not external monsters but kin of Zeus who have to be expelled from the society of heaven. Not all foes can be so easily identified or conquered. Other myths might explore the limits of rule by one man. In the story of Oedipus, that his name is derived from his lameness suggests the unsoundness of his royal rule. Similar stories of left-handedness or lameness circulated concerning Greek tyrants of the seventh century BC, which shows the durability of some patterns of thought.[29] In addition, major members of the Panhellenic pantheon were female, an obvious fact, but one whose implications for a patriarchal society are surely surprising and far reaching. Athena or Demeter were at least sometimes classified as 'female' rather than simply as 'divine', and myths involving goddesses sometimes address social issues such as the definition of gender roles.[30] Myths also relate to local rituals, but even so their interest is not merely aetiological, and they too have their own structure of meaning.[31]

One example of the way a myth can incorporate contemporary meanings is provided by the myth of Demeter and Persephone as told in the sixth-century BC *Hymn to Demeter*.[32] The hymn tells of the seizure of Demeter's daughter Kore ('maiden') or Persephone by Hades, and Demeter's search for her. It has an oblique relation to the mysteries of Demeter and Persephone celebrated at Eleusis (below, pp. 102–7) in that the mourning Demeter disguised as an old woman is given hospitality by the king of Eleusis and, when she reveals her true identity, bids a temple to be built to her there and later teaches her secret mysteries to the leaders of the Eleusinians.[33] But the hymn is not a narrowly local aetiological myth; it concerns general Panhellenic themes. Demeter in her anger at the theft of Persephone prevented the crops from growing,

---

[29] Vernant 1982; Ogden 1997; Ginzburg 1990: 226–95 speculates on this pattern.

[30] Loraux 1992; below, pp. 98–100.    [31] Introduction: Tyrrell and Brown 1991.

[32] Parker 1991; compare below, p. 45 on Homeric Hymns. Trans. in Foley 1994 (or Loeb *Hesiod and Homeric Hymns*).

[33] Clinton 1992: 28–37 argues that the *Hymn* was an aetiology for the Thesmophoria, but this view does not account for the overall thrust of the piece.

an appropriate action by the deity whose name included the words Ge (earth) and Meter (mother) and whose specific sphere of responsibility was agriculture. The resulting famine would have led to the end of the human race and would hence have robbed the Olympians of the rites offered to them by mortals. That roused Zeus to action and he persuaded Hades to let Persephone return to her mother and the Olympians, though by a ruse Hades ensured that she would stay with him under the earth for a third of each year. The power of the female god was immense, but it was ultimately circumvented by that of the male gods. An analogy is established between the fertility of Demeter and that of the soil with a further suggestion that her mysteries were connected with human mortality and afterlife.[34]

### LOCAL MYTHS

The Panhellenic myths of Homer, Hesiod and the Homeric Hymns also had their local versions which either rooted the myths in the local community or elaborated significantly different versions of the myth. Local myths might concern the Olympians or they might relate to a further order of beings, 'heroes', normally conceived as mortals who had died and who received cult at their tomb or at a specific sanctuary. Heroes were very numerous (in Attica alone over 170 heroes were worshipped). They ranged from major Attic heroes like Erechtheus or Kekrops, worshipped in the Erechtheion on the Akropolis, down to minor and sometimes even anonymous heroes worshipped only in a particular deme (like Hyttenios at Marathon, or Heros Iatros, the hero physician, near the Athenian Agora).[35]

Pausanias' *Guide book* is a wonderful repository of the stories told to him in the second century AD and thus a neat refutation of the view that the Greeks somehow outgrew mythology with the growth of 'rational' thought.[36] For example, the Athenians told of a contest between Athena and Poseidon for the control of Attica; the event was depicted on the west pediment of the Parthenon (Fig. 2.2). Poseidon created with a blow of his trident a salt spring on the Akropolis, while Athena planted there the first ever olive tree. Athena was adjudged the victor, but Poseidon in pique flooded a plain north-west of Athens, until a final reconciliation was brought about. Athena Polias became the guardian deity of the city, but the mythical contest left its material remains (Fig. 2.3). The unique

---

[34] See Nixon 1995.  [35] Kearns 1989; 1992; Larson 1995.  [36] Veyne 1988.

Fig. 2.2. A montage of the west front of the Parthenon, Athens. In the pediment is a restoration of the sculpture showing (in the centre) the struggle between Athena (left) and Poseidon (right). On the left (after two unknown figures) are Kekrops, Pandrosos, Herse, Erysichthon and Aglauros. (No. 4 on Fig. 2.14.)

plan of the Erechtheion was due in part to the need to incorporate the spring within the building where Poseidon and Erechtheus, the second king of Athens, were both worshipped, and when Pausanias visited the Akropolis he was shown both the salt spring and the olive tree behind the Erechtheion, which had regenerated miraculously after the Persians had burned it in 480 BC.[37]

[37] 1.26.5, 27.2; Herodotos 8.55. Parker 1987b. Below, p. 40, on the Akropolis.

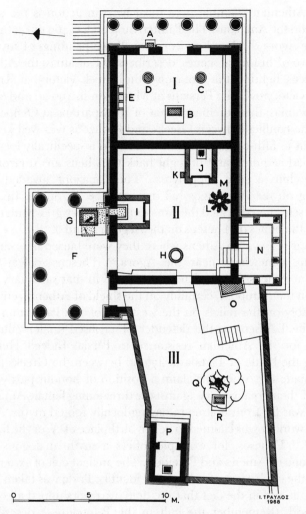

Fig. 2.3. Restored plan of the Erechtheion (421–405 BC) (No. 6 on Fig. 2.14).

  I Eastern section: A. Altar of Zeus Hypatos; B. Altar of Poseidon and
    Erechtheus; C. Altar of the Hero Boutes; D. Altar of Hephaistos; E. Thrones
    of the priests.

 II Western section: F. North porch; G. Altar of Thyechoos, with marks of the
    thunderbolt on the rocks below; H. Prostomiaion, salt sea and the trident
    marks; I. *Aduton* for the tomb of Erechtheus and the sacred snake; J. *Aduton* or
    *megaron* for the wooden cult statue of Athena Polias; K. Wooden statue of
    Hermes; L. Kallimachus' lamp with eternal fire and bronze palm tree
    chimney; M. Booty from the Persian Wars; N. Porch of the Maidens.

III Pandroseion: O. Tomb of Kekrops; P. Temple of Pandrosos; Q. Olive tree of
    Athena; R. Altar of Zeus Herkeios.

A fine Athenian example of a local hero in action is the story of Theseus and the Amazons. The Painted Stoa built c. 460 BC on the north side of the Agora displayed on its rear wall two paintings of mythological and two of historical scenes, described by Pausanias: the Athenians and Theseus fighting the Amazons, the Greek victory at Troy, the Athenian victory over the Persians at Marathon in 490 BC and (according to Pausanias) the Athenian defeat of the Spartans at Oenoe.[38] The story of the conflict between Greeks and Amazons was well known in Greece, but in fifth-century Athens it received a specifically local twist. Theseus had acquired and brought back to Athens an Amazon bride (who bore him a son, Hippolytus). The Amazons invaded Attica, encamping on the Areopagos hill opposite the Akropolis. In a great battle Theseus then defeated the Amazons. The story grew with the 'discovery' of the bones of Theseus on the Aegean island of Skyros in 476/5 BC and their removal to Athens where they were buried in a sanctuary to Theseus somewhere near the Agora.[39] Theseus' defeat of the Amazons at Athens was depicted in a mural in that sanctuary and in carvings on the Akropolis, certainly on the shield of Athena's cult statue and probably on the reliefs on the west end of the Parthenon.[40] The story glorified Athens as the defender of civilised (male) values as a prototype for the Athenian resistance to Persia. Indeed Herodotos describing the battle of Plataia in 479 BC between the Greeks and the Persians made the Athenians claim a position of honour partly on the grounds of their great victory against the threatening female Amazons.[41]

Athens was far from unique in having locally rooted myths. All over the Greek world towns claimed to be the birthplace of $X$, or the favoured spot of $\Upsilon$.[42] Ephesos, for example, offers a myth analogous to the Athenian one of Athena and Poseidon. The ancient cult of Artemis was central to the city's sense of communal identity. Pride was taken both in the local cult and in the fact that the deity was worshipped all over the Greek world. (Remember the cult in the Peloponnese described by Xenophon.) The point comes over most vividly in the confrontation

---

[38] Pausanias 1.15; Camp 1986: 66–72; Castriota 1992: 76–89. In fact Pausanias may have been misinformed about the otherwise unattested battle at Oenoe; the scene may rather have shown the marshalling of Athenian forces at the Attic village of Oenoe before Marathon.

[39] Koumanoudis 1976; Castriota 1992: 33–63.

[40] Theseion: Pausanias 1.17.2. Cf. Barron 1972, esp. 33–40 for alleged influence of the painting on vase-paintings. Parthenon: Castriota 1992: 143–51.

[41] 9.27. Amazons on the Athenian treasury at Delphi: Robertson 1975: 167–70. Amazons and Theseus: Dubois 1982; Tyrrell 1984; Tyrrell and Brown 1991: 159–88; John Henderson 1994; Blok 1995; Walker 1995; Parker 1996: 168–70; Mills 1997.

[42] See, for example, Chuvin 1987 on Hierapolis and Lindner 1994 on Nysa.

Fig. 2.4. Part of frieze from temple of Artemis and Hadrian, Ephesos (early fourth century AD). Greeks under Herakles (marked by his club and lion's cape) scare off four Amazons, who seek sanctuary with Artemis (on block to right, not preserved).

dramatised in the Acts of the Apostles when Paul preached in the theatre at Ephesos only to be shouted down by the crowd chanting 'Great is Artemis of the Ephesians.'[43] Not only was Ephesos guardian of a unique image of Artemis, which had supposedly fallen from heaven, but Ephesos also claimed that Artemis had been born there (and not as was often claimed on the Aegean island of Delos). The Ephesians also sometimes claimed that her cult had been established by Amazons, who thus sometimes had a much more positive significance at Ephesos than at Athens (Fig. 2.4).[44] The benevolence of Artemis towards the Amazons is also illustrated in the local story of how the Amazons successfully sought refuge in the sanctuary of Artemis, both from Herakles and from Dionysos.[45] Artemis remained the protector both of the Amazons and of the city right through antiquity.

Some local myths did not simply invoke Panhellenic deities in actions affecting particular communities, they offered a refraction of the

[43] Acts of the Apostles 19.23–41; Oster 1976.
[44] Birth: Strabo 14.1.20; Appendix no. 15. Rogers 1991: 68–9, 144–51. Amazons: Bammer 1976, though the 'tradition' was disputed (Weiss 1984: 201 n.52).
[45] Fleischer in Bammer 1974: 78–82; Price 1984a: 255–6. Other scenes in *LIMC* 1.603 no. 249, 1.765 nos. 1 and 4. On city foundations see Tacitus, *Annals* 4.55–6; Weiss 1984; below, p. 156.

Fig. 2.5. Seizure of Persephone by mature, bearded Hades.

Panhellenic deity through the lens of local concerns. For Greek gods existed at both the Panhellenic and the local level, and the Panhellenic structures of the pantheon varied with different local selections and emphases. Though all accepted the ultimate supremacy of Zeus, the view from Athens or Ephesos where Athena and Artemis were the chief civic deities looked very different. The case of the cult of Persephone at the Greek city of Locri in southern Italy illustrates the point very nicely.[46] Seven series of clay relief plaques from the first half of the fifth century BC have been found in the sanctuary of Persephone at Locri (Figs. 2.5–2.8). The scenes depicted and particular symbols in them not only reflect the Panhellenic myth of Persephone's seizure by Hades, but moreover emphasise her sphere by extending it into that of marriage, which was in other Greek cities normally under the protection of Hera. One series adds an entirely new dimension to the cult, namely

[46] Sourvinou-Inwood 1978. For data see also Prückner 1968.

Fig. 2.6. Girl voluntarily entering chariot of young man; her female friends say goodbye. This series may have been dedicated by women on marriage.

Persephone as a protector of children (as Demeter was elsewhere). At Locri Persephone lacks the usual Panhellenic association with Demeter, but has incorporated the spheres of marriage and children, that is those female activities which were central to the community.

### FESTIVALS AND SACRIFICES

For the Greeks, one way of dealing with the multiplicity of their gods was a firm structure of various calendars of festivals and sacrifices.[47] For us, however, the 'Greek Calendar' is something of a nightmare, because the names of the months varied in the different ethnic regions of Greece, and because the alignment of lunar and solar years by intercalation (as our 29 February) was done haphazardly by different cities. However, there were some common principles. There were twelve months, each divided into three groups of ten days; the individual months were generally named after a festival celebrated during that month: Lenaeon was

---

[47] Deubner 1932 is the basic study (in German) of Attic festivals. Parke 1977 and E. Simon 1983 offer introductions in English, though both works are unsatisfactory in their interpretations. Neils 1992 and 1996 include good studies of one festival, the Panathenaia.

Fig. 2.7. Procession of female priest and four young women carrying a robe (which may be a bridal robe to be dedicated to Persephone).

the month in which the Lenaia, a Dionysiac festival, was celebrated (Fig. 2.9). At the Panhellenic level, there was agreement as to the years in which the Panhellenic festivals should be held; the Olympia and the Pythia (at Delphi) every four years, the Isthmia and Nemea every two years. But the uncertainties of calibration meant that sacred heralds had to be sent out each cycle to announce exactly when the festival would begin so that people could attend the festival and to prevent open hostilities by or against the host city and competitors.[48] The Athenians also proclaimed by heralds twice a year, in spring and autumn, a truce of fifty-five days both for the Lesser and for the Greater Eleusinian Mysteries; they protested vigorously when in 367 BC the heralds, members of the clans of the Eumolpidae and Kerykes, were arrested by a town in Aetolia in central Greece 'contrary to the laws common to the

[48] On these and other 'sacred periods' (*hieromeniai*) see Rougemont 1973; Dillon 1997: 1–11; Appendix no. 15.

Fig. 2.8. Persephone seated, opening box, within which is the young Dionysos. This series was probably dedicated by parents on the occasion of their child's ritual presentation to Persephone.

Greeks'.[49] There was also agreement that certain months were 'sacred periods', not to be profaned by military action. When the Argives began to ravage Epidaurus just before the Karneia, they called each day of the invasion the 27th of the previous month, thus postponing the Karneia until their task was completed.[50] Conversely a generation later, when the

[49] *IG* 1³ 6.B 17–27, 36–47, trans. Fornara 1983: no. 75 (before 460 BC); ML 73.21–6, trans. Fornara 1983: no. 140 (c. 422 BC); Tod 2.137, trans. Harding 1985: no. 54 (367 BC).

[50] Thucydides 5.54 (419 BC).

| Months of the Athenian civil calendar, with modern equivalents ||
|---|---|
| Hekatombaion | June–July |
| Metageitnion | July–August |
| Boedromion | August–September |
| Pyanopsion | September–October |
| Maimakterion | October–November |
| Posideion | November–December |
| Gamelion | December–January |
| Anthesterion | January–February |
| Elaphebolion | February–March |
| Mounuchion | March–April |
| Thargelion | April–May |
| Skirophorion | May–June |

Fig. 2.9. Calendar of Athenian festivals.

Argives were themselves under threat of Spartan invasion they proclaimed a sacred truce every time the Spartans invaded. This worked until the Spartan king obtained a ruling from the oracles at Olympia (Zeus) and Delphi (Apollo – his son) that he need not be bound by such a truce.[51]

Within any given city the calendar specified exactly when each festival was to occur. At Athens, for example, the temple of Dionysos at Limnai had to be opened once a year on the 12th of Anthesterion (Demosthenes 59.76), while the Great or City Dionysia at which our tragedies were staged was a three- or four-day festival, beginning on the 10th of Elaphebolion. All this was spelled out in a great calendar inscribed on the walls of the Portico of the Basileus in the Agora.[52] So rooted was the fixed date that, when in 270 BC it proved necessary to postpone the performance by four days, four days were inserted after the 9th of Elaphebolion; the Great Dionysia could thus still begin on 10th of Elaphebolion. When the Macedonian king Demetrios Poliorketes

---

[51] Xenophon, *Hellenica* 4.7.2–3 and 5.1.29 (388 BC).
[52] Below, p. 78. Longest sacrificial calendar from outside Attica from Erythrae: *LSAM* 26 = *Inschriften von Erythrae* 207, second century BC. Cf. *Syll.*³ 1024 = *LSCG* no. 96, trans. Austin 1981: no. 128 (Myconos). For earlier examples see Parker 1996: 43 n.1. Cf. timetable at Magnesia on the Maeander: Appendix no. 3.

was briefly in Athens (302 BC), the Athenians renamed the actual month Mounuchion first Anthesterion and then Boedromion to permit him to be initiated in a single ceremony into the Lesser Mysteries of Eleusis celebrated in Anthesterion, and in the Greater Mysteries celebrated in Boedromion.[53] A city's calendar thus expressed in linear fashion the deities of the city.[54]

The calendar of the Athenian state was complemented at local level by calendars of the 'demes' or villages that constituted the state.[55] Demes formed their own religious community and as such celebrated their own festivals and performed their own sacrifices. From the late fifth and fourth centuries BC, a period of peak deme self-consciousness, there survive fragments of five calendars. Nevertheless, these calendars relate to the central calendar in various ways. As Pausanias noted, 'Even those who in their demes have established worship of the gods nevertheless hold Athena in honour' (1.26.6). The fact that there were no deme festivals on the date of the Panathenaia, the principal festival in honour of Athena, shows that she was not a remote political deity of no concern to the ordinary Athenian: everyone was, in principle, free to attend the festival in Athens itself, at which the meat of sacrificial victims was distributed deme by deme among those sent by each deme.[56] Some central festivals had their deme analogues. The festival of the Arrhephoria, performed on the Akropolis largely in private, perhaps had a corresponding festival 'on the Akropolis' at one deme (Erchia), presumably because the festival related to issues of fertility and marriage which also concerned the deme. The demes also celebrated festivals which had no central parallel. The rural Dionysia celebrated by most demes was a riotous affair held during the winter, when plays were performed as at the Great Dionysia in Athens itself.[57] Some deme calendars include the worship of heroes peculiar to that locality. For example, at the deme of Thorikos sacrifices were made to the local hero Thorikos; to Kephalos and to Prokris (Thorikos was the home of Kephalos, who accidentally shot his wife Prokris); to Philonis (a nymph who lived at Thorikos); and to two Panhellenic figures with local

---

[53] Plutarch, *Demetrios* 26; Habicht 1997: 79. This passage suggests, *pace* Deubner 1932: 91 and Mikalson 1975: 46, that the Greater Eleusinia were held not in late Metageitnion but in early Boedromion. For later honours at Athens see above, p. 7.

[54] Beard, North and Price 1998: II ch. 3 on Rome; Markus 1990: 85–135 on Christian transformations.

[55] Mikalson 1977; Whitehead 1986: 176–222; Parker 1987a; Rosivach 1994: 14–34. Cf. briefly Sourvinou-Inwood 1990: 313–16. [56] For the Thesmophoria see below, p. 98.

[57] The benign face of the Dionysos of these and other cults has to be set alongside, and in tension with, the savage, wild Dionysos of Euripides' *Bacchae*. Henrichs 1990; *SEG* 43.26 for deme Dionysia.

associations, Demeter, who landed at Thorikos on arrival in Attica; and Helen, after whom an island lying off Thorikos was named, where she allegedly first slept with Paris on her way from Sparta to Troy.[58] The Attic demes were thus integrated into the religious life of the Athenian state while preserving their own individuality.

Attica was unique in Greece in the size of its territory (c. 2400 km²) and in the degree of political integration attempted at least during the fifth and fourth centuries BC, and there is no exact equivalent from other states for these Attic deme calendars. But other states did have their own sub-divisions depending upon their own scale and complexity, and these sub-divisions did sometimes participate as units in central state festivals (as the phratries in the Karneia at Sparta) and also had their own religious life, as phratries in Thasos, Delphi and indeed in Athens.[59] It is only the poverty of extant epigraphy outside Attica that keeps the details of the calendars of the civic sub-divisions from us.

The festivals whose sequence was fixed in the calendars were central to the piety of Greek cities.[60] They vary greatly in scale and content depending upon the context and on the deity, but they have some common features. The festivals often opened with a grand procession through the town leading to the sanctuary of the god (Fig. 2.10). A vivid picture of a procession at Ephesos is given in a Greek novel of the second century AD, where it serves to link the hero (Habrocomas) and heroine (Anthia):

The local festival of Artemis was in progress with its procession from the city to the temple nearly a mile away. All the local girls had to march in procession richly dressed as well as the young men of Habrocomas' age. He was around sixteen, already a member of the ephebes, and took first place in the procession. There was a great crowd of Ephesians and visitors alike to see the festival, for it was the custom at this festival to find husbands for the girls and wives for the young men. So the procession filed past, first the sacred objects, the torches, the baskets and the incense; and horses, dogs, hunting equipment, some for war, most for peace . . . Each of the girls was dressed as if to receive a lover. Anthia led the line of girls.[61]

At Athens the processions, especially at the Panathenaia, were so lavish that a special marshalling building, the Pompeion (*pompe* = procession),

---

[58] Appendix no. 1; Parker 1987a; Kearns 1989: 177, 195, 203. The claim about Helen and Paris was also made by Gytheum, the port of Sparta, the islet being Kranae.

[59] Sourvinou-Inwood 1990: 312–13 and 316–20. See more generally N.F. Jones 1987; Osborne 1990.

[60] Price 1984a: 101; Connor 1987; Parker 1996: 79–80.

[61] Xenophon of Ephesos 1.2, trans. of whole in B.P. Reardon, *Collected Ancient Greek Novels* (Berkeley and London, 1989). Cf. Price 1984a: 110–11 and procession at Magnesia: Appendix no. 3.

Fig. 2.10. Sacrificial procession on Attic black-figure band-cup, c. 560–550 BC (height of cup 0.18m). The procession, which leads to Athena on the far left, is an image of the new Panathenaia (cf. also Fig. 2.15). A female and male stand either side of a flaming altar. They are approached by: a *kanephoros* bearing a *kanoun* (with sacrificial materials); three sacrificial animals (heifer, sow and ewe); three musicians (two shawm-players, one lyre-player); worshippers (three olive-branch bearers; three hoplite warriors with shields; one marshal (?); one horseman).

Fig. 2.11. Three youths leading sacrificial cow, on south frieze of the Parthenon, Athens (width 1.22m).

was constructed on the north-west outskirts of the city. The surviving building, circa 70 by 35 metres, dates to around 400 BC, but it replaced an abandoned predecessor of the fifth century BC.[62] From there the procession made its way a thousand metres along a special route ten metres wide through the Agora and up the steep hill to the temple of Athena on the Akropolis.[63] As at Ephesos, the procession consisted both of religious objects (here a new robe woven for the ancient image of Athena) and of participants representing the state. An idealised version of the procession was carved on a frieze round the main building (*cella*) of the Parthenon (Fig. 2.11).[64] The relief was and remained unique in that no other Greek temple, so far as we know, featured a representation of a religious ritual. On the south and north sides of the frieze are horsemen and chariots emphasising the aristocratic tradition at Athens, preceded by elders, animals for sacrifice and ritual objects. The west side has

[62] Knigge 1988: 79–82.

[63] Travlos 1971: fig. 540. The route, initially gravelled, was paved in the first and second centuries AD: Thompson 1960: 328–33; *Archaeological Reports for 1995–96* (London, 1996) 2–3. For cults on the Akropolis see Herington 1955, Hooker 1963 and Neils 1996.

[64] Jenkins 1994. Connelly 1996 offers a mythological interpretation of the frieze.

further horsemen. The climax of the frieze is on the east side: two processions of maidens lead towards the handling of the robe; the heroes
who gave their names to the ten Attic tribes and the twelve Olympians
are displayed to either side of the robe scene.

The robe itself displayed and (literally) paraded a mythological story.[65]
Indeed it seems that Athena's robe was so important that not one (as used
to be thought) but two robes were regularly woven. The new robe for the
cult statue of Athena Polias woven each year for the annual Panathenaia
by girls, the *arrhephoroi*, and women included a traditional design of the
battle of the Olympians against the Titans. It may be the presentation of
this annual robe which is shown in the east frieze of the Parthenon. In
addition, from perhaps the 470s onwards, a second, and much larger,
robe was woven by professional (male) weavers for the quadrennial
Greater Panathenaia and featured Athena and Zeus as saviours of the
divine order.[66] Weaving a figured cloth was extremely time-consuming
and required the highest degree of skill; the annual robe will have taken
most of the nine months allocated for its production, and the quadrennial robe was made as the result of an officially judged competition.

One of the components of processions including that of the
Panathenaia were the animals which were to be sacrificed to the god.[67] A
civic decree which formed part of the reorganisation of the annual festival in 335/4 BC specified the details.[68] The cattle bought with rent from
land sacred to Athena, once they had reached the Akropolis, were sacrificed on the great altar of Athena in front of the Parthenon, with the finest
reserved for a sacrifice on the nearby altar of Athena Nike 'Victory'. The
sacrificial meat from two of the sacrifices was distributed there to various
civic officials and participants in the sacrifice: the prutaneis, the chief
magistrates, the treasurer of the goddess, the sacrificial officials, the board
of generals and division commanders and also Athenians who partici-
pated in the procession and the maidens who acted as *kanephoroi* (Vessel
Bearers). The meat from the other sacrifices was distributed to the
Athenian people in the vicinity of the Pompeion, portions assigned to
each deme in proportion to the number of participants in the procession
from that deme. That is, under a democratic system all citizens were

---

[65] Mansfield 1985; Barber 1991: ch. 16, the relevance of which was pointed out to me by L.F. Nixon;
Barber in Neils 1992: 103–17. Compare gifts of cloth to Artemis Brauronia below, p. 95.

[66] For the addition of Demetrios Poliorketes, see Plutarch, *Demetrios* 10.5, 12.3 (and above, p. 29);
below, p. 128, for Plato's criticisms; below, pp. 90–2, for the *arrhephoroi*.

[67] Introduction to sacrifice: Jameson 1988a; Bremmer 1996a.

[68] *IG* 2[2] 334 = *Syll.*[3] 271, trans. Rice and Stambaugh 1979: 119–20; *LSCG* 33 and Schwenk 1985: no.
17 include a new fragment; below, p. 65 on the land, p. 81 on the context. Cf. Appendix no. 3.

eligible to a portion of the sacrificial meal, at public expense. Honoured civic officials (numbering up to sixty-six) dined in special rooms inside the Pompeion. Formal rules, varying from cult to cult, specified who could participate in the sacrifice. Sacred officials (both male and female) would receive their perquisites; both men and women attending the festival might receive portions of the roast meat. The rules were thus a reflection of the social groupings involved in a particular cult.[69]

The Panathenaic sacrifices, when 100 oxen were killed, were unusual in their scale: smaller communities would not expect to kill so many animals. Cattle were the most prestigious sacrificial animal, no doubt because of their expense. Athenian state sacrifices in the fourth century involved at least 850 oxen, but cattle were rarely offered by Attic demes or by smaller cities. Sheep, goats and pigs were the normal victims for some deities and on lesser occasions: the animals and their prices are duly specified in, for example, deme calendars (Appendix no. 1). Private sacrifices usually involved these cheaper victims, as is illustrated on votive offerings.[70] Otherwise the sacrifices to Athena are exemplary of normal civic sacrifices. The meat derived from such sacrifices offered a modest addition to the normal Greek diet based on plant and milk products.[71]

Sacrifices were always accompanied by prayers which explained the purpose of the sacrifice and specified what was desired in return from the relevant deity. The combination of sacrifice and prayer in a private setting is brought out very clearly by a fourth-century Athenian legal speech arguing that the speaker was the son of a legitimate daughter of one Kiron. Kiron, it is claimed, never offered sacrifices without the speaker's participation:

This applied not only to rites to which we were invited, but also to the rural Dionysia, to which he took us; we attended performances seated beside him, and we celebrated all the festivals at his house. When he sacrificed to Zeus Ktesios [of Property], a sacrifice to which he gave especial attention, to which he did not invite either slaves or non-slaves not part of the family, and at which he performed everything personally, we used to participate in the sacrifice, we used to touch the offerings with him, put them on the altar with him, and do everything else with him; he used to pray that it would give us health and prosperity, as a grandfather would naturally do.[72]

---

[69] Osborne 1993, against Detienne 1989, who argues for the complete exclusion of women from sacrifice.      [70] Figs. 3.3 and 3.5.

[71] Jameson 1988b; Rosivach 1994. On costs of sacrifices, at Delos: Jacquemin 1991.

[72] Isaeus 8.15–16. For nice examples of public prayers see Aristophanes, *Thesmophoriazusae* 312–71 (parody of prayer at Assembly); Thucydides 6.32 (at libations). Cf. Versnel 1981b; Pulleyn 1997. Below, p. 97, on Zeus Ktesios.

Fig. 2.12. Drawing of sacrificial scene on Attic mixing bowl (a column krater),
c. 460 BC (height of image 0.20m). On the left an older man pours a libation over the
altar, and a youth holds the *kanoun* (with sacrificial materials). On the right another
youth cooks the innards (*splankhna*) of the sacrifical animal over the flames of the altar.
Behind him is a herm. On the far right stands another spit with *splankhna*. At the top
right, part of goat's skull with horns.

The handling of the animal and the distribution of the meat as prescribed in the Panathenaic decree followed conventional rules and also
belonged in a religious setting.[73] The painting on a vase made in Etruria
around 540 BC by an artist originally from east Greece depicts in detail the
different stages of the sacrifice, the handling of the body after it is killed,
the dismemberment of the body and the placing of sections of the meat
on skewers prior to roasting.[74] The edible portions were served to the
humans, while the inedible portions were burnt for the god, whose presence at the sacrifice is sometimes emphasised iconographically (Fig. 2.12).

The aetiology for the division of the animal in this way between
humans and gods can be found in Hesiod's *Theogony* (535–57). The story
comes as part of a sequence concerning the sons of a Titan who
rebelled against Zeus. One son, Prometheus, at a time when gods and

[73] Durand 1986; Detienne and Vernant 1989; Durand and Schnapp in Bérard 1989: 53–70; Peirce
1993; van Straten 1995. Cf. Price 1984a: 207–33.
[74] *CAH* 3 2nd edn Plates vol. no. 324; Durand in Detienne and Vernant 1989: 87–118.

mortals still lived together, tried to deceive Zeus by giving him the white bones of a slaughtered ox wrapped in succulent fat, and the flesh and offal to mortals covered with the paunch so that it looked unappetising. Though Zeus saw through the trick, he went along with it and, 'because of this, the tribes of men upon earth burn white bones to the deathless gods on fragrant altars'. The event is taken to mark the division between mortals and immortals, and leads to a complex chain of events. Zeus in his anger deprived mortals of fire which Prometheus stole back, and Zeus, angry again, created woman as a curse to man. The story of the origins of sacrifice thus treats the division of the animal both as a marker of the distance between mortals and immortals and as a means of bridging that divide. It is also connected by an extension of the story (in the *Works and Days* 42–105) with the need for humans to cultivate crops (rather than live off what grew spontaneously) and with the creation of woman as a bane to man, two key aspects of Greek civilisation.[75]

Sacrifices are to modern Judaeo-Christian eyes a rather peculiar practice.[76] Judaism has not practised animal sacrifice since the destruction of the temple in Jerusalem by Rome in AD 70, and the ideology of Christianity is intimately bound up with the theory that the death of Christ superseded animal sacrifice. As an early Christian explained when writing to Jews who had converted to Christianity:

> The blood of his [Christ's] sacrifice is his own blood, not the blood of goats and calves and thus he has entered the sanctuary once and for all and secured an eternal deliverance. For if the blood of goats and bulls and the sprinkled ashes of a heifer have power to hallow those who have been defiled and restore their external purity, how much greater is the power of the blood of Christ . . .[77]

This text expresses very forcefully the view that animal sacrifice is a form of religious worship inferior to the more spiritual practices of modern religions.[78] Sacrifices were no doubt noisy and rather messy affairs (but not particularly smelly, as anyone knows who has been present at the butchering of an animal by the roadside in Greece today). However, they were not just the pretext for a good meal, they were major religious events.

---

[75] Rudhardt 1970; Vernant 1980: 168–85.
[76] For very different modern approaches see Burkert 1966: 102–13 (more fully in Burkert 1983); Detienne and Vernant 1989. Cf. above, p. 17, on Burkert's search for origins.
[77] Letter to the Hebrews 9.12–13, ascribed to Paul.
[78] Sacrifice has an ambiguous position in modern Islam. Sanctioned by the Koran (Surah 22.32–7) and practised at the time of the annual pilgrimage to Mecca, sacrifice nonetheless has no place in official Islamic worship.

During festivals, in addition to sacrifices, hymns were sometimes sung. The standard structure was invocation of the god, honouring the god through recounting of one or more divine deeds, and finally a prayer for divine favour.[79] At Miletos there was a special association of singers (*molpoi*): on the 'Sacred Way', the processional route over twenty kilometres from Miletos to the temple of Apollo at Didyma, they stopped at six designated shrines to perform their hymn in honour of Apollo Delphinios.[80] Elsewhere in the Hellenistic and Roman periods there were special choirs to sing hymns to the god.[81] Some of these cult hymns were inscribed on stone and survive to this day; two hymns at Delphi include a full musical notation.[82] Cult hymns naturally deployed mythology, often with local emphasis; that from Palaikastro on Crete invokes Zeus and refers to his birth on Crete.[83] Such hymns were, from the start, a fundamental and autonomous mode of religious action – a well-performed hymn was in itself a 'gift' to the god.

Sacrifices, hymns and other offerings to the gods had a common purpose, namely to please the gods. The standard term for what we call 'cult statue', and indeed for other images, was an *agalma*, an object in a sanctuary which was a glory or a delight to the gods.[84] And the gods were certainly supposed to savour the offering of sacrifices to them. Conversely, the proper performance of cult could be drawn on in the future by the individual or the community.[85] A typical example is found at the beginning of Homer's *Iliad*, where Chryses, the priest of Apollo, prays to Apollo Smintheus:

Smintheus, if ever I roofed a temple that pleased you or if ever I burnt for you rich thighs of bulls or goats, fulfil this prayer for me. (1.39–41)

Though this form of prayer, 'if I ever . . . will you now . . .', is attested only in works of high literature, as here, most Greeks probably shared the assumption that previous offerings gave them some claim on the gods' attention. The point is made explicit in two verses inscribed on the thighs of a small bronze statue of a warrior:

---

[79] Bremer 1981; Furley 1995.
[80] *Syll.*³ 57 = *LSAM* 50; *RE* Supp.6.509–20; Gödecken 1986 and Schneider 1987 on route. Cf. Appendix no. 7.     [81] Nilsson 1955–67: II.377–81; Price 1984a: 88.
[82] West 1992: 279–80, 288–301.
[83] West 1965, with comment of Versnel 1990: 32–3 (trans. Rice and Stambaugh 1979: 29–30). Cf. below, pp. 118–19, for 'Orphic' hymns.     [84] Price 1984a: 178.
[85] Pulleyn 1997: 16–38; Parker 1998, on the importance of *charis* or reciprocity; Appendix no. 9.

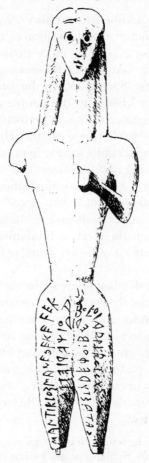

Fig. 2.13. Drawing of bronze statuette (height 0.20m) from Thebes, perhaps from the sanctuary of Apollo Ismenios (early seventh century BC). The figure may originally have worn a helmet, carried a spear in his right hand and a shield in his left.

Mantiklos dedicated me to the silver-bowed far-shooter [i.e. Apollo] from his tithe. Phoibos [Apollo], grant him grateful recompense. (Fig. 2.13)[86]

That is, mortals and gods were in a relationship defined in terms of an exchange of favours. Moderns of an anti-ritualistic bent criticise this as merely *do ut des*, 'I give that you may give', but such criticism misses the point. Like other systems of gifts and counter-gifts, the Greek ritual system assumed choice on both sides. Gifts to the gods were not a way

---

[86] P.A. Hansen, *Carmina Epigraphica Graeca* (Berlin and New York 1983), no. 326.

of buying the gods, but of creating goodwill from which humans might hope to benefit in the future.[87]

Festivals also often included competitions of various sorts. The most prestigious of these competitions, at the Panhellenic festivals at Olympia, Delphi, Nemea and the Isthmia, drew competitors from all over the Greek world in chariot racing, horse racing, athletics and, at Delphi and the Isthmia, musical events.[88] 'Sport' in the ancient world involved as much fervour and local pride as today, but it belonged overtly within a religious framework. In due course other cities sought to promote their own festivals to Panhellenic status, thus hoping to attract top rank competitors from all over Greece. The Athenians established the Greater Panathenaia as a Panhellenic festival in about 566/5, and in the Roman period in numerous cities there were 'sacred and crowned games', which operated on the cycles of the four ancient Panhellenic games and whose competitions and privileges were modelled on them.[89] This period marked the greatest flowering of competitions in the Greek world, in part because rivalry between cities under Rome found its outlet in civic display.

The Panathenaia, whatever its Panhellenic status, retained the structure of a civic festival.[90] In the Greater Panathenaia, every fifth year (on inclusive counting), there were competitions (for men, youths and boys) in reciting Homer, music, athletics, equestrian events, team events for tribes, a torch race, and a boat race. Some of the athletic and equestrian events probably took place along the Panathenaic Way, especially in the Agora; some remained there even after a special stadium for racing was built in 330 BC and a hippodrome in the Peiraeus.[91] The musical events were also held in the Agora until the building in the mid-fifth century BC of a concert hall (*odeion*) on the south slope of the Akropolis (Fig. 2.14 no. 23). Whereas victors at Panhellenic games won only a crown and subsequently a pension from their own city, victors at Athens won substantial sums. In the fourth century BC first prize in the lyre competition was a crown of gold leaf worth 1,000 drachmas and

---

[87] For a comic application of this idea, involving Athena remembering the gift of the robe, see Aristophanes, *Knights* 1178–80. For another use of the analogy of gift-exchange see Price 1984a: 65–77. For philosophical criticism see below, p. 133, and Parker 1998.

[88] Finley and Pleket 1976; Raschke 1988; Tzachou-Alexandri 1989; Golden 1998.

[89] Establishment: Fornara 1983: no. 26. Fig. 2.10 is a response to the new festival. Appendix no. 11 for a new Hellenistic festival. Roman period: Cartledge and Spawforth 1989: 184–9.

[90] Tracy 1991; Neils 1992; Parker 1996: 75, 89–92; Neils 1996.

[91] The stadium was rebuilt in the early 140s AD by the Athenian dignitary Herodes Atticus: Tobin 1997: 162–73.

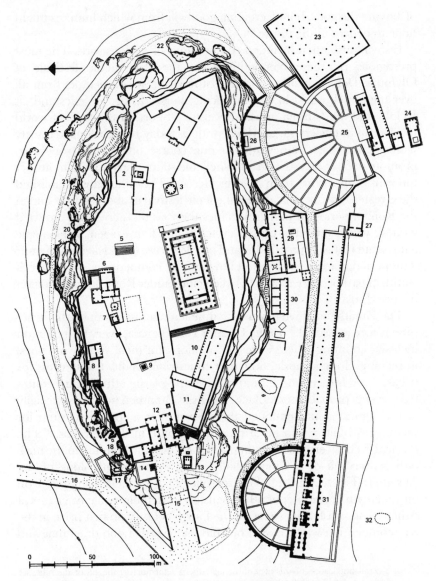

Fig. 2.14. The Athenian Akropolis and adjacent buildings in the second century AD
1. So-called Ergasterion. 2. Shrine of Zeus Polieus. 3. Temple of Roma and Augustus.
4. Parthenon. 5. Altar of Athena. 6. Erechtheion. 7. Pandroseion. 8. House of the
Arrhephoroi. 9. Athena Promachos. 10. Chalkotheke. 11. Artemis Brauronia.
12. Propylaia. 13. Temple of Athena Nike. 14. Agrippa monument. 15. Beulé Gate.
16. Top of Panathenaic Way. 17. Klepsydra Spring House. 18. Apollo Hypoakrios.
19. Cave of Pan. 20. Sanctuary of Eros and Aphrodite. 21. Peripatos inscription.

500 silver drachmas at a time when a skilled labourer's daily wage was one drachma, and prizes in the athletic competitions were jars of olive oil, for example forty for the winners of the youths' wrestling, worth about 480 drachmas. Oil was produced from special olive trees sacred to Athena levied by a magistrate on the owner of the fields where the trees were located, stored on the Akropolis and placed in special oil jars by 'the commissioners of the games'. These oil jars were substantial in size, usually 60 to 70 cm high, and contained 38 to 39 litres on average. They were unique in design and decorated with scenes of, on the front, Athena and, on the rear, the competition concerned, with the legend 'for the games at Athens'. The canonical shape and decoration established by around 530 BC were preserved through the third and second centuries BC, even though the design of a black figure on a red background had gone out of use on other Athenian pottery in the early fifth century (Fig. 2.15). Over 1,400 such vases were needed for prizes in each games but only about 300 in total survive today, a useful sidelight on the survival rate of our most plentiful material evidence for archaic and classical Greece.[92]

Victories in the games were also celebrated and commemorated in poems specially commissioned for the occasion. The first known composers of such works were Simonides and perhaps Ibycus, in the sixth to early fifth centuries, but their poems do not survive intact. In the fifth century the most famous authors of this genre were Pindar and Bacchylides, whose works give a unique insight into aristocratic culture throughout the Greek world. The poems were performed, sometimes by the poet himself (or another solo voice), sometimes by a chorus, in various settings in the victor's native city: sanctuaries, where sacrifices were offered, perhaps in a victory procession, and at the victor's house. A nice example of the victory poem is one written by Pindar for a victory in a wrestling match by one Theaios of Argos at a festival of Hera at Argos.[93] The poem opens with praise for the mythical heroes of the city,

[92] Beazley 1951: 88–100; Boardman 1974: 167–77. Compare Bérard 1989: 109–14 for various images of the Panathenaia.

[93] Pindar, *Nemean* 10. Performance: Heath 1988; Carey 1989 argues for choral performances.

Fig. 2.14 (*cont.*)
22. Sanctuary of Aglauros. 23. Odeion of Pericles. 24. Temple of Dionysos.
25. Theatre of Dionysos. 26. Thrasyllus monument. 27. Nikias monument. 28. Portico of Eumenes. 29. Asklepieion. 30. Ionic portico. 31. Odeion of Herodes Atticus.
32. Shrine of Nymphs.

Fig. 2.15. The earliest surviving prize amphora, dating (on stylistic grounds) to the 560s, the decade in which the Panathenaia was reorganised (height 0.61m) (cf. 2.10). The main scene is of a two-horse chariot race, the specific competition for which this amphora was awarded. On the neck is a siren. On the other side is a representation of Athena, which is constant over many generations.

and then moves on to praise of Theaios, who had also won Panhellenic victories at Delphi, Isthmia, Nemea and Athens, where he had twice been awarded 'in earth baked by the fire olive oil in richly painted vases' (lines 35–6), that is Panathenaic oil jars. Praise of Theaios' family leads to a further, standard element of these poems, adaptation of local mythology in honour of the victor. Here Pindar tells the story of the friendship of the divine twins Castor and Polydeuces, who had once been entertained by ancestors of Theaios and whose patronage of his family might enable him to win a victory at Olympia. The poems in deploying myths in an allusive manner often assume knowledge by the audience of local mythology.[94]

Drama, like 'sport', always occurred within a religious context. At Athens the major dramatic festivals were two festivals of Dionysos, the Great or City Dionysia and the Lenaia. Here all Athenian tragedies and comedies were performed during the festivals from the later sixth century in special seating in the Agora and then from the fifth century in a new theatre of Dionysos on the slopes of the Akropolis.[95] There is much dispute as to the extent to which the context should affect our interpretation of the plays.[96] Some have seen tragedy as essentially religious, while others have argued that the festivals were really just a holiday and merely the occasion for the plays. Both extremes are probably untenable. On the one hand, plays are not 'cultic' like the hymns sung in honour of the gods. Some plays do include aetiological myths for the cities where the action is set, for example Corinth, Thebes, Athens. For Athens Aeschylus' *Oresteia* trilogy closes with an Athena who is Athena Polias founding the venerable Athenian law-court of the Areopagus and establishing a shrine on the Areopagus hill for the Erinyes or Furies, now placated as the Semnai 'revered ones' or Eumenides who will grant blessings to the Athenians.[97] Euripides' *Ion*, set at Delphi, refers to the aetiology of the Athenian Arrhephoria,[98] and his *Iphigenia at Tauris* ends with Athena commanding the foundation of

---

[94] See, for example, Calame 1990, revised in 1996: 57–169; Dougherty 1993. On Pindar's social values see Kurke 1991.

[95] Fig. 2.14 no. 24. See Gebhardt 1974: 432–4; Polacco 1990, without reference to the work of the Greek Archaeological Service (*Arkhaiologikon Deltion* Khronika 40 (1985 [1990], 9–11). It was rebuilt in the fourth century under Lycurgus (cf. below, p. 81).

[96] Goldhill 1987; Connor 1990; Mikalson 1991; Seaford 1994: 235–80; Sourvinou-Inwood 1994 and 1997b; for the setting see Pickard-Cambridge 1988.

[97] *Eumenides* 681–706, 794–1047. Aeschylus was probably the first to identify the Panhellenic Erinyes with the local Semnai. For their cult, performed by an Athenian lineage, see Polemo in Scholiast on *Sophocles, Oedipus at Colonus* 489; Parker 1996: 298–9; cf. Lardinois 1992; Clinton 1996: 165–70.

[98] 8–27, 267–82; cf. below, p. 94.

the Attic cults of Artemis at Halae and Brauron.[99] But in general the relationship to Athenian or other local cults is not so close. The Athena of Sophocles' *Ajax* or Euripides' *Troades* is not the Athena Polias worshipped on the Akropolis nor was the Dionysos of Euripides' *Bacchae*, written in exile in Macedonia, the same as the Dionysos at whose festivals the plays were performed.[100] The gods represented in the tragedies operate in the first instance at the level of the Homeric/Hesiodic pantheon, and secondarily from time to time at the level of local cults.

Although the plays are not primarily cultic, the religious framework of procession and sacrifice and the civic setting of the festivals for Dionysos are important. They permit both tragedy and comedy to offer licensed commentaries on commonly held values, both religious and political. Thus tragedies can meditate on the nature and limits of divine justice, and sometimes explore general issues through particular focus on local cults.[101] Similarly comedies can use explicitly religious settings for their own purposes. In Aristophanes' comedy *The Frogs* a drunken Dionysos on his way to the underworld meets a group of Eleusinian initiates who sing movingly of Persephone, Demeter and Iacchus (316–459), and in his *The Women at the Thesmophoria* the women debate formally at the festival of the Thesmophoria what punishments should be given to Euripides for his alleged slanders of women (373–519).[102] There is no sharp divide between the gods of drama and the gods of Athens and other states. Rather, drama was one medium for exploring the religious ideas of the polis.

Tragedies and comedies were not exclusively Athenian, and not exclusively classical. The works of the Athenian dramatists, both tragic and comic, were staged not only in Athens but also in other Greek cities, as far west as Sicily and south Italy, in the fifth and fourth centuries.[103] They continued to be revived throughout the Hellenistic and Roman periods. Respect for the great masters did not mean the end of new work. New plays, tragic and comic, were composed for festivals until at least the late second century AD.[104] For example, new comedies were still being performed at the Dionysia of Smyrna (on the west coast of Asia Minor) in the mid-second century; a contemporary attests their popularity: the songs were sung later by everyone, including women

---

[99] 1449–67; cf. pp. 90–3 on Brauron.
[100] Cf. below, p. 115 for the absence of maenads in this or other Athenian festivals of Dionysos.
[101] Parker 1997.
[102] Cf. pp. 102–7 on Eleusis, pp. 98–100 for the Thesmophoria. Below, p. 52, on Dionysos' statue.
[103] Taplin 1993.       [104] C.P. Jones 1993.

and slaves, 'in the baths, in the alleyways, in the market-place, and at home'.[105]

A particularly full record of the range of competitions in a festival of the Roman period happens to survive from Oenoanda, a small town in south-west Asia Minor.[106] This new festival, founded in AD 124–5, stretching over three weeks, included seventeen days of competitions and other events: musical competitions (singers accompanied by the *kithara* 'lyre', players of the shawm with a choir or *khorauloi*, trumpeters and heralds); dramatic competitions (poets, writers of encomia in prose, comic actors, tragic actors); mime acts outside the competition; and gymnasium competitions for the local citizens. These competitions are typical of the festivals of this period and demonstrate the continued vitality of the classical tradition.

The competitions involving words develop a tradition that goes back to the archaic period. From at least the sixth century BC onwards, poets wrote special hymns for performance in competition at festivals. The so-called Homeric hymns, some thirty-three in number, are a compilation of hymns of which at least some were originally sung competitively at festivals.[107] The extant hymns date to the seventh and sixth centuries BC (and perhaps later), and are called 'Homeric' only because their language stood in the Homeric tradition. The hymn to Delian Apollo itself refers to the festival at which the long-robed Ionians gather in honour of Apollo with their children and diffident wives:

The girls of Delos handmaidens of the Far Shooter [Apollo], when they have praised Apollo first and also Leto [his mother] and Artemis [his sister] who delights in arrows, they sing a hymn telling of men and women of past days, and charm the tribes of people. (146–61)

The singer of the Homeric Hymn also describes himself for the singers of the cult hymn and claims to be the one whom the girls most appreciate. Another Homeric Hymn, to Aphrodite (6.19–21), hopes that the god will grant him victory in the competition, though it is in fact hard to identify at what festival this might have occurred.

There were also competitions, at for example the Athenian Panathenaia, for the performance of epic, by *rhapsodoi*, and of lyric 'epic', by *kitharodoi*, who accompanied themselves with a *kithara*.[108] Such

---

[105] Aelius Aristides 29.30, trans. in C.A. Behr, Leiden 1981–6.

[106] *SEG* 38. 1962; Mitchell 1990, with translation.

[107] The collection may have been made in the fifth century AD by Proclus, on whom see below, pp. 168–9. See generally Parker 1991: 1–4; Calame 1995.

[108] Neils 1992: 69–75.

competitions are still found in second-century AD Oenoanda. Here, as
elsewhere in the Roman period, we also find competitions for encomia
of the gods in prose.[109] In addition, Greek orators of the Roman period
also composed prose hymns to the gods, not for competitions, but for vir-
tuoso performances, whether at festivals or in other settings. Ten such
speeches by the second century AD orator Aelius Aristides survive, and
rules for their composition were formulated in rhetorical handbooks.[110]
Competitive and epideictic praise of the gods was one of the enduring
ways in which Greek mythology was deployed and constantly adapted
and recreated for local circumstances.

[109] Price 1984b: 90 on encomia to gods and emperors.
[110] Aelius Aristides, *Orations* 37–46 Keil, trans. C.A. Behr, Leiden 1981–6; cf. Russell 1990.
Quintilian 3.7.7–8 (Latin, first century AD); Alexander Numenius, in Spengel, *Rhetores Graeci* 3.
4–6 (second century AD); 'Menander Rhetor', trans. in Russell and Wilson 1981: 6–29 and (in
part) in MacMullen and Lane 1992: 59–62 (third century AD).

# CHAPTER 3

# *Religious places*

Greek temples are among the most familiar surviving objects of antiquity. Thousands of visitors a year gaze at the Parthenon, and the influence of the temples, direct or indirect, is visible all the way from the White House in Washington DC to the Opera House in Ulan Bator, Mongolia. In antiquity too they were prestigious buildings. Architects around the Greek world rivalled one another in building bigger and finer temples, and cities were extremely proud of their religious architecture. Herodotos, who was fond of Samos, includes the temple of Hera there among the three architectural wonders that justified his writing at length about the Samians (the other two were an aqueduct one kilometre long through a mountain, and a harbour mole) (3.60). This temple of Hera on Samos was planned in the earlier sixth century BC on a colossal scale and, a generation later, probably because of marshy conditions, rebuilt on a similar scale. Work continued for the next five hundred years until hope of actually completing the temple was abandoned, but the temple was still an impressive sight. Bronze coins produced by Greek cities in the Roman period often feature their temples as matters of local pride; for example, coins of Samos from the first to the mid-third centuries AD proudly display the ancient cult statue of Hera in its temple.[1] Temples, however, are only the most prominent component of a Greek sanctuary and must be seen as secondary to the functions of the sacrificial altar, which was indispensable, and in the context of an area of sacred space surrounding both altar and temple.[2] An antiquarian writer of about 200 BC described the marvels of the Samian sanctuary of Hera (including her peacocks) in his treatise on the wonders of Samos.[3]

---

[1] Temple: Kyrieleis 1981; 1993. Coins: Price and Trell 1977: 133–5.
[2] Price 1984a: 133–7; Schachter 1992; Marinatos and Hägg 1993. For general introductions see Melas 1973, Tomlinson 1976 and Osborne 1987: 165–92. On the Athenian Akropolis see Hopper 1971; Korres in Economakis 1994: 35–51; and on Athens generally Wycherley 1978.
[3] Menodotos in Athenaeus 14.655a, 15.671d-674a (Tresp 1914: 151–8; *FGH* 541).

### LOCATION

When Greeks from the eighth century BC onwards founded new colonies, one of their principal acts was the definition of sacred space.[4] We find an example in Homer's *Odyssey*, which reflects many aspects of eighth-century Greece,

> Nausithoös settled them [the Phaeacians] in Scheria far from men who live by toil. About the city he had drawn a wall, he had built houses and made shrines to the gods and divided the plough land. (*Odyssey* 6.7–10)

Some five hundred years later, Alexander the Great is said to have displayed similar concern when founding Alexandria in Egypt:

> He himself marked out the ground plan of the city: where the market place was to be laid out, how many temples were to be built and in honour of what gods, both Greek and Isis the Egyptian, and where the wall was to be built round it. With this in view he offered sacrifice, which proved favourable. (Arrian, *Anabasis* 3.1.5)

Some sanctuaries in mainland Greece were sited in relation to divine intervention, for example those of Poseidon and Athena at Athens (above, p. 19), or at a particularly awesome spot like Delphi. But when founding new communities the Greeks assumed that the founder would locate sanctuaries as part of his overall urban planning. The assumptions of the colonial founders no doubt formalised views current at home. Although there was no divine sanction for the siting of most new Greek temples in the archaic and classical periods, no community could exist without temples to its gods.

The official assignment of sacred space was equally important when cities were refounded. Colophon, an ancient city on the west coast of Asia Minor, regained its freedom (from Persia) at the hands of Alexander the Great and his successors, and decided at the very end of the fourth century BC to incorporate within its walls the 'ancient city'. It seems to have been long ruined and abandoned. The decree of the city includes the following provision:

> Resolved by the people to enclose within the same walls in addition to the present city the ancient city which, on receipt from the gods, our ancestors founded and where they set up temples and altars, our ancestors who were held in high esteem among all the Greeks. In order that this could be achieved quickly, the priest of Apollo and the other priests and priestesses and the chief

---

[4] Malkin 1987: 135–86. See also the theoretical divisions of Hippodamus, criticised by Aristotle, *Politics* 1267b22–1269a28.

magistrate with the help of the council and the others listed in this decree should go down to the ancient Agora on the fourth of the next month and upon the altars of the gods which our ancestors bequeathed to us should pray to Zeus the Saviour, Poseidon the Securer, Apollo the Clarian, Mother Antaia ['appearing face to face'], Athena Polias and to all the other male and female gods and to the heroes who occupy our city and territory since we enjoy complete prosperity, to make a solemn procession and sacrifice in the manner the people decided.[5]

The revival of the old sacred places, which did not have to be freshly allocated, is marked by means of procession, sacrifice and prayer. God-given places as they were, the ten land-commissioners and the architect had to work around them when laying down the line of the roads, the building lots reserving the agora, the work-places and the other necessary public land.

Greek sanctuaries were carefully placed, within an urban, suburban or rural context. The urban sanctuaries were situated in a variety of contexts. Though the Parthenon stood out at Athens and 'makes a great impression on sightseers' as the author of a guidebook to Greece noted in the third century BC, this was unusual.[6] Most urban sanctuaries did not tower over their towns like medieval cathedrals; rather they were integrated into the fabric of urban life, especially with the development in the classical period of imposing secular architecture.

The locating of urban sanctuaries may be illustrated archaeologically from the excavations of Megara Hyblaia, a Greek town founded on the east coast of Sicily in about 725 BC. In and around the agora were built a series of temples and shrines during the first phase of the settlement down to circa 650 BC (Fig. 3.1).[7] Megara Hyblaia gradually grew into the division of space appointed by the founder: temples were built in and adjacent to existing sanctuaries and within the agora itself; other buildings came to sharpen the boundaries of the civic space, and the founder himself probably received heroic honours perhaps next to the house in which he had once lived.

Selinus, on the south-west coast of Sicily (founded in about 628 BC) followed the model of her mother city, Megara Hyblaia. There was a walled Akropolis, a grid plan of streets, and sanctuaries going back to the seventh century.[8] Although the city possessed several temples on the

---

[5] Maier 1959: no. 69, lines 9–21 (311–306 BC).

[6] Heraclides of Crete ?, ed. F. Pfister, Vienna 1951, trans. in Austin 1981: no. 83, 1.1.

[7] Vallet, Villard and Auberson 1976; 1983. For sanctuaries in and around the Athenian agora see Camp 1986.

[8] Fifth-century listing of the gods of Selinus: ML 38, trans. in Appendix no. 10.

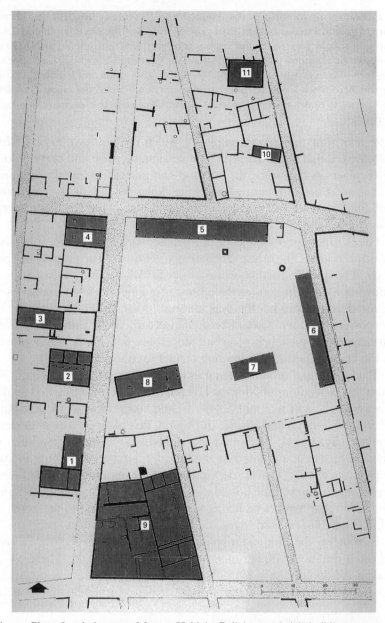

Fig. 3.1. Plan of archaic agora, Megara Hyblaia. Religious and civic buildings are shaded. 1. Secular public building (sixth century BC). 2. Hestiatorion (c. 530 BC). 3. Temple built c. 600 BC at rear of earlier sanctuary, destroying earlier buildings. 4. Building added c. 630 BC to house dating to period of foundation of colony.

[cont. on p. 51]

Akropolis, in addition there was a contemporary and no less important sanctuary of Demeter Malophoros 'apple bearer' about 750 metres to the west of the city outside which was probably the main gate.[9] There is no reason to suggest that the complex perpetuated local cults predating the arrival of the Greek colonists. The sanctuary of Demeter Malophoros was probably designed to replicate a sanctuary to the same goddess at mainland Greek Megara, the 'grandmother' of Selinus. The founder of the city had been sent out from Megara, where too the sanctuary was sited just outside a gate on the way down to water, in this case the sea of the Saronic Gulf (Pausanias 1.44.3), and at Selinus the several thousands of terracotta votives of a goddess holding a pomegranate belong within a Greek iconographical tradition.[10] The goddess was simply one of the major protectors of the community. The sanctuary consists of a large *temenos* (sacred precinct) roughly 110 by 80 metres, with an inner precinct about 60 by 50 metres (Fig. 3.2). The latter included an altar dating back to the mid-seventh century, and a shrine of the late seventh century, rebuilt in the sixth, and a large altar replacing the earlier one in the late sixth century. The chthonic elements of the cult are picked up by the sanctuary of Zeus Meilichios that lies in the north-east corner of the main precinct; a sanctuary of Hekate may be next to the main entrance.

The placing of this sanctuary on the periphery of the town fits into a pattern of 'suburban' sanctuaries.[11] The deities whose sanctuaries lay on a city's akropolis or agora were normally ordinary Olympian deities, central both physically and metaphysically. But the sanctuary of Demeter Malophoros, though important, was concerned with rites of transition and women, who were not politically central to the city.[12] Similarly the sanctuary of Persephone at Locri in south Italy, which as we have seen was especially concerned with women, marriage and

---

[9] Original publication: Gàbrici 1927; see briefly Coarelli and Torelli 1984: 97–103. Recent work synthesised: Jameson, Jordan and Kotansky 1993: 132–6.

[10] See above, pp. 49–50. Merging of Greek and Punic traditions in the fourth century: Jameson, Jordan and Kotansky 1993: 137–41.

[11] Cole 1994 surveys the evidence on Demeter. See in general Vallet 1968: 81–8; de Polignac 1995: 21–5.     [12] Below, pp. 98–100, for festivals of Demeter.

---

Fig. 3.1 (*cont.*)
Pits inside, probably for chthonic sacrifice, suggest it was a 'heroon' for the city's founder, who will have received after his death the heroic sacrifices that were normal for founders. 5–6. Porticoes (650–600 BC). 7. Temple (650–625 BC). 8. Temple (625–600 BC). 9. Building for civic administration (640–630 BC). 10. Small temple (650–625 BC) built in large sanctuary. 11. Sacred building (550–500 BC).

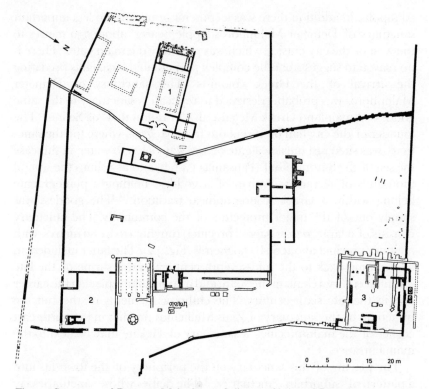

Fig. 3.2. Sanctuary of Demeter Malophoros, Selinus. 1. Shrine of Demeter Malophoros; 2. Sanctuary of Hekate? 3. Sanctuary of Zeus Meilichios.

child-rearing, lay on a large terrace, about 100 by 40 metres, on the north edge of the town outside the walls. Sanctuaries of Dionysos were also characteristically suburban: in some cities he bore the telling name 'in front of the city'.[13] At Athens one sanctuary of Dionysos was outside the original city 'in the Marshes',[14] the other was on the south slopes of the Akropolis (Fig. 2.14, nos. 24–5), but an annual ritual recalled that the statue of Dionysos displayed there during the Dionysia had been brought to Athens from outside, from Eleutherae on the borders of Attica and Boeotia.[15] The outsider-status of Dionysos made it appropri-

<hr />

[13] Gernet and Boulanger 1932: 105; cf. Robert 1948: 79 on the meaning of the phrase.

[14] Thucydides 2.15.4. Probably in the Ilissus area but the precise location is unknown: Pickard-Cambridge 1968: 19–25; below, p. 117.

[15] On the sixth-century origins of Great/City Dionysia: Connor 1990: 8–16; Sourvinou-Inwood 1994; Parker 1996: 92–6. Above, p. 44, on tragedies.

ate for the sanctuaries to be away from the centre, either physically or in terms of mythical origins. Deities associated with fertility often had their sanctuaries in a suburban location.

Sanctuaries are also found well away from the nucleated centre of the polis. Some were small shrines, perhaps dedicated by local groups or by individual families.[16] Others were major civic sanctuaries.[17] The reasons for the precise location of these rural sanctuaries must be varied, but one common reason was the definition of boundaries.[18] The Argive Heraion, some eight kilometres from the city of Argos, lay at the edge of the fertile plain disputed by Argos, Mycenae, Tiryns and Asine. The sanctuary, which may go back to the eighth century BC, may originally have been more in the orbit of Mycenae, and become decisively 'Argive' only after the destruction by Argos of Mycenae and Tiryns in the 460s.[19] The role of sanctuaries on boundaries is clearer in, for example, Pausanias' account of Mantinea in the southern Peloponnese. The city was ringed by a series of sanctuaries at or near boundaries with the various neighbouring city states: a sanctuary of Poseidon Hippios near the frontier with Tegea, one of Zeus Kharmos on the way to Pallantion, one of Artemis on the way to Orchomenos, and at Anchisia also on the way to Orchomenos are 'the ruins of a sanctuary of Aphrodite and the boundary between Mantinea and Orchomenos'.[20] Such sanctuaries were not forts, they were symbolic markers laying claim to and hopefully defining the outer limits of a city's territory. Given that marginal areas were often important for grazing and that most Greek wars were fought over disputed border lands, such definitions were a matter of no mean importance.

In some cases at least a major procession as part of an annual festival served to make manifest the links between city and sanctuary. At Argos, for example, a major procession led from the city to the Heraion.[21] The sanctuary of Demeter and Kore at Eleusis on the western edge of Attica was also closely tied to Athens. At the foot of the Akropolis at the edge of the Agora was a sanctuary, the Eleusinion, where special rites took place and any Athenian business concerning the Mysteries was carried out. From it there started the great procession of initiates and future

---

[16] Edlund 1987: 98–102, 141–2.
[17] Vallet 1968: 88–94; Edlund 1987; Osborne 1987: 165–71; Alcock 1993: 200–10; de Polignac 1995.
[18] de Polignac 1994; 1995: 98–106; Nixon 1990 applies de Polignac's ideas to Crete.
[19] Hall 1995; cf. de Polignac 1995: 52–3.
[20] 8.10–12. Cf. Bruit Zaidman and Schmitt Pantel 1992: 207–14, with fig. 11; and on Arcadia generally Jost 1994.
[21] de Polignac 1995: 41–3, 46; Hall 1995: 594–6, arguing for a fifth-century origin.

initiates and youths (ephebes) who walked the seven kilometres from Athens to celebrate the Mysteries at Eleusis.[22] During the latter stages of the Peloponnesian War, at a time when the Spartans controlled access to Attica, the Athenians had had to skip the procession to Eleusis, omitting the customary sacrifices, dances and rites which were performed on the road to Eleusis. In 407 BC Alcibiades, although found guilty of profaning the Mysteries in 415 BC, was able to assert his piety and to raise Athenian morale by leading the procession by land. 'He posted sentries on the heights, sent out an advance guard at daybreak, and then, marshalling the priests, novices and initiates, and placing them in the centre of his column, he led them along the road to Eleusis in solemn and complete silence.'[23] Ephebes, who were formally organised in the 330s under Lycurgus (below, p. 95), came to have a prominent and enduring role in the procession. In the third century AD the Athenian people gave fresh instructions to the official in charge of the ephebes to organise 'in accordance with ancestral custom' the procession escorting the sacred objects from Eleusis to the Eleusinion in Athens and the return procession six days later.[24] No doubt the organisation of the procession was very different from that of the classical period, but this and other similar processions long formalised and defined the ties between centre and periphery. Processions leading to popular festivities at sanctuaries outside the urban centre were normal in the Greek world.[25]

### APPEARANCE AND SETTING

Sanctuaries varied not only in location but also in appearance. Pausanias described the full range. On Mount Lykaion in Arcadia, central Peloponnese, known locally as Olympos or 'Sacred Peak', where (rather than on Crete) Zeus was believed by the Arcadians to have been born, was a sanctuary of Zeus Lykaios

into which people are not allowed to enter; if anyone ignores the rules and enters he inevitably lives no more than a year ... On the mountain top is a mound of earth forming an altar of Zeus Lykaios, from which most of the Peloponnese can be seen. Before the altar on the east stand two pillars on which there used to be gilded eagles. On this altar they sacrifice in secret to Zeus Lykaios.[26]

---

[22] Travlos 1971: 198–203.    [23] Plutarch, *Alcibiades* 34.3–6; cf. below, pp. 82–5 on 415 BC; Graf 1996.    [24] *IG* 2² 1078 = *Syll.*³ 885, c. AD 220. Cf. Pélékidis 1962: 220–5.

[25] Note their discussion in Aeneas Tacticus 17.1 (trans. D. Whitehead, Oxford 1990; also Loeb).

[26] 8.38.6–7. Pausanias here alludes to the alleged local practice of human sacrifice: Bonnechere 1994: 85–96.

Some woods were sacred; indeed Pausanias is particularly interested in woods with a religious (or political) significance. On a mountain south-west of Argos at Lerna was a sacred wood consisting largely of plane trees bounded by two rivers stretching down to the sea.

Within the grove are cult images of Demeter Prosymne and of Dionysos. Of Demeter there is also a seated image of no great size. These are of stone, but elsewhere in a temple is a seated wooden image of Dionysos Saviour.[27]

The god Pan and his associated nymphs were normally worshipped in caves, at least outside his 'home' in Arcadia. Pausanias mentions one on the slopes of the Athenian Akropolis; the cult was founded by the Athenians after Pan had appeared to the runner Philippides returning to Athens with the news that the Spartans could not help fight the Persians at Marathon in 490 BC (1.28.4, No. 19 on Fig. 2.14);[28] he also mentions an important one in the Attic countryside (1.32.7), which along with other such cave cults probably developed after that on the Akropolis. Caves were the perfect symbol for this god of the wild who could steal people's wits away. Then there were sanctuaries on level or terraced ground, defined perhaps by boundary stones or a wall, as the sanctuaries of Megara Hyblaia or Selinus. Take for example the sanctuary of Asclepius at Sicyon on the north coast of the Peloponnese,

On passing within the enclosure you see on the left a building with two rooms. In the outer one lies a figure of Sleep, of which nothing now remains except the head. The inner room is given over to Apollo Karneios. Into it no one may enter except the priests. In the portico lies a huge bone of a sea monster, and after it an image of the Dream-God, and Sleep, surnamed Epidotes ('Bountiful') lulling to sleep a lion. Within the temple of Asclepius on either side of the entrance is an image, on the one side Pan seated, on the other Artemis standing. When you have entered you see the god, a beardless figure of gold and ivory made by Kalamis [fifth-century sculptor]. He holds a staff in one hand and a cone of the cultivated pine in the other. (2.10.2–3)

Defining and analysing sanctuaries archaeologically without the aid of Pausanias or other texts is rather challenging. While excavators of pre-historic sites have begun to formulate explicit criteria for deciding that particular sites are 'sanctuaries' and explicit questions that may be answered archaeologically (see above, p. 9, n. 21), classical archaeologists have so far not been so ready to be explicit about their methods. They have often identified their buildings on the basis of Pausanias'

---

[27] 2.36.8–37.2. Cf. Herodotos 6.75–82 for violation of the woods sacred to the hero Argos by the Spartan king Cleomenes: Jacob 1993; Birge 1994.

[28] Borgeaud 1988 explores his cults; Parker 1996: 163–8.

descriptions or other texts, and they have not always been as ready to present evidence for the whole sanctuary as for the more prestigious architecture and sculpture.[29]

The most prestigious building in a sanctuary was of course the temple. These were of different types. The most complex type looked inwards, it incorporated different elements of religious landscape within its walls. The Erechtheion on the Akropolis in Athens (above, Fig. 2.3) included a whole series of altars to various gods and heroes, marks resulting from the contest between Poseidon and Athena, and a shrine with the original wooden cult statue of Athena Polias, which was believed to have fallen from heaven.[30] Similarly the temple of Apollo at Delphi, though more regular in plan, was also replete with sacred objects.[31] In the innermost part of the far end of the temple was the *omphalos* or navel which was believed to mark the centre of the world. A gold statue of Apollo probably stood beside it, another of wood was elsewhere in the temple. Beside it was the tomb of Dionysos, who was another important god at Delphi. Then there were the oracular items: Apollo's sacred laurel and the tripod with its 'oracular chasm' beneath it. Moreover the temple also housed the eternal flame of Hestia and an altar of Poseidon. The temple as a whole articulates the complex pantheon of Delphi.

More commonly temples had a much simpler design.[32] A colonnade surrounds a rectangular room opening east, at the far end of which was a cult statue of the deity. It might be decorated in the pediment and on the architrave with sculpture depicting mythical scenes. The Parthenon, exceptionally, also has a frieze along the wall of the inner building. Being a dwelling place for the deity, it was the principal objective of the temple to house the cult image.

The image of the deity in the 'normal' temple might be of colossal size, of prestigious material, and by a famous craftsman. The statue of Athena Polias in the Parthenon was by Pheidias, the best known craftsman of the fifth century. It was some ten metres tall, adorned with gold and ivory; the gold weighed perhaps forty-four talents, which is more than a metric ton, and the total cost was about 750 talents, roughly

---

[29] For some interesting work on pre-Roman Gaul, see Brunaux 1988.

[30] The Parthenon itself is also abnormal in design (fig. 2.14 no. 4): the two chambers probably each had a cult purpose (the west chamber was called not a 'treasury' but 'parthenon', and the north aisle sheltered a small shrine and a round altar). Fig. 2.2; Korres in Tournikiotis 1994: 56–97; Harris 1995: 2–5.

[31] Plan: Price 1985: fig. 28. Dionysos: Roux 1976: 175–84; West 1983: 150–2.

[32] For plans, see Coulton 1977: 191 fig. 72, and Bruit Zaidman and Schmitt Pantel 1992: 236–8.

equivalent to the yearly income of 12,750 skilled labourers. The chamber in which the statue stood was specially designed to permit views of the statue not only from the front, but from all sides.[33] The image of Asclepius at Sicyon was no doubt smaller, but it too was of gold and ivory, and Pausanias was able to give the name of the fifth-century crafts-man. Such images were very prestigious and excited strong feelings. In the second century AD people would travel to Olympia to see the work of Pheidias, his colossal statue of Zeus, and indeed deemed it a mis-fortune to die without seeing these sights.[34] Also noteworthy were the simpler wooden images, many of which were to be seen in the second century AD Pausanias describes wooden images (*xoana*) at, for example, the sacred grove near Argos or the eight-foot high cypress image of Hermes on a mountain peak in Arcadia (8.17.2). Some of these *xoana* were deemed by Pausanias to be of considerable antiquity, and pres-tige.[35] But even better were the images that had fallen from the sky and were not the work of human hands.[36]

The cult statue in the temple was not supposed to be a literally accu-rate image of the deity. Despite the prestige of Pheidias' statue of Athena Polias, much copied by later sculptors throughout the Greek world, it was felt to be only a conventional representation. So in the early second century AD the orator Dio of Prusa delivered a great speech at Olympia in the sight of Pheidias' statue of Zeus explaining, in accor-dance with Stoic philosophy, how the statue was a representation of Zeus, based in part on his description in the *Iliad* (1.528–30).[37] That par-ticular deities had their normal guises – old man, young woman, etc. – and their own attributes – thunderbolt, trident, etc. – was a matter of convention. The anthropomorphism of Greek cult statues does not mean that the Greeks thought that their gods actually were people.[38]

The point of the cult statues was not to serve as the object of private devotions inside the temple, nor indeed normally of any public ritual. 'Normal' temples were not congregational buildings; rather, the deity, imagined to be temporarily present at festival time, looked out through

---

[33] See Robertson 1975: 311–22; Ridgway in Neils 1992: 131–5; Korres in Tournikiotis 1994: 93. Cf. ML 54 = *IG* I³ 458, trans. Fornara 1983: no. 114. Below, pp. 63–4, on building costs.

[34] The philosopher Epictetos (1.6.23) criticises such folly.

[35] Pausanias' usage of *xoanon* has developed into the misleading modern notion of *xoana* as primi-tive, aniconic, cult statues; cf. Price 1984a: 176; Donohue 1988; Appendix no. 3.

[36] Pausanias 1.26.6 on the Athenian image of Athena Polias, housed in the Erechtheion on the Akropolis; Ridgway in Neils 1992: 120–7. Above, p. 23, on the Ephesian image of Artemis.

[37] Dio, *Oration* 12. Below, pp. 138–9 on Stoicism.

[38] Gordon 1979; Vernant 1983: 328–30. Above, p. 13, on Homer.

the doors of the temple especially opened for the occasion at the ritual happening outside.[39]

Some deities, however, it was not thought proper to honour in this manner. In sanctuaries of Demeter there was generally no 'normal' temple, though there were some buildings. For example, the sanctuary of Demeter and Kore at Corinth was laid out on three terraces, on the lower slope of the hill overlooking the city. The lowest terrace, which was used for dining, had thirty dining rooms, with couches for 200 people; the middle terrace had pits for sacrifice and other offerings, but neither a temple nor a normal altar; the highest terrace had two theatre areas cut into the rocks, with space for 80 to 90 spectators.[40]

The offering of sacrifices normally took place outside the temple on an altar; altars, not temples, were in fact the key element of sanctuaries. At Olympia the altar of Zeus where 100 oxen were sacrificed during the Olympic games consisted of a mound of ashes that accumulated over the centuries. Pausanias reported that in his day it was 6.5 metres high (5.13.8–9). When there was a temple, the standard design of an altar from the seventh century BC onwards was a square or rectangular stone structure placed in front of the temple at the east end where the sacrifice would be performed in sight of the deity.[41] Raised altars and temples formed a single unit. Offerings to chthonic deities, who often lacked a regular temple, took a different form. Sacrifices to heroes often involved low hearths and the burial of objects in pits, as probably for the heroic founder of Megara Hyblaia, and in Demeter sanctuaries such as that at Corinth there were also pits for ritual purposes.

## VOTIVES

Sanctuaries were not just places for the performance of ritual; they were also places where communities and individuals could display their gratitude and piety toward the god. From the earliest to the latest times offerings were made to the gods, though the nature of these offerings changed over time. Some were of marble or bronze, and were thus relatively durable (and familiar); others were of more perishable materials, such as ivory or wood (Fig. 3.3).[42] We have to imagine that sanctuaries

---

[39] For access to temples see Corbett 1970.
[40] Nixon 1995: 77–85. The sanctuary of Demeter Malophoros at Selinus (above, p. 51) had a shrine, but not a full temple.    [41] Cf. Rupp 1983.
[42] For other votives see Figs 2.5–8, 8.2 (terracotta); 2.13 (small bronze); 3.5 (relief), 5.2 (pottery); 1.1 and 5.3 (marble statues). Cf. Appendix nos. 9–10.

Fig. 3.3. Painted wooden plaque, from a cave sanctuary at Pitsà (near Sicyon), 550–500 BC (length c. 0.30m). A family prepares to sacrifice. On the right, a lighted altar. Next to it, a woman carries on her head a *kanoun* (with objects for the sacrifice), and in her left hand a vessel for libations. A boy leads the sacrificial sheep. There follow two other youths, playing a lyre and a double shawm. Three women advance, in time to the music, carrying branches. All the figures are wearing garlands. The four women are named, and were perhaps a mother with her three daughters. They are described as making a dedication to the Nymphs (to whom the cave was sacred).

which to today's visitor seem an empty expanse of open ground were cluttered with votive offerings: sanctuary inscriptions recorded, often in meticulous detail, the proper transfer of the votives from one board of annual magistrates to the next.[43] Sometimes the numbers grew so great that the old ones had to be cleared away to make room for new dedications. Particularly in sanctuaries of Asclepius and other healing gods, special sacred regulations governed the removal and disposal of such objects.[44] Some survive to this day, sometimes because old or damaged offerings were piously buried, others are attested by the inscriptions which survive from their bases, yet more are described by Pausanias. This abundant information on votives makes them important for our understanding of Greek religions.[45]

In the Panhellenic sanctuaries cities from all over the Greek world

[43] Linders 1988.
[44] *LSCG* nos 41–3, 70, *LSCG* Supp. 43, 107, *LSAM* 59 = *Inschriften von Iasos* 220. Cf. Appendix no. 8.
[45] Rouse 1902 remains a good starting point; see briefly Osborne 1987: 185–8. Above, pp. 24, 51, on Locri and Selinus. Neumann 1979; van Straten 1981, 1992; Simon 1986; Linders and Nordquist 1987; Alroth 1989; Morgan 1990: 194–203, 225–33; Jackson 1991; Muller 1996 on the Thesmophorion at Thasos.

made offerings to the gods. After defeating the Persian invasion of
480–479 BC, the Greeks made collective dedications. Pausanias reports
that at Delphi 'the Greeks in common dedicated from the spoils taken at
the battle of Plataia a gold tripod set on a bronze serpent' (10.13.9). By
his day the gold tripod had been removed, but the bronze serpent
column, which was about 5.5 metres high, remained until the early
fourth century AD, when Constantine took it to his new city of
Constantinople (modern Istanbul), where the remains of it stand to this
day. Dedications by communities and individual citizens were often kept
in special buildings or 'treasuries'.[46] At Olympia eleven treasuries stand
in a line overlooking the altar of Zeus and the end of the stadium. At
Delphi treasuries, about thirty in total, mainly flank the Sacred Way that
leads up through the sanctuary to the temple. The Delphic treasuries
were erected by cities from all over the Greek world: mainland Greece
(Corinth, Sicyon, Thebes, Athens), northern Greece (Potidaea), the
Aegean islands (Siphnos), eastern Greece (Knidos), north Africa
(Cyrene) and the west (Syracuse and Massilia). They range in date from
the mid-seventh century through into the mid-fourth century BC. Those
of the archaic period are themselves adorned with sculpted reliefs of the
highest quality. By the time of Pausanias most if not all the treasuries
were empty, the lavish offerings having been removed in the passage of
time by other Greek states and by Romans.

Fortunately for us, the contents of one treasury which seems to have
been damaged by fire were carefully buried under the Sacred Way at
Delphi, to be rediscovered only in 1939. The cache dates mostly to the
seventh and sixth centuries, though there are also some fifth-century
pieces. Gold, silver and ivory were used in great abundance as well as
bronze. The cache included three beautiful anthropomorphic statues,
the flesh in ivory with gold plates for the clothing, perhaps of Apollo, his
mother Leto and his sister Artemis; a life-size bull in gold and silver and
a large number of ivory reliefs of mythological scenes, which once
adorned either the side of a throne or a separate votive, perhaps a
chest.[47] Evidently, an extraordinary amount of wealth went into these
dedications (Fig. 3.4).

At Delphi monuments and objects were also dedicated outside the
treasuries. The Naxians around 560 BC dedicated just below the temple
a marble column about 10 metres high surmounted by a sphinx a further

---

[46] Roux 1984.
[47] Amandry 1939; 1977; Robertson 1975: 140–1. On gifts of gold and silver to sanctuaries see Lewis
     1986; Linders 1987; Harris 1990–1.

Fig. 3.4. Gold and silver statue of bull (on wooden frame), Delphi (sixth century BC) (height 1.45m).

2.3 metres high. The Athenians built not only a treasury, perhaps around 500 BC, but also a monument from the spoils of victory against the Persians at Marathon in 490 BC and a portico from spoils taken during the Peloponnesian war. From the late fourth century BC such monuments replaced the building of treasuries. One commemorated a lion hunt by Alexander the Great, and from the early third century BC victory dedications, by Hellenistic kings and others, took the form of lavish buildings.

In civic sanctuaries dedications were made both by the local community and by individual men and women, both in their own names and as members of families.[48] One of the best known assemblages happens to survive from the Athenian Akropolis. After the sack of the Akropolis by the Persians in 480 BC the damaged dedications were gathered up and carefully buried together. Subsequently votives accumulated again in abundance. One Polemon composed four books about them in the second century BC, and Pausanias also described many dedications. The surviving archaic votives, while not as lavish as the Delphic cache, include some of the finest extant works of archaic Greek sculpture and the picture is filled out by the inscriptions on the votives' bases.[49] The

[48] Van Straten 1992: 274–84 stresses the representation of women in votives as members of families, but the point is also true for men. On dedications by women see Kron 1996: 155–71.
[49] Sculpture: Schrader 1939; Payne and Mackworth-Young 1950. Inscriptions: Raubitschek and Jeffery 1949; *IG* I³ 526–947; some trans. in Rice and Stambaugh 1979: 150–1.

sculpture ranges in date from around 560 BC down to the years immediately preceding the Persian attack.

The most common surviving type of dedication was statues of young women, *korai*. As we have seen, dedications of similar statues of young men (*kouroi*) were common in the Greek world (above p. 4), but no true *kouroi* it seems were dedicated on the Akropolis. Seventy-five *korai* survive, some only in small fragments, dating mainly between 530 and 480 BC. The statues, around life size or less, stood sometimes on bases and sometimes mounted on columns for greater visibility. The women are always shown holding an offering in one or both hands (principally pomegranates and apples). Though these statues have long been studied by art historians, the reasons for their dedication remain uncertain.[50] *Korai* might predominate over other types of sculptural dedication because of the importance of women in the cult of Athena. In general the extant groups of *kouroi/korai* in sanctuaries parallel the gender of the deity: *kouroi* in the sanctuary of Apollo Ptoios in Boeotia, and of Apollo at Didyma; *korai* in the sanctuary of Hera on Samos, though there are some cross-gender dedications. But the statues were not necessarily put up by women. In the two cases on the Akropolis where inscribed statue bases can plausibly be associated with *korai* it was men who dedicated the statues. For example, 'Nearchos the potter (?) dedicated the work from the first fruits (*aparkhe*) to Athena.'[51]

A wide range of dedications was made by non-aristocrats. The inscribed bases record potters and painters (in addition to Nearchos and a relief showing a seated potter), a tanner, an architect, a shipbuilder, a fuller and a washerwoman. The dedicatory inscriptions regularly indicated that the offerings were made 'from the first fruits' or 'from a tithe'. It is unclear if there was a real difference in meaning between the two terms, but in any case they both draw attention to wealth as the source of the dedications. The Akropolis *korai* would thus be signs of the piety of the wealthy (but not necessarily aristocratic) class of archaic Athens.[52]

Another range of sculpture is to be associated with aristocrats. The magnificent statue of a man bearing a calf on his shoulders for sacrifice is surely aristocratic, and the most common representations of men are those of horsemen and charioteers, both free standing and in relief. One surviving horseman wears a wreath of wild celery, the prize in two of the Panhellenic games, at Nemea and at Isthmia. As extant inscribed bases

---

[50] Holloway 1992.    [51] *IG* 1³ 628.
[52] Cf. the assumption of the author of the Hippocratic treatise *Airs, Waters, Places* 22 that the wealthy are more able than the poor to make sacrifices to the god and to set up votive offerings.

show, this group commemorates victories in games, Panhellenic and local, in the most prestigious and expensive of the sports.

Individuals also commemorate themselves in exceptional ways. There is a free-standing sculpture of a man with a writing tablet on his lap (a Treasurer of Athena? or a democratic official?); a relief of a family (mother, father, two boys and a girl) making a sacrifice to Athena. Nor was only marble sculpture dedicated: there were numerous bronze figurines, such as a youth probably holding jumping weights, presumably commemorating an athletic victory, and vases. Some of these were quite modest offerings, a world apart from the lavish marble statues of *korai* or horsemen.[53]

Sanctuaries of Asclepius and other healing gods were much used by individuals in search of healing, who often made personal votive offerings.[54] Many votive objects, of stone and clay, survive from such sanctuaries.[55] In the sanctuary on the south side of the Akropolis of Athens stone reliefs form about a fifth of all the dedications recorded in the (extensive) inscribed inventories; the extant ones often feature Asclepius (Fig. 3.5). The other principal categories of dedication in the sanctuary were of anatomical objects, or of gold or silver coins destined to be melted down to form new cult equipment.[56] Asclepius continued to be popular through into the Roman period, and the sanctuary at Pergamon was one of the most famous (below, pp. 110–12).

EXPENSES

The costs of building and running Greek sanctuaries could be considerable. The only detailed extant figures for the building of a Greek temple relate to the temple of Asclepius at Epidauros 375–370 BC. This cost something over twenty-three talents. Accounts also survive for most of the twenty-five other items, the cult's buildings, the cult statues, the structures in the sanctuary that were constructed in the period 370–250 BC The total expenditure was probably in the region of 250 to 300 talents.[57]

---

[53] Later, in the fifth and fourth centuries, Akropolis temple inventories record dedications by (male) citizens, wives/daughters of citizens, resident (male) foreigners, other (male) foreigners, and women (unspecified): Harris 1995: 223–38.

[54] A visit to such a sanctuary is vividly described by Herodas, *Mimiambi* 4, c. 280–265 BC. Cunningham 1966: 115–17 argues that the sanctuary is *not* specifically that on Kos, but see Sherwin-White 1978: 349–52.    [55] For paintings, see *LIMC* 2.1, 891 (cf. above, fig. 3.3).

[56] Aleshire 1989; 1992; cf. also Rouse 1902: 208–27. Below, fig. 8.2.

[57] Burford 1969. Cf. the contract price of 300 talents for rebuilding the temple of Apollo at Delphi, burnt in 548 BC: Herodotos 2.180; 5.62.2. For contributions to a rebuilding in 360 BC see Tod 2.140, trans. in Harding 1985: no. 60. Introduction: Tomlinson 1976: 49–53.

Fig. 3.5. Votive plaque from sanctuary of Asclepius, probably in Athens (350–300 BC)
(height 0.50m). On the left, Asclepius seated; Hygieia standing, her right hand
resting on a disc on top of a votive pillar. In the centre an altar, to which a slave leads
a bull. On the right a family: the man places on the altar an offering from the basket
carried by a naked servant; then two women, one with a little girl; finally, a servant
carrying a baby.

This figure does not reflect the level of expenditure we can normally
expect from a modest city (for comparison, Athens received circa 400
talents per year as tribute in the mid-fifth century BC). Epidauros being
a Panhellenic sanctuary, some of the money was in this case donated by
other states and individuals. Fifth-century Athens, too, was certainly
atypical, with her resources including her Aegean empire. Extrapolation
has been made from the Epidauros figures to Athenian building projects,
but it is difficult to control the key variables, cost of marble and cost of
transport. In fact the accounts for the Parthenon, Pheidias' cult statue
and the entrance gateway, the Propylaea, suggest that the total there may
have been as high as 2,000 talents.[58]

These and other costs to do with the upkeep of cults were met by
public subscriptions as well as – especially in the Hellenistic and Roman
periods – private individuals. In the case of the fifth-century Athenian
Akropolis building programme, the revenues of the empire were
employed too. Many of the regular expenses, however, were paid for by

[58] ML pp. 164–5. For some accounts see ML 59 and *IG* 1³ 436–51, partially trans. in Fornara 1983:
no. 120. The contribution of allied tribute should not be exaggerated: Kallet-Marx 1989;
Giovannini 1990. See in general Burford 1963; Coulton 1977: 18–23.

the so-called sacred revenues of the gods themselves. During the Athenian empire Athena's income was exceptional, again, in that 'first fruits' (*aparkhai*), one-sixtieth of the regular tribute of the cities, was paid to her; the so-called 'Athenian tribute lists' are in fact massive inscribed records of the quotas, set up on the Akropolis. Like other deities elsewhere, Athena also owned large areas of land which were leased out for profit. It has been guessed that 5 to 10 per cent of all Attica was sacred land of one sort or another.[59] Mass leases of sacred property (houses, fields, orchards etc.) were established in 343–2, and repeated ten years later, one aspect of the regularisation of public finances in this period.[60] A similar picture is implied in the civic decision, probably in the late first century BC, to restore Attic sanctuaries and to lease out their properties.[61] When 'new land', perhaps in the newly restored territory of Oropos on the border between Attica and Boeotia, became available in the 330s BC, it was leased to provide revenues particularly earmarked to meet the costs of the Lesser Panathenaia.[62] In the previous century during the Athenian empire boundary stones of 'Athena ruler of the Athenians' are found in three Greek states (Samos, Kos and Chalcis); they probably mark lands confiscated by the Athenians whose revenues went to Athena. Land sacred to Demeter lay near the border of Attica with Megara, its alleged cultivation by Megarians being one of the pretexts for the outbreak of the Peloponnesian war, and also nearly the cause of Athenian military action in the late 350s.[63]

Although sacred lands existed everywhere in the Greek world, their extent and size would have varied from state to state.[64] In Aristotle's ideal state the revenues of a quarter of the territory were dedicated to cover the expenses of the worship of the gods, while in Hippodamus' ideal state the proportion of the territory devoted to this purpose was as high as a third.[65] In a number of cases the survival of boundary stones helps us to trace the evolution of a particular deity's lands. In the case of Artemis of Ephesos we can actually plot her extensive estates all the way

---

[59] Cf. Lewis 1973: 198–9. See survey of Faraguna 1992: 341–6.

[60] Walbank 1983: 100–35, 177–23; on the reforms of Lycurgus, below, p. 81.

[61] *IG* 2² 1035 = *SEG* 26.121. Cf. Culley 1977.

[62] Above, p. 33. Robert 1960: 189–203 identified the 'New Land' with Oropos; Langdon 1987 identified it with an Aegean island. In democratic Athens festivals were financed partially through 'liturgies', a system of para-taxation falling on the rich: J.K. Davies 1967; 1971: xvii–xxxi; Parker 1996: 128.

[63] Boundary stones: see now Parker 1996: 144–5. Megara: *LSCG* 32, trans. in Harding 1985: no. 78; de Ste. Croix 1972: 254–6.

[64] Debord 1982: 127–80; Ampolo 1992; Isager and Skydsgaard 1992: 181–98.

[65] Aristotle, *Politics* 1330a8–16, 1267b33–7.

up the river valley running east from Ephesos. Artemis' estates included two lakes which afforded the goddess good revenues. Not that they were untouched. Our sources also tell us that the Attalid kings despoiled the goddess of these revenues, that the Romans restored them before the Roman tax-gatherers claimed them again for themselves, but that finally Artemis recovered them when an Ephesian embassy appealed to Rome.[66] Sacred lands were vulnerable not only with respect to central rulers, but also to forces within the communities themselves. A story is told that in the fifth century the Byzantines were so pressed for money that they sold off publicly owned sacred lands, the fertile land for a period, the infertile in perpetuity. They also dealt in a similar manner with the sacred lands belonging to religious associations and phratries (especially when they were sited in the midst of the property of a private individual, who would pay a high price for this land); only in the case of the lands belonging to religious associations and phratries was there any form of compensation.[67]

Sacred revenues derived from various sources were stored in cash in the sanctuaries, at Athens in the Parthenon.[68] The money was, in principle, the deity's, though in the fifth century the Athenians felt able to borrow it for secular purposes so long as they paid interest on it, and in the last decade of the Peloponnesian War golden dedications to Athena were converted into coins. However, theft of sacred property was a capital crime, and the temple-robber might be denied burial.[69] The pillaging of the Delphic sanctuary by the Phocians in 356 BC to pay for mercenaries sent shock waves through the Greek world. It was noted piously that the subsequent war was waged for ten years until the annihilation of those who had divided among themselves the sacred property; the Phocians were then condemned as temple-robbers to pay a huge indemnity to the sanctuary, which they did for some twenty years.[70] Despite occasional pillaging, temple properties survived into late antiquity, when they faced new threats from the rise of Christianity in the fourth and fifth centuries AD.[71]

---

[66] Strabo 14.1.27, 642c; *Inschriften von Ephesos* 7.2.3501–16.

[67] Ps.-Aristotle, *Oeconomica* 2, 1346b13–21.

[68] Tod 1.69 = *IG* I³ 351, trans. in Fornara 1983: no. 141; ML 76 = *IG* I³ 329, trans. in Fornara 1983: no. 143; *IG* 2² 1388, trans. in Harding 1985: no. 10. Harris 1995 analyses (and translates) the inventories. Eleusinian revenues: Cavanaugh 1996: 211–12 (on *IG* I³ 386–7).

[69] Thucydides 2.13.4–5; ML 72 = *IG* I³ 369, trans. in Fornara 1983: no. 134; Linders 1987: 115; cf. Parker 1983: ch. 5.

[70] Diodorus Siculus 16.14.3; Tod 2.172, trans. in Harding 1985: no. 88; contributions to 'Sacred War': Tod 2.160, trans. in Harding 1985: no. 74; Linders 1987: 117; Bousquet 1988.

[71] See below, pp. 164–71.

# CHAPTER 4

# Authority, control and crisis

'Polytheism', in contrast to Christianity or Islam, is often seen as a toler-
ant and open religious system. It is associated with amateur priests, who
lacked authority, and with an absence of dogma, orthodoxy and heresy.
Already having many gods, it is attributed the capacity to accommodate
even more at any time. This romantic view of Greek religious liberalism
has little to commend it. The absence of dogmas did not entail that anything was permitted, nor was the pluralism of gods open-ended. In fact
the terms 'polytheism' and 'monotheism' are unsatisfactory (above,
p. 11), and the issue of tolerance/intolerance is anachronistic. As a
matter of state policy, religious toleration does not predate the eight-
eenth century.[1] The best way forward to understand this issue is to
examine religious authority and responses to religious crisis. The chapter
sets the scene for Greek cities in general, and then concentrates on
Athens, largely because the Athenian evidence best illuminates the
issues.

## RELIGIOUS OFFICIALS

Priests were an essential component of every Greek state.[2] Aristotle's
*Politics*, an analytic study of the fourth-century Greek political community, includes among the necessary offices of the state superintendents of
religion, namely priests and, especially in larger states, a range of
officials concerned with the performance of rites, the upkeep of temples
and religious accounts, and also civic magistrates who were responsible
for religious festivals (1322 b.18–29; cf. 1328 b.11–13). Aristotle's assumption that there was a clear category of 'priests' runs counter to the
suggestion of modern scholars that the category is a Judaeo-Christian

---

[1] Garnsey 1984.
[2] Burkert 1985: 95–8; Jordan 1989; Sourvinou-Inwood 1990: 320–1; Garland 1984 catalogues
Athenian religious officials; Garland 1990b; Kron 1996: 139–55 on female priests.

one which has limited correspondence with Graeco-Roman patterns of thought.[3] *Hiereis* or *hiereiai* may not be Christian priests and do not constitute a unified 'clergy', but equally they are a recognised ancient category with a wide range of functions. Though those appointed as priests did not necessarily serve full-time or life-long, their office might be a privileged aspect of their life.

Both men and women could be priests. The presence of women here is surprising, given that all other public offices were occupied by men. Nevertheless, priesthood was not a field of equal opportunities for men and women. Priesthoods were to some extent homologous to the pantheon, so that priesthoods of female gods such as Demeter, Athena or Artemis were normally held by women, while those of the male gods, Zeus or Hephaistos, were normally held by men; exceptionally the priest of Apollo at Delphi, the Pythia, was always a woman. The corresponding gender was chosen to represent the community in its relations with the particular deity, while divine possession of the Pythia by Apollo was facilitated by her gender.

The function of priests was principally ritual.[4] They might preside over sacrifices, though their presence was not always necessary. Although other officials were responsible for the actual killing and dismemberment of the sacrificial animals, the priests commonly received special parts of the sacrificial animals as the perquisites of their office, normally the skins, which could be sold. More generally, priests were central figures in most festivals. In their special clothing they were prominent in processions and they took part in the main ritual actions. We can see this, for example, in the Parthenon frieze, which represents at the centre of the climactic panel on the east side the priestess receiving a ritual stool from a young girl and the king archon receiving Athena's robe from another girl. Despite their ritual importance, priests are often said to be not professionals, the implication being that they were somehow not very important. This is untenable. Priests were absolutely essential for the proper working of the religious system. Classifying them as 'amateurs' is very misleading. Some priesthoods were limited to members of particular 'lineages' (*gene*).[5] The Eleusinian Mysteries were run both by civic magistrates and by members of two Athenian 'lineages', the Kerykes and the Eumolpidai, and the role of these 'lineages' continues throughout antiquity from the archaic period down to the ending of the Mysteries at the end of the fourth century AD.[6]

---

[3] Beard and North 1990.     [4] Appendix nos. 3, 6.
[5] Feaver 1957 studies the 'lineage' and 'democratic' priesthoods.     [6] Clinton 1974.

Similarly at Pergamon the cult of Asclepius was introduced by one Archias; it subsequently became a civic cult, but the priesthood remained in the 'lineage' of Archias. In the second or third century AD one Flavius Aristomachus was honoured as the priest of Asclepius, twenty-second in line from Archias.[7] Limitation to particular 'lineages' was understood as a traditional privilege, but may have created a degree of specialisation. Admittedly in democratic Athens when new cults were established or old ones reorganised the priesthoods were open to all Athenians appointed by lot.[8] This procedure is parallel to the democratic procedure for appointment to political office and implies that religious and political competence is shared by all citizens. Thus the first female priest of the new fifth-century sanctuary of Athena Nike (which developed a cult going back to the sixth century BC) was appointed by lot 'from all Athenian women'.[9] In some cases (though not necessarily in the case of Athena Nike) priesthoods might be held for long periods or for life. One fifth-century female priest of Hera at Argos actually served for fifty-six and a half years before accidentally burning the temple down and being deposed from office.[10]

Priests were appointed by various means: lot, election, birth or sale. Whatever the mode of appointment or duration of office, they often had to follow particular rules which set them apart from ordinary citizens and made them appropriate intermediaries with the divine. The priest of Athena Polias at Athens could not eat cheese from Attica, for reasons that are unknown, and priests of Poseidon generally abstained from eating fish from Poseidon's realm of the sea. Sexual abstinence was sometimes prescribed, either, for men, immediately before entering the sanctuary or, in the case of women, long term. Some female priests held office only until they reached marriageable age, others remained unmarried and held office for life. One of the most famous of the latter group was the Pythia, who was required to remain a virgin. Male priests who were not expected to be unmarried could prepare themselves for a festival by temporary abstinence but women had to be perpetually pure in order to be open to the divine.[11]

---

[7] Pausanias 2.26.8; *LSAM* 13, trans. Edelstein 1945: I.280–2; Habicht 1969: no. 45; below, pp. 109–12. For other hereditary priesthoods see Horsley 1992: 122–4.

[8] Cf. Isocrates 2.6. On appointment (by lot) see Aleshire 1994.

[9] ML 44 = *IG* I³ 35, trans. Appendix no. 4 (c. 448 BC); *SEG* 12.80 = *IG* I³ 1330 (trans. Appendix no. 5) is the tombstone of the first priest. Cf. Parker 1996: 125–7. On the uses made of the name of this priest in Aristophanes' *Lysistrata* see Lewis 1955; Loraux 1993: 176–83.

[10] Thucydides 2.2.1, 4.133.     [11] For purity rules for worshippers see Appendix no. 6.

Such regulations necessarily marked out the holders of priesthood as distinct from the rest of society. The distinction of priests was echoed and emphasised iconographically. Priests, male and female, were honoured in the Hellenistic and Roman periods in sanctuaries with statues of themselves as priests. For example, in the sanctuary of Athena Polias at Priene on the west coast of Asia Minor were a statue of Niko, a female priest of the fourth century BC, and an early imperial statue of a male priest of Rome and Augustus; there also survives the bust of a young girl, also of the fourth century BC, who may have taken part in the cult of Athena.[12] Tombstones also feature priestly office. For example, classical Attic tombstones show men in distinctive dress holding a knife, and women with a huge key (of a temple): their office was the distinctive feature of their personal identity (Figs. 4.1–2).[13]

Priests were not the only authority within the religious sphere. Complementing their ritual authority were people with particular expertise in interpreting the sacred laws. At Athens special officials (*exegetai*) were appointed for the task, at least from the fourth century BC onwards. They are to us somewhat shadowy figures, but they were presumably important upholders and (re-)interpreters of traditional practices.[14] They could also give advice to individuals especially on problems arising from pollution and murder. Plato presents a paradoxical case in which a son prosecuted his father for murder of a murderer. The original murderer, perhaps a hired agricultural workman, had killed a household slave and then been left tied up in a ditch while the father enquired of one of the official interpreters what should be done. The murderer died before a reply came back from the interpreter.[15] For Plato the story sets off a dialogue about the role of piety. For us the enquiry of the interpreter reveals the possible importance of an official religious expert.

Whereas these *exegetai* were officially appointed, other religious experts of a similar kind were not. According to Plato:

Vagrant priests and diviners (*manteis*) go to the doors of the wealthy and as if they possessed a power provided to them from the gods because of their sacrifices and incantations they persuade the wealthy person that they can remedy

---

[12] *Inschriften von Priene* 160, 222; Carter 1983: 276 no. 86; Price 1984a: 179. Cf. below, pp. 92–3 for other representations of young girls.

[13] Clairmont 1993, men: no. 1.186, 1.250, 2.341b, 2.412a, 3.297–297a, 3.305, 3.320b, 4.781–2; women: no. 1.248, 1.350a, 1.934, 3.390b, 4.358. Cf. further, index 6.147–8. Mantis 1990: 28–65, 82–96, 114–15. Cf. Connelly in Ridgway 1994: 28–31. For an inscribed tombstone see Appendix no. 5.

[14] Jacoby 1949: 8–51; Oliver 1950; Clinton 1974: 89–93. Their early history is obscure: Parker 1996: 49 n. 26. For other officials see Appendix nos. 2, 6, 7.    [15] *Euthyphro* 4 b–d; below, p. 128.

Fig. 4.1. Grave relief from Athens, of an elderly man, 'Simos of the deme Myrrhinous' (c. 400 BC) (height 0.62m). The clothing (a long *chiton* with short sleeves) and the prominent knife are characteristic of male priests.

Fig. 4.2. Grave relief from Kerameikos cemetery, Athens (height 1.01m). A young woman 'Polystrate' carries in her right hand a long key; her left hand may originally have carried a smaller (painted) object. The key marks her as a female priest.

with rejoicings and religious celebrations any injustice which the wealthy man himself or his ancestors may have committed, and if the wealthy man wishes to harm some enemy they say that at little cost they will harm a just man as well as an unjust with some invocations and spells. They do this as they say by persuading the gods to serve them. (*Republic* 2.364 b–c)

Plato's depiction of the priests and diviners is part of an argument about the nature of true justice and virtue (which cannot be bought) and is sharply hostile, but diviners could be prominent and prestigious figures. In the *Anabasis* Xenophon regularly turned to diviners for help in the interpretation of sacrifices, dreams and omens (above, p. 1). They were often itinerant figures who moved from place to place as occasion demanded.[16] In the fifth century a certain Lampon was a prominent Athenian religious expert. He was not only influential as far as measures of a religious character were concerned, but also the first signatory of the peace between Athens and Sparta in 421 BC. When the Athenians decided to reorganise the first fruits given to Eleusis an amendment on various technical matters proposed by Lampon was passed,[17] and he was sufficiently well known to be the butt of jokes in the comic poets.[18] However, he was an exceptional figure and the more normal standing of the diviner is described by Euthyphro, the son prosecuting his father for murder:

> The people laugh at me and say I am an enemy when I say anything in the assembly about divine things and forecast the future to them, and yet there is not one of those things I have foretold that is not true, but they are jealous of all such men as you are [Socrates] and I am. (Plato, *Euthyphro* 3c)

What for the diviner seemed to be jealousy was experienced differently by the members of the assembly. They could prefer detailed arguments over religious expertise, though speakers always appealed to the general benevolence of the gods for the city.[19]

### ORACLES

The consultation of oracles by the state represented an appeal to religious authority of a rather different kind. In the archaic period it seems from the narrative of Herodotos that it was perfectly normal for states to consult oracles, especially the oracle at Delphi, on a wide variety of issues.[20] Indeed the consultations about founding a new city were so standard that Herodotos is not surprised when a Spartan, Dorieus, who omitted to consult Delphi failed the first time and, when he went beyond his oracular brief the second time, lost his life.[21] About the founding of

---

[16] For exceptional Athenian honours for a diviner (in 394–3 BC) see M.J. Osborne 1970, repeated in M.J. Osborne 1981–3; 1.43–5, 2.45–8. Cf. Herodotos 9.33–6. See further on *manteis* Bremmer 1996b. On other mobile skilled workers see McKechnie 1989: 142–77.

[17] ML 73, trans. Fornara 1983: no. 140 (? c. 422 BC).

[18] Cratinus in Athenaeus 8.344E = fr. 62 Kassel–Austin, Eupolis fr. 319 Kassel–Austin; cf. below, pp. 129–30. For another Athenian diviner see *SEG* 16.193.

[19] See Parker 1997 for assumption in oratory of divine benevolence.

[20] Parke 1967 and 1985; Vernant 1974; Price 1985; Parker 1985. On attitudes to oracles see Nock 1942. Cf. Appendix nos. 11–12.

[21] 5.42–5. Sparta had four Pythioi, whom Dorieus bypassed: Herodotos 6.57.

Cyrene by Thera in circa 630 BC Herodotos tells two different and incompatible stories which he has heard in the two cities. Delphi plays a role in each but is especially prominent in the Cyrene version. A century after Herodotos heard this story, the people of Cyrene decided to inscribe what purports to be the original seventh-century document, starting with a reference to the special role of Apollo in instigating the foundation.[22]

The authenticity of such consultations has been doubted, but is supported, for example, by the Athenian consultation in 481 BC about their response to the threat of Persian attack (Herodotos 7.140–4). The Athenian envoys first received a bleak oracle advising the Athenians to flee to the ends of the earth, as other Greek cities had done, rather than capitulate to Persia. The envoys were dismayed at the advice and returned as suppliants to ask Apollo if the future need be so bleak. The Pythia replied that Athena could not prevail upon the will of Zeus but that a wooden wall would ultimately protect the Athenians and divine Salamis would bring death to women's sons. On their return to Athens the envoys reported the oracle to an assembly of the people where a spirited debate occurred as to its meaning. Herodotos' report of this public debate, which should have occurred within his own lifetime, has strong claims to historicity. If the debate and the oracle are rejected as fictitious, we open up serious general problems with our major ancient account of archaic Greece. The debate centred on the interpretation of the text: was the wooden wall a wall round the Akropolis, or ships? If the latter, why was Salamis to be a place of death? The final interpretation, by the Athenian politician Themistocles, claims that the unofficial interpreters of oracles (*khresmologoi*) are wrong to take the deaths to be of Athenians, for Salamis was called 'divine' and he therefore persuaded the Athenians to hope for victory by sea. Rational argument, based on a close reading of the oracular text, carried the day.

Consultations of oracles on major political issues were less common in the classical period. This was not because of a loss of faith in Delphic authority, or in the gods generally, but because of the development of political institutions that could reach political decisions within the state. The Athenians, after 481 BC, did not again consult an oracle on an overtly political matter. The development of democratic debate made that unnecessary.[23] But even the Athenians consulted an oracle, that of

[22] Herodotos 4.150–8. ML 5, trans. Fornara 1983: no. 18 (first half of fourth century).

[23] The consultation in 352 about Megarian cultivation of sacred land (above, p. 65) blended 'political' and 'religious' factors.

Zeus at Dodona, perhaps in 430, and perhaps about how they should respond to the plague devastating Athens.[24] Some states did continue to consult Delphi and other oracles, but they were states where internal debate was less developed. So Sparta consulted Delphi in 432 BC as to whether it would be better or worse for her to go to war with Athens (Thucydides 1.118), and any state could find itself in a real quandary. Should a state on the borders of Macedon make an alliance with Macedon's mighty Philip II? The Chalcidians consulted Delphi.[25] And what was a city to do about the incursion of pirates? In the first century BC the city of Syedra in southern Turkey had to ask Apollo for his advice.[26]

Although by AD 100 Delphi was perhaps a shadow of its former self, oracles did not fade away.[27] Elsewhere in the Greek world they certainly did flourish in the Hellenistic and Roman periods. The oracle of Apollo at Didyma, in the territory of Miletos on the west coast of Asia Minor, continued to issue divine responses until its sack by the Persians in 494 BC. The revival of the oracle and the rebuilding of the temple, on a grand scale, began in the late fourth century BC, and oracles continued to be issued there until the mid-third or even early fourth century AD.[28] One hundred kilometres to the north was the oracle of Clarian Apollo. This too probably went back to the archaic period, but the temple was redesigned in the early Hellenistic period and, in the first century AD, colossal statues of three gods (Apollo seated between his mother Leto and his sister Artemis) were added, and the temple at least was completed in the second century AD by the emperor Hadrian. In the second and third centuries AD delegates came from numerous Greek cities of inland Asia Minor and the west coast of the Black Sea to consult the oracle, some every year, some only at times of public crisis (like the city of Syedra).[29] Consultation of all oracles about matters of religious propriety remained perfectly normal, and it was always possible to argue that an external crisis (plague or brigands) had a religious cause and so could best be solved by asking an oracle which god should be placated. For example, a series of cities asked the oracle of Clarian Apollo how

[24] Cf. below, p. 77 for the recommendation to create an official cult of Bendis.
[25] Tod 2.158, trans. Harding 1985: no. 67.
[26] *SEG* 41.1411, trans. Appendix no. 12. Cf. Robert 1966: 91–100; Parke 1985: 157–9; see Faraone 1992: 74–93 on binding images.
[27] Plutarch, *The Obsolescence of Oracles* (*Moralia* 410E–438E), explained the diminution of Delphic importance in terms of population decline.
[28] Archaeology: Tuchelt 1991. Above, p. 37 on the route between Miletos and Didyma.
[29] Parke 1985; Lane Fox 1986: 168–261.

they should handle the great plague which devastated the Roman empire after AD 165.[30] Oracles remained through antiquity pre-eminent sources of religious authority.

### THE CITY AND RELIGIOUS CHANGE

On the one hand, the observance of religious guidelines impinged on the political life of the community in many ways. Meetings of the Athenian assembly began with the purification of the auditorium by the sacrifice of a pig and the carrying of its body round the auditorium, the reading of a prayer and a curse against speakers who spoke and acted against the interests of the city, and the making of offerings to various gods. The Athenian council probably also opened in a similar fashion.[31] Religious items were privileged in the conduct of assembly business. Sacred matters were taken first at two of the four monthly meetings of the assembly, at any rate after 350 BC, followed by questions concerning heralds and embassies and then questions concerning secular matters.[32] This privileging of religious items was normal in Greek cities. On the other hand, the overall control of the religious life of the community lay with the citizens and their magistrates and political leaders. While the assembly considered religious items that required decision, the council held a watching brief over religious matters as over all other aspects of civic life. The council assisted the treasurers of the gods when necessary and was involved in temple-building and repair. It often provided from its members boards of religious officials (*hieropoioi*) for particular festivals and it heard reports from priests and others on the performance of their religious duties.[33] The role of the state was to co-ordinate the sacred and the human spheres, to ensure that the community flourish.[34]

One of the matters regulated by the assembly was the introduction of new cults.[35] Foreigners living in Athens who wished to establish shrines to their native deities sought the permission of the assembly. In 333 BC Phoenician merchants from Kition on Cyprus gained permission to found a sanctuary of their ancestral deity Astarte/Aphrodite (who had

---

[30] Graf 1992, with trans., on *SEG* 41.981. Cf. Faraone 1992: 54–73 on Apollo's statues as protectors.
[31] Rhodes 1972: 36–7; Hansen 1987: 90–1.
[32] Aeschines 1.23; Aristotle, *Ath. Pol.* 43.6; cf. 30.5. For the particular importance of speeches on 'rites' see a fourth-century rhetorical handbook, probably by Anaximenes, ascribed to Aristotle: *Rhetoric to Alexander* 3.1423a20–1424a8 (trans. Loeb Aristotle vol. 16).
[33] Rhodes 1972: 127–34. Appendix no. 11 for *hieropoioi* elsewhere.
[34] Connor 1988, rejecting the sacred/profane dichotomy.
[35] Garland 1992; Parker 1996: 214–17.

Fig. 4.3. Bendis on an Attic red-figured cup (430–420 BC) (height 0.18m). On the left, Themis with a torch in her right hand, and a *kanoun* (for sacrifices) in her left. On the right, Bendis in exotic Thracian dress carrying two spears, accompanied by a doe. Themis, as the god of order, stands for the recent placing of Bendis among the state cults; her attributes allude to the new festival, with its sacrifice and torch race.

a temple at Kition) on the analogy of the permission given to Egyptians for the sanctuary of Isis.[36] As they were not citizens, they could not own land in Attica, but rather than merely rent land they obtained the special right of land ownership for their sanctuary. In the fifth century similar permission seems to have been granted to Thracians for a sanctuary in the Peiraeus of their native (female) god Bendis, perhaps in accordance with an oracle from Zeus at Dodona. In this case the assembly took a subsequent interest in the cult. On making a second enquiry to Dodona, the assembly was told for reasons that are entirely unclear to placate Bendis. The Athenians negotiated with the Thracians and instituted their cult as a state cult. Payment for the cult was made from at least 429/8 BC by the Treasurers of the Other Gods (that is of the gods other than Athena); at some stage the festival was expanded and the nocturnal torch race at the festival in the Peiraeus became a notable event (Fig. 4.3). Plato's *Republic* opens with Socrates recounting that (in about 410 BC) he went down to the Peiraeus the previous day to pray to Bendis and to see the inauguration of her new festival. He was impressed by the

---

[36] Tod 2 189 = *LSCG* 34, trans. Harding 1985: no. 111. Cf. Parker 1996: 160–1.

procession of Athenian citizens and also that of the Thracians.[37] The establishment of this foreign cult as a civic cult is often condemned as a symptom of religious decay in Athens. In fact the assembly's action was prompted by oracular advice, and the civic adoption of the foreign cult remained almost unique at Athens in the following centuries.[38] Though in practice individual citizens may have introduced new gods without seeking permission, they might be called to account, if their actions were found objectionable (cf. below, p. 85); foreigners, who had to tread more warily, could have merely rented accommodation for their shrines, but in fact sought official permission for them, by asking for permission to buy the necessary land. The introduction of new deities at Athens whether for private or for civic worship was in principle tightly controlled by the Athenian people.

Given that there was a religious setting for public business and that the council and the assembly organised the religious life of the state, it is hardly surprising that political and religious change often went hand in hand. At Athens a religious reorganisation did indeed accompany political change. The reforms of Solon in 594 BC, which are often seen as purely politico-economic, had an important religious dimension. Solon apparently established a scale of rewards for victors in the games at the Isthmia and at Olympia and a scale of values for sacrificial offerings, and the publication of his laws included publication of the sacrificial calendar of the state.[39] This calendar remained intimately connected with Solon's laws. At the end of the fifth century BC political strife between oligarchs and democrats centred on claims to the 'ancestral constitution' which they both wished to (re-)establish. After the overthrow of an oligarchy in 410, the restored democracy created a commission including one Nikomakhos to republish Solon's laws. This complex task was probably unfinished when the democracy was overthrown in 404 by Sparta and another oligarchy established. After the restoration of democracy in 403, the commission was reappointed to republish a revised Solonian code, which was achieved in 399. The whole law code including the sacrificial calendar was inscribed on large marble tablets and displayed in the Portico of the Basileus (Archon) in the Agora.

The republication of the sacrificial calendar was part of a claim by

---

[37] *Republic* 327a. The principal epigraphic evidence (*IG* $1^3$ 136 and $2^2$ 1283) is very difficult to interpret. Cf. Simms 1988; Parker 1996: 170–5. On literary representations see Montepaone 1990.

[38] The cult of Isis seems to have become official, or at least in the hands of the Athenians, by the end of the third century BC: Dow 1937; Dunand 1973: 2.4–17. See further below, pp. 123–5.

[39] Plutarch, *Solon* 23 (though the Isthmian games were by tradition founded only in 582/580). Lysias 30.17–20. Parker 1996: 43–55, 218–20. Above, p. 28, for the calendar.

the restored democracy to legitimacy: traditional sacrifices were an important part of the 'ancestral constitution'. But Nikomakhos was challenged in court, partly on the grounds that he had tampered with the sacrificial code by introducing some new (and expensive) sacrifices and deleting others.[40] The speaker argued firmly for the importance of tradition:

Now our ancestors by sacrificing in accordance with the tablets [of Solon] have handed down to us a city superior in greatness and prosperity to any other in Greece so that it behoves us to perform the same sacrifices as they did if for no other reason than that of the success which has resulted from those rites. (Lysias 30.18)

Nikomakhos and his fellow commissioners did indeed change the sacrificial calendar: the law code published after 403 includes a revised calendar of sacrifices, which was itself revised once. But the speaker's claim that nothing should have been changed was weak. Nikomakhos had the trust of the people, having just been reappointed for a second term, and the remit of the commission permitted a degree of rationalisation: the commissioners were to ensure that the city offered the sacrifices as specified by Solon and also the sacrifices subsequently determined by decrees of the people. Change was thus possible in the name of tradition.

The democratic reforms of Kleisthenes in 507 BC also entailed religious change. Kleisthenes is often seen as a radical who swept away the old, but in fact his strategy was to create new structures parallel to the old. The four ancient Ionic tribes were not abolished in favour of his ten new tribes; they remained in existence for religious purposes, and are duly mentioned in the sacrificial calendar as revised by Nikomakhos. The ancient brotherhoods (phratries) were also not abolished. People given citizenship in the classical period are given the choice of phratry in which to enrol, and the phratries were the basis for the annual celebration of the Apatouria in the phratries' local sanctuaries throughout Attica (below, p. 90). But Kleisthenes also made villages (demes) the basic units of the state and they, as we have seen, proudly celebrated their own cycles of sacrifices.[41]

The development of Athens' empire in the fifth century BC also had religious aspects, though they were not the product of a single reform.[42]

---

[40] Rhodes 1991 on the code; Todd 1996 on Nikomakhos.

[41] Above, pp. 29–30, on demes. Cf. Aristotle, *Politics* 1319b20–8 on Kleisthenes' tactics. Kearns 1985; Parker 1996: 112–21; Sourvinou-Inwood 1990: 316–20 and Parker 1996: 104–8 on religious roles of phratries.    [42] Meiggs 1972: 290–305; Parker 1996: 142–5.

After the transfer of the Delian League's treasury from Delos to Athens in 454 BC, representatives of the allies were expected to bring their tribute to Athens each year at the time of the Great Dionysia, when they could take part in the festival and watch the performance of tragedy and comedy. Every fourth year the allies were also expected to send representatives to Athens, along with a cow and panoply, to take part in the Greater Panathenaia (eight months before the Dionysia).[43] The order to send the cow and panoply which would be paraded in the Panathenaic procession was peculiar. Normally only citizens took part in their city's festivals. The exceptions were colonists, who did not retain citizenship of their mother city but who were expected to continue participating in that city's festivals. Thus an Athenian colony founded in Thrace in the 440s was to send a cow and panoply to the Greater Panathenaia as well as a phallos to the Great Dionysia.[44] The Athenians were therefore exploiting the belief that the Ionian cities who formed the core of the allies had originally been founded from Athens; they extended the participation to other non-Ionian cities and established severe penalties for the breach of an alleged convention.[45]

Athens also exploited the religious value of Eleusis. The Eleusinian Mysteries were unique at Athens: though a civic cult, initiation in them was open to all Greeks, and to Greek-speaking non-Greeks. The Athenians had traditionally offered first fruits of grain to Demeter, goddess of agriculture. Perhaps in the mid-430s BC they decided to extend the scope of the offerings: Athenian allies were ordered to appoint local collectors of grain who would take the first fruits to Eleusis; other Greek cities were invited but not obliged to do likewise. The increased volume of grain presented to Demeter necessitated the building of new storehouses in the sanctuary.[46] The Athenians claimed it was ancestral custom, sanctioned by the Delphic oracle, for other Greek cities to give first fruits to Eleusis; as rulers of an empire, they could insist on observance of the custom by their allies. In the fourth century, with the ending of Athens' centralised empire, Athenians and Athenian citizens living in settlements overseas (cleruchs) continued to send grain to

[43] ML 40.2–8 = *IG* I³ 14, trans. Fornara 1983: no. 71; ML 46.41–3 = *IG* I³ 34, trans. Fornara 1983: no. 98; ML 69.55–8 = *IG* I³ 71, trans. Fornara 1983: no. 136.

[44] ML 49.11–13 = *IG* I³ 46, trans. Fornara 1983: no. 100. Cf. Parker 1994 for the cults of such colonies.

[45] Ionian cities in the fourth to second centuries BC again sent representatives (*theoroi*) to the Panathenaia, by now without Athenian compulsion: Habicht 1991: 329; Parker 1996: 221.

[46] ML 73 = *IG* I³ 78, trans. Fornara 1983: no. 140. Cf. Mylonas 1961: 125–7; Clinton 1987 and Cavanaugh 1996: 73–95 on date; below, pp. 102–7, Fig. 5.4 no. 5.

Eleusis. No obligation was or could be imposed on other states but many Greek states apparently did send first fruits each year. Laggards were chastised by the Delphic oracle.[47]

The reorganisation of Athenian finances at a time of financial crisis in the 330s BC involved considerable reorganisation of the financing of festivals; over a period of twelve years from 338 to 326 BC the politician Lycurgus succeeded in restructuring all aspects of Athenian finances and gradually increasing Athenian revenues.[48] This reorganisation included religious expenditure, and was designed to maintain or even to enhance the celebration of traditional cults. A series of laws allocated specific revenues for specific festivals and was designed to ensure that money was not wasted and that traditional sacrifices could be carried out. One law concerned the regulations for festivals, the money raised by selling the hides of sacrificial victims and the making of the appropriate cult vessels for processions. Oracular approval, presumably that of Delphi, was to be sought for these changes, which involved the melting down of many old offerings.[49] Another law, on the leasing of newly acquired land on the northern border of Attica to provide revenues for the Lesser Panathenaia, entailed a complete revision of both the Lesser and the Greater Panathenaia.[50] Financial concerns were accompanied by and were directed towards general changes in the civic cults.

The guiding spirit behind the whole series of reforms was that of democratic patriotism, a strong sense of attachment to the gods of the land of Attica. As Lycurgus himself said in a speech prosecuting one Leocrates for abandoning the city after its defeat at the hands of Philip of Macedon:

I pray to Athena and the other gods and heroes established in the city and its territory, if I have acted justly in denouncing and bringing to trial Leocrates, who betrayed their temples and images and sanctuaries and the rites and sacrifices laid down by law and handed down by your forefathers, make me today a fit prosecutor of Leocrates' crimes.[51]

Lycurgus' reforms constitute a great period of Athenian religious consolidation and revitalisation, which left as its heritage a system of 'traditional' cults which endured for centuries to come.

---

[47] Isocrates 4.31. The law on the Mysteries was revised at this time: *SEG* 30.61. Cf. Clinton 1994b.
[48] Mitchel 1970: 34–52; Humphreys 1985; Faraguna 1992: 355–80; Parker 1996: 242–55.
[49] *IG* 2² 333 = Schwenk 1985: no. 21, 335–4 BC    [50] Above, p. 33.
[51] Lycurgus, *Against Leocrates* 15 (trans. Loeb, *Minor Attic Orators* 2). See below, p. 95, on the oath of the ephebes.

### RESPONSES TO RELIGIOUS THREATS

The protective concern of the Athenian demos in religious matters comes over very clearly in cases where the religion of the state was allegedly threatened or challenged. Two episodes from the later fifth century illustrate the mechanisms of control and the appeals to popular religious belief: the profanation of the Mysteries and the mutilation of the herms in 415 BC, and responses to Socrates.[52] Both episodes illustrate the scope of the law against impiety (*asebeia*). Though the law, like other Athenian laws, did not offer an extensive definition of impiety but rested on ordinary usage, it applied (as we shall see) both to actions that offended the gods (415 BC) and also to the promulgation of scandalous beliefs concerning the gods (Socrates). That is, both episodes refute the common modern view that democratic Athens was basically liberal and open-minded in relation to deviant actions and opinions.[53]

The affair of 415 BC involved two religious scandals that were separate, though it was believed that the same group of people was involved in both. Establishing what actually happened is not possible; apart from Thucydides' brief narrative, the main evidence is a speech of defence delivered by Andocides in (probably) 400 BC which is, naturally, very tendentious. He was standing trial for alleged breach of a decree of 415 banning him from the Athenians' Agora and sanctuaries. We also have part of a speech for the prosecution (one of the handful of cases in ancient history when arguments on both sides survive). Both speeches are suspect as to matters of fact, but very important in terms of their arguments and assumptions.[54]

One night shortly before the Athenian expedition to Sicily set out, a gang of men mutilated most of the herms in Athens. The herms were plain rectangular shafts with a head of the god Hermes on top and a set of male genitalia half way up (cf. Fig. 2.13). Following customs that went back to the later sixth century BC these herms were dedicated throughout Athens in large numbers outside houses and shrines, and in the Agora in a special Stoa of the Herms.[55] The mutilation of the faces was deeply shocking and an ill omen for the expedition (Fig. 4.4). Thucydides (6.27) and Andocides (1.36) agree that it was also generally taken to have been done as part of a conspiracy designed to overthrow the democracy

---

[52] See generally on impiety Cohen 1991: 203–17; Parker 1996: 162–3; Parker 1983: 144–90 on sacrilege.      [53] See below, pp. 133–4, for Plato's impiety law.
[54] Cf. MacDowell 1962; Dover 1970; Osborne 1985; Murray 1990; Furley 1996.
[55] Thompson and Wycherley 1972: 94–6; Parker 1996: 80–3.

Fig. 4.4. Head of herm found in the Athenian Agora (height 0.23m). It was buried in the late fifth century BC, and may have been one of those mutilated in 415 BC.

and install an oligarchy. The logic of this anxiety, which has worried some scholars, is perfectly clear. The connection of religion and politics was so close that to attack one was automatically to undermine the other.

Andocides in 400 was defending himself against accusations of being involved in the mutilation and of thus having turned informer to save his own skin. He had opposed the mutilation, which took place while he was incapacitated by injury. Only one herm in the city escaped mutilation, that near his house, which the conspirators had expected him to mutilate. Apparently, on his return to Athens from exile in 403, he had instituted proceedings for impiety against someone for mutilating a herm belonging to his own family. This ploy to clear his own name disgusted his prosecutor in 400, who argued that it showed contempt for the gods. Andocides' own speech and that of the prosecution concur in their condemnation of the impious nature of the crime.

The profanation of the Eleusinian Mysteries came to light immediately before the Sicilian expedition set off. It was alleged that Alcibiades and others had celebrated the Mysteries in at least five private houses in the presence of non-initiates. Some scholars assume that the profanation was a parody and exceedingly funny to the participants, but the prosecution of 400 stressed that the rite was performed by the wrong person and that in imitation of the rites sacred things were revealed to the uninitiated (Lysias 6.51). This celebration was even more shocking than the mutilation of the herms and challenged one of Athens' central religious rites. So sensitive was the matter that the assembly in 415 to which news of the profanation was brought was cleared of non-initiates before matters could proceed and Andocides' jury in 400 again consisted only of Eleusinian initiates. Others might inadvertently have learned some of the secrets of the Mysteries.[56]

Those implicated in the scandal, including Andocides, were the subject of an awesome curse by male and female priests.[57] Andocides himself was excluded by a special decree of 415 from the Athenian Agora and sanctuaries. He thus wandered the Greek world for thirteen years until his return in 402. At his trial in 400 Andocides denied that he had acted impiously or had turned informer, especially not on his own father. He also argued that the exile decree of 415 was no longer valid because of subsequent constitutional changes. He stressed his performance of religious functions for the state since his return in 402 and argued that his safe passage over the seas in the years of exile demonstrated that the gods did not seek his death. Conversely, the prosecution argued for the continuing validity of the exile decree, expressed horror at the impious nature of his advising the council on religious matters and the possibility of his being appointed magistrate in charge of the Mysteries, and claimed that he had been preserved from the sea specifically to stand trial in Athens. But the central event which had brought about the trial was Andocides' alleged participation in the Mysteries while still debarred. The prosecution argued for the absolute necessity of punishing impiety: the gods were capable of punishing impiety themselves, but the jury should here act as agents of the gods. Andocides

---

[56] Andocides 1.12, 29, 31.    [57] Lysias 6.51; Plutarch, *Alcibiades* 22.

evaded the issue of his alleged participation in the Mysteries, obfuscated the events of 415 and appealed successfully for leniency. But he entirely agreed with the prosecution that those actually guilty of impiety deserved death (1.30).

Threats to the religious system were not always unreligious *acts*, like the mutilation of the herms; they might also be more conceptual, but no less repugnant to the Athenian people. In the second half of the fifth century BC Athens was the centre towards which thinkers from all over the Greek world gravitated. Their free thinking about the gods and about the world, so exciting to those interested in 'progress', was checked by a series of trials. The evidence for all the fifth-century trials is late and has been rejected in part as mere inferences from jokes in comedy,[58] but it is no weaker than many sources for the fifth century BC and perhaps should not all be dismissed. However, only with Socrates are Athenian responses to these thinkers well attested and clear. The evidence for attitudes to Socrates is principally Aristophanes' comedy, *The Clouds*, first performed unsuccessfully in 423 BC but substantially revised a few years later to meet popular criticism, though not actually staged again.[59] The play, often seen as merely comic, in fact articulates a set of profound objections to the free thinkers. Possible defences of Socrates are found in *Apologies* by Plato and Xenophon. Plato's version, because it is more surprising and less conciliatory than Xenophon's, is likely to be nearer to what Socrates said, but both stand as possible lines of defence against the accusation of impiety.[60]

The actual charge sheet at Socrates' trial in 399 consisted of the following points. Socrates is guilty:

(1a) Of refusing to recognise the gods (*theoi*) recognised by the state;
(1b) Of introducing other new divinities (*daimonia*);
(2) He is also guilty of corrupting the youth. The penalty demanded is death.[61]

The first charge (1a), that Socrates does not recognise the gods of the state is explicitly stated in the *Clouds*. In the play a father, Strepsiades, overwhelmed by the debts run up by his son Pheidippides, urges his son

---

[58] Dover 1975 demonstrates the weak evidential base for the decree of Diopeithes (allegedly c. 432 BC), and for the trials of Anaxagoras, Diagoras, Protagoras and Euripides, against (for example) Dodds 1951: 189–91. For later trials at Athens see Parker 1996: 276–8; below, p. 127.
[59] Dover 1968; Jeffrey Henderson 1993 on revision.
[60] Versnel 1990a: 123–31; Connor 1991: 203–17; Cohen 1991; Parker 1996: 199–217; Burnyeat 1996 stresses the provocativeness of Plato's *Apology*. Hansen 1995 argues for the historicity of both speeches. See also below, p. 128, on Plato's *Euthyphro*.
[61] Diogenes Laertius 2.40; cf. Plato, *Apology* 24B and Xenophon, *Apology* 10.

to learn at Socrates' think tank how to make the Right Argument lose so that he could evade his debts. Pheidippides refuses and Strepsiades himself goes, a comic reversal of the age of Socrates' normal pupils. There he finds an institution devoted to science (including geometry and astronomy), he hears of enquiry into alleged trivia, how far can a flea jump, the sort of research still pilloried by those hostile to universities, and he finds Socrates hanging in a basket to contemplate the sun. Strepsiades immediately takes this to mean that he looks down on the gods, which Socrates confirms: gods like Zeus do not exist, and are not responsible for the workings of nature, like rain or thunder. Later Strepsiades passes on the lesson and reproves his son for believing that Zeus exists.

The defence against these charges differs in Xenophon and Plato. Xenophon simply claims that Socrates was conventionally pious; everyone could have seen him sacrifice at the public festivals and at the state altars. Xenophon's Socrates could thus sanction Xenophon's own religious actions described in the *Anabasis* (above, p. 1). Plato goes deeper into the charge, seeking to distinguish between old prejudices against Socrates articulated long ago by Aristophanes and the arguments of the actual prosecution: standard charges against all philosophers about teaching things up in the clouds and under the earth, having no gods and making the worse appear the better cause are inapplicable to Socrates. He was not interested in science, and it was the philosopher Anaxagoras who claimed that the sun was stone and the moon earth and that they were not therefore gods. Here Socrates accepts the logic of the prosecution, but denies that it happens to be true of himself. He also rejects the idea that he was completely godless (*atheos*). He did recognise the gods, though not in the same way as the prosecution (a surprising admission that charge (1a) was at least half true).[62]

The counterpart of the alleged denial of civic gods (1a), was the introduction of new deities (1b). In the *Clouds* the admission of Strepsiades to the think tank takes the form of initiation into the mysteries. Strepsiades sits on a sacred bed, is crowned with a garland and is sprinkled with a special substance and finally sees a vision of the only true gods, the Clouds, who of course are responsible for rain and thunder. He decides that he will now not pour a libation or sacrifice to any other gods but these. Xenophon and Plato both deny that Socrates had any interest in

[62] Fahr 1969; Yunis 1988: 62–6. For the unconventional nature of Socrates' piety see Vlastos 1991: 157–78.

new gods, but both admit that he had privileged access to the divine through a special voice or divine being (*daimonion*) that spoke to him. Socrates' claim to have his personal divine being, which no doubt underlay the prosecution's argument, was paradoxical. The man who claimed to know least had a hot line to the divine. It was also threatening to the principles of communal life in which access to wisdom and knowledge was supposed to be evenly distributed.

The consequences of the religious charges were supposed to be the corruption of the youth (2). The whole purpose of Strepsiades' education was to enable him not to pay his son's debts. The Clouds are said by Socrates to teach all the sophistical skills of logic and persuasion, and Strepsiades later watches a debate in which the Wrong Argument triumphs over the Right. Strepsiades puts his lesson into practice by forswearing himself by Zeus, Hermes and Poseidon that he owes a creditor any money: after all, he has been taught that Zeus does not send thunderbolts to strike down perjurers.[63] Later, however, Pheidippides turns his own skills in logic on Strepsiades and starts to beat up his father, at which point Strepsiades repents of his rejection of the gods and sets the think tank on fire:

For with what aim did you insult the gods
And pry into the seat of the moon?
Chase them, hit them, pelt them for many reasons
But most because they have wronged the gods. (1506–9)

This act of violence which closes the play may be an alteration to the original version, but it has the same logic as that of the prosecution of 399: the elimination of Socrates from the community.[64]

The moral consequences of Socrates' teaching were a serious issue in 399. Socrates himself had acted honourably during the vicious oligarchy of 404–403, but he had been associated with Critias, one of those oligarchs, and with Alcibiades, the aristocratic playboy implicated in the scandal of 415, who had eventually betrayed his city.[65] Because of an amnesty passed on the restoration of democracy in 403, political accusations against suspected oligarchs could not be brought, but it is wrong to see the actual charges against Socrates merely as a device to circumvent the amnesty. The charges did have their own logic and their own force.

---

[63] The issue of oaths and perjury also recurs in Athenian tragedies: Mikalson 1991: 80–7. For a civic oath see Appendix no. 1.
[64] M. Davies 1990 shows that the ending of *Clouds* does not imply the actual killing of Socrates.
[65] Xenophon, *Memorabilia* 1.2.9–12; Aeschines 1.173.

Xenophon and Plato both deny that Socrates actually corrupted anyone, but Xenophon makes Socrates claim it was sensible for young men to obey him rather than their parents because of his wisdom. Plato offers the defence that he was educating the young, but offers a vignette of the idle sons of the rich picking up his philosophical teaching and undermining the alleged expertise and knowledge of others. Both arguments concur with Aristophanes' horror of perjury: oaths were the foundation of civil society and anyone who undermined their authority deserved to be punished. Impiety necessarily had social implications and had to be punished by the Athenian people. Socrates was found guilty, and though he could presumably have 'escaped' – either by flight or by paying a huge fine – he was put to death.

# CHAPTER 5

# Girls and boys, women and men

Greek religion was certainly not a formality affecting only the public life of the community, but rather it was embedded in all aspects of ancient life. This does not mean, however, that it gave all these aspects an all-embracing religious significance. It is also a mistake to imagine that areas which possess such a significance for Christianity today can be assigned their ancient equivalents. The modern Christian services for birth, marriage and death have no exact ancient equivalent. Furthermore, it is unhelpful to search for 'the religion of the Greek household' as the prime locus of Greek religiosity. Archaeologically, Greek houses had no separate room for a household shrine and rarely had special permanent altars.[1] And the literary evidence, by its silence on this subject, also suggests strongly that the family is not the basic ideological unit of Greek religion. Rather one should see the individual as a basic unit operating within the overall framework of the private and public worship of the gods.[2] This chapter will therefore focus on the individual citizen from birth to death, distinguishing throughout between the rituals appropriate for males and those for females.

## CHILDREN

The birth of a child was not marked by a formal religious service, like modern christenings. Though our evidence is meagre and mainly poor in quality, it seems that (so long as the father had agreed the child should be reared) the five-day-old child was carried around the hearth, the symbolic centre of the house, perhaps by its parents and that five days later a party was held to celebrate the birth. Though a formalised character of the first event can be seen in the fixed term Amphidromia (Running Around), neither event had a firm religious context. However, there was

---

[1] Jameson 1990: 192–4.     [2] Sourvinou-Inwood 1988a, 1990. Cf. above, p. 61, on votives.

an important ritual occasion in the first few years of the child's life. At the annual festival of the Apatouria the father presented his new child or children to the fellow members of his brotherhood (phratry). The sons of citizens were always so presented, daughters were probably sometimes presented but they did not subsequently become full members of the phratry.[3] The Apatouria was a state festival at Athens and in all the Ionian cities of the Aegean and the west coast of Asia Minor,[4] but it was celebrated not by the citizens collectively nor on their behalf by officials, but by all the phratries of the city, each at its own cult centre. It was the first transition in a citizen's life and, as we shall see, also important for the next two transitions.

The important roles of children in particular cults were linked to ritual transitions from one stage of life to the next.[5] I begin with the ritual transitions that helped to transform girls into women. At Athens every fourth year a number of girls aged between five and ten (perhaps mainly nearly ten) was selected, perhaps from each tribe, to serve as 'bears' (*arktoi*) at the sanctuary of Artemis at Brauron on the east coast of Attica (Fig. 5.1).[6] Excavations of the sanctuary have revealed a series of cheap pots of the sixth and fifth centuries BC with scenes representing the girls' procession, race and dance and a series of marble statues of girls, dating to the fourth and third centuries BC (Figs. 5.2–3). The mythical explanation of the ritual was probably that a bear living in the area was killed after she had hurt a girl. Artemis got angry and sent a plague on the Athenians. The Delphic oracle then ordered that Athenian girls should 'play the bear'; the Athenians established the 'bear-ritual' (*arkteia*). There was also a variant version which held that Agamemnon was to have killed his daughter Iphigeneia, in order to get a fair wind to sail to Troy, not at Aulis (as the normal Panhellenic version held) but at Brauron; in place of her he sacrificed a bear (not a deer, as in the usual version), and Iphigeneia's 'tomb' was shown at Brauron. Each of these stories is held to be the explanation of why the *arktoi* served the god Artemis at Brauron.[7]

On the Athenian Akropolis two girls aged between seven and eleven

---

[3] Golden 1985; 1990: 25–9; Lambert 1993: 143–89. Above, p. 79, on the phratry.

[4] The equivalent festival for north west Greeks was the Apellai: Burkert 1985: 255.

[5] Burkert 1985: 98; Garland 1990a: 144–7.

[6] Kahil 1983; Brulé 1987: 179–283; Sourvinou-Inwood 1988b; Kahil 1988; Dowden 1989: 9–47; Lonsdale 1993: 169–93. Fig. 2.14 no. 11 for Artemis Brauronia on the Athenian Akropolis.

[7] There is also another Attic version of the myth, which relates to the cult of Artemis at Mounichia, which should be kept distinct: Brelich 1969: 247–79; in English, Sale 1975; Brulé 1987: 179–86. For a series of pots like those from Brauron see Palaiokrassa 1991.

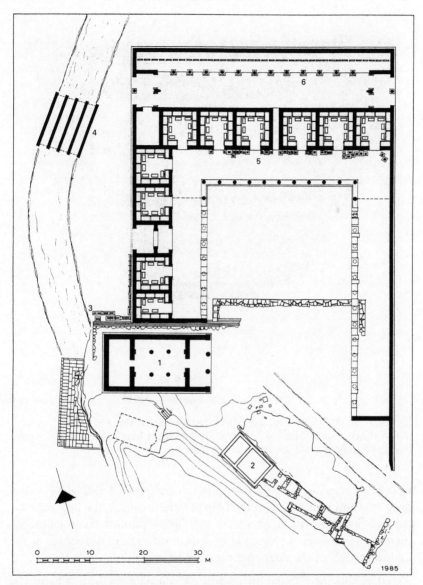

Fig. 5.1. Plan of sanctuary of Artemis, Brauron (fourth century BC). 1. Temple of Artemis, probably with altar in front. 2. The 'old temple'. 3. Sacred spring. 4. Bridge for processions coming from Athens. 5. Building with ten rooms for dining. 6. Portico.

Fig. 5.2. A pot of characteristic shape from the sanctuary at Brauron. It depicts a race of naked girls (or *arktoi*). Pots of this shape (dubbed *krateriskoi* by modern scholars) are found only in Attica, and principally at sanctuaries of Artemis.

were elected to live for a year at a time as *arrhephoroi*, tending the sacred olive tree and weaving, with the help of other women, the new robe for Athena (Fig. 2.14 no. 8; above, p. 33). Proud parents commemorated their daughters' service by making dedications on the Akropolis. At the annual festival of the Arrhephoria the girls (according to Pausanias),

placed on their heads what the priestess of Athena gives them to carry and neither the priestess knows what it is she is giving them nor do the girls who carry it. In the city there is a sacred precinct not far from that of Aphrodite in the Garden and through it there runs a natural underground passage. Here the virgins descend. Down below they leave behind what they have brought and take something else and carry it, veiled as it is. These two virgins are discharged forthwith and others are taken up to the Akropolis in their place. (1.27.3)

Fig. 5.3. Marble statue of a girl (or *arktos*) from the sanctuary at Brauron (350–300 BC) (height 0.77m).

Interpretation of the festival is problematic, but it is clear that the virginal *arrhephoroi* are deployed in a context of impregnation (dew), sexual power (Aphrodite and Eros), and birth (Erichthonios). The word 'arrhephoros' etymologically probably means 'dew carrier', which at first sight does not help. Archaeological evidence reveals that from near the Erechtheion a secret stairway led down off the Akropolis past a small rock-cut shrine of Eros and Aphrodite, near which was the precinct to which they were going (cf. no. 20 on Fig. 2.14). The mythical associations of the *arrhephoroi* are with their starting-point the Erechtheion. Kekrops, the first king of Athens, whose tomb was in the complex (Fig. 2.3, O on plan) had three daughters, Aglauros, Herse and Pandrosos.[8] They were given a closed basket by Athena who forbade them to open it. One night Aglauros and Herse did so and saw Erichthonios, the mysterious child of Hephaistos. Snakes also appeared out of the basket, and in terror the two girls jumped off the Akropolis to their deaths. The sanctuary of Aglauros lies at the foot of the cliff; it may have been this precinct to which the *arrhephoroi* descended.[9] Pandrosos (Alldew), who did not succumb to this fatal curiosity, has a shrine next to the sacred olive tree on the Akropolis itself (Fig. 2.3, P on plan). The myth demands that they be themselves untouched.

At one time scholars believed that there was a normal progression for girls from *arrhephoros* to *arktos* to *kanephoros* (Vessel Bearer) in the Panathenaia and other festivals;[10] a passage of Aristophanes (*Lysistrata* 638–47), the basis for this belief, does put the three in sequence but the ages at which the three positions were held make it difficult for anyone to be able to hold all three, and in any case the fact that there were only two *arrhephoroi* per year immediately shows that Aristophanes is characteristically exploring the limits of what was possible. Some have seen both the *arktoi* and the *arrhephoroi* as 'initiation rituals' for girls before they reach menarche, but the term 'initiation ritual' is too general to be helpful (cf. above, p. 17). We might rather think of the religious symbolism afforded by girls. Both boys and girls could be useful symbols: at sacrifices children with both parents alive were especially important, combining purity with wholeness.[11] But boys were less appropriate symbols of purity because of the expectation that they might be sexually active (and hence impure) even before puberty. In addition, the *arktoi*

---

[8] Parker 1987b: 193–7; Brulé 1987: 79–123. On the route see Pirenne-Delforge 1994: 48–62.

[9] No. 22 on Fig. 2.14 (incorporating correction of Dontas 1983).

[10] On the prominence of *kanephoroi* see Thucydides 6.56.1; images, Figs 2.10, 2.12 and 3.3.

[11] Cf. Appendix no. 3.

and the *arrhephoroi* can be seen to represent the progress of their age cohort towards menarche, the start of nubility, and marriage.[12] Thus at Brauron the dedications, known both from inscribed records and from archaeology, are made exclusively by women, and consist of feminine objects (perfume boxes, jewels, mirrors), and especially implements for spinning and weaving, the archetypal 'women's work', which was of course of major economic importance to the household. More than twenty sorts of clothing appear in the records, including clothing marking both successful birth and the death of the mother in child-birth.[13] The *arktoi* served a god who was probably associated with the experience of women.[14] So girls required ritual transformation to become women, but did not connect with political structures until marriage, and even then only indirectly.

For a boy the next important step after initial presentation to the phratry was becoming a man. When he reached puberty, he was again presented by his father (perhaps at around age sixteen) to the phratry at the Apatouria and a sacrifice performed, at the sanctuary of the specific phratry.[15] In Athens from the fourth century BC onwards a boy also underwent two years' special training with his age cohort of *epheboi* (aged eighteen to twenty), at least if he came from a well-off family. This institution continued the process of socialisation into local religious traditions that began earlier, at the knees of mother and nurses, and at the side of father or grandfather (above, pp. 12, 34). At the outset the ephebes were taken round a series of civic sanctuaries, to instil devotion to the ancestral cults, and swore a special oath to defend their native land.[16] The oath, taken in the sanctuary of Aglauros on the slopes of the Akropolis (above, Fig. 2.14, no. 22), called upon a series of deities begin-ning with Aglauros.[17] According to the politician Lycurgus, under whose guidance a major reorganisation of the ephebic system occurred, this

---

[12] Cole 1984a. The conventional age of marriage for women, fifteen, followed soon after menar-che.

[13] Kahil 1983: 240; Brulé 1987: 226–37, though he wrongly revives the idea that some of the offerings marked a girl's first menstrual period (cf. Linders 1972: 58–9. E.g. *IG* 2² 1514.49 shows that the word at issue (*rakos*) is an adjective, meaning 'damaged'). See C.G. Simon 1986: 198–210, 411–15 on parallels in Ionian cults of Artemis and Hera. On production of cloth see Barber 1991. See Appendix no. 9 for a woman's votive offering to Demeter.    [14] King 1983.

[15] Golden 1990: 26–9; Garland 1990a: 179–87; Lambert 1993: 161–78. Sanctuaries: Hedrick 1991.

[16] Aristotle, *Athenian Constitution* 42.3. At Teos in Asia Minor sacrifices to a Hellenistic king were designed to instil in the ephebes the importance of gratitude: *SEG* 41.1003, Block 2.38–44 (c. 204/3 or 197/6 BC; on the context see Price 1984a: 30–2).

[17] Tod 2.204, trans. Harding 1985: no. 109, a fourth-century inscription. For its traditional charac-ter see Siewert 1977. Above, p. 54, for participation in festivals.

was one of the oaths which bound together the democracy;[18] like other oaths, it had been called into question in the Aristophanic version of Socrates' teaching.

An aetiological myth of the Apatouria talks of a conflict over the borders between Athens and Boeotia.[19] It was to be settled by a single contest between the Boeotian king, Xanthos, 'the fair one', and an Athenian volunteer, Melanthos, 'the black one'. During the combat Melanthos distracted Xanthos by shouting that there was someone else fighting at his side; when Xanthos turned to look, Melanthos killed him and then became the next king of Athens. One aspect of the Apatouria thus commemorates this 'trick', *apate* (though the etymologising may not be correct). According to one modern theory, there is here an inversion of the straight fighting of the heavy-armed warrior or hoplite that the ephebe will become. The hero Melanthos is 'dark' fighting 'light', an outsider hoping for the throne of Athens, who wins by trickery. The inversion of normal codes makes this myth paradigmatic of the life of the ephebes: they were (temporary) marginal figures serving on the frontiers, transitional between the status of children and full adults.

Marriage was important for both women and men, but had a different significance for them. For men, conventionally aged about thirty, it followed their full incorporation into the political community; for girls, conventionally aged about fifteen, it marked their attainment of full adult status. At betrothal the bride's father pledged her to the groom 'for the ploughing of legitimate children', and the dowry was arranged. At the subsequent wedding, there was no marriage service, no one religious ritual which sanctified the occasion. Instead various rituals called on various gods. At Locri in south Italy women dedicated plaques to Persephone when they were married (above, pp. 24–5), on the isle of Kos dining rooms in the sanctuary of Herakles were used for wedding feasts, so long as the god's statue was also invited,[20] and at Athens the parents of a bride made a preliminary sacrifice to Aphrodite Ourania, at her sanctuary on the north slope of the Akropolis.[21] Various mythical models were available: at Locri the role of Persephone as bride; Hera as a wife of Zeus; on fifth-century Athenian vases the bride is depicted as being adorned by other women with the help of Eros and other companions of Aphrodite and some-

---

[18] Lycurgus, *Against Leocrates* 76; above, p. 81.
[19] Vidal-Naquet 1986: 106–28. Lambert 1993: 144–52 shows the problems with this theory.
[20] Sherwin-White 1978: 318 discusses his connection with marriages on Kos.
[21] No. 20 on Fig. 2.14. Deubner 1932: 16; *SEG* 41.182.

times by Aphrodite herself.[22] Both bride and groom would take purificatory baths. At Athens the water was traditionally drawn from a special spring, Enneakrounos (Thucydides 2.15.4). A nocturnal procession marked the transition from one household to the next. Bride and groom went in a cart, flanked by relatives carrying torches, from the bride's to the groom's house. Then the bride was handed over from her mother to her mother-in-law (if they were alive).[23] At the new house bride and groom would go to the hearth for offerings. The bride's incorporation into the new family was marked both by a marriage feast in her new house, and by the special sacrifice and wedding feast offered by her husband to fellow members of his phratry at the Apatouria. She did not thereby become a member of the phratry, but the sacrifice and feast could be taken in a court of law as proof of the legitimate nature of the marriage.[24]

## WOMEN AND MEN

As adults, males and females continued to have different religious roles and experiences. This is clear both at the level of the household and at that of the city. In the household a common cult was of Zeus Ktesios (of Property). A writer on religious antiquities recorded that as special symbols of Zeus Ktesios jars appropriately adorned and filled were kept in the house.[25] The normality of sacrifices to Zeus Ktesios comes over very clearly in a legal oration in which the speaker is prosecuting his stepmother for poisoning his father.[26] Philoneos, a friend of his father's, who had a house in the Peiraeus but who used when necessary to stay with them in Athens, needed to return to the Peiraeus in order to perform a sacrifice to Zeus Ktesios at his house there. The speaker's father, who was about to sail off to Naxos, accompanied him.

After they had had dinner, the two of course set about pouring libations and sprinkling some incense to secure divine favour for themselves, as the one of them was offering sacrifice to Zeus Ktesios and entertaining the other, and his companion was having dinner with a friend and on the point of setting out to sea.

---

[22] Lissarrague 1992: 142–63; Oakley and Sinos 1993: 16–21; Golden 1998. For girls' races at the festival of Hera at Olympia as a 'prenuptial initiation rite' see Serwint 1993.

[23] Nixon 1995: 88–92 on the importance of the mother–daughter relationship.

[24] E.g. Isaeus 3.76, 8.18. Cf. on phratries elsewhere Sourvinou-Inwood 1990: 316–20.

[25] Antikleides (?), *FGH* 140 F 22 (from Athenaeus 11.473B), with Tresp 1914: 44–7 and Cook 1914–40: 2.1054–68.     [26] Antiphon 1.16–20.

But Philoneos' slave mistress put poison in the wine, which she pour for them. After the two men had made the libations, they drank the wir and were killed. It is notable that the only woman present at this hous hold sacrifice, for which Philoneos had travelled specially from Athe down to the Peiraeus, was his slave mistress, who had travelled with hi from Athens. The speaker's step-mother had not made the journey, b the speaker alleged that it was she who had told the slave to put pois in the wine. This domestic cult seems to be one dominated by the m of the household.[27]

Civic festivals also pointed to gender roles. While by convention woman's place was in the home and she was (if of good birth) invisil or anonymous outside it, and a man's place was in the public doma festivals offered roles for both sexes. At the Athenian festival of t Oschophoria, young men dressed as women processed in honour of Dionysos and Ariadne. By the fourth century BC the story went that the ritual had been founded by Theseus, who had disguised two young men among the virgins destined for the Minotaur on Crete, who would help him in slaying the monster, and thus in rescuing Ariadne. 'On their return Theseus and the young men processed through Athens in the same manner as those who now bear vine branches with bunches of grapes' (*oschoi*). Women too took part in the procession, representing the mothers of the girls who were being sent to the Minotaur.[28]

Conversely, the festival of the Thesmophoria, the most widespread Greek festival, was celebrated entirely by women.[29] The undoubted fantasy of Aristophanes' comedy *Women at the Thesmophoria* may evoke the impression that the whole setting is fantastical. But other evidence refers to the peculiar features of the festival. In Attica, the wives of citizens were chosen by fellow women of the deme to represent the deme at the festival in Athens.[30] The women who assembled in Athens at the sanctuary of Demeter, perhaps near the Pnyx where the assembly usually met, constituted a para-assembly;[31] the official (male) assembly almost never met on the days of the Thesmophoria.[32] Inscriptions use

---

[27] Cf. above, p. 34, for another oration in which the male head of the family is responsible for sacrifices to Zeus Ktesios.

[28] Plutarch, *Theseus* 23 (from Demon, late fourth century BC: *FGH* 327 F 6). Cf. Vidal-Naquet 1986: 114–16; Parker 1996: 169, 270.

[29] Cf. Detienne 1989, with Osborne 1993; above, p. 29. Appendix no. 14 for the Thesmophoria as a focus for women.    [30] Isaeus 8.19; cf. 3.80, 6.49–50.

[31] Thompson 1936 locates the sanctuary immediately south of the Pnyx; this remains a possible location, despite Broneer 1942 and Clinton 1996b.

[32] Mikalson 1975: 71–4, 187, 189, with Clinton 1996b: 119n. 29.

the form of male political language for decrees of the women: 'It was decided by the women', rather than 'It was decided by the council and people',[33] and refer to *Archousai*, female equivalents of male magistrates, *Archontes*.[34] This women's festival was located very firmly in the context of the male institutions of the city.

The festival of the Thesmophoria lasted three days. At Athens on the first day the women processed up to the sanctuary near the Pnyx, and performed sacrifices of piglets in the pits of Demeter and Kore; we have already noted these pits in some Demeter sanctuaries,[35] and the swallowing up of the piglets was supposed to correspond to the loss of the pigs of the mythical swineherd Eubouleus when Kore disappears into the earth. On the second day, the women fasted, sitting on the ground on a plant (vitex) believed to affect menstruation among other things;[36] like Demeter after the rape of Kore, the women grieved, wearing no garlands. On day three, the women celebrated Kalligeneia, the goddess of Good Birth, with sacrifices and feasting. The women here break the usual rules prohibiting them from performing animal sacrifices; a cautionary tale in Pausanias (4.17.1) reveals the threat that lurked behind this reversal: one Aristomenes of Messenia in the Peloponnese and his men, on entering a sanctuary of Demeter knowing that the women were celebrating the festival there, were assaulted and wounded by the women with their sacrificial knives and spits used for roasting the sacrificial meat; Aristomenes was hit by their torches and captured.

The festival's symbolism centres on the notions of fertility. There are hints of agrarian fertility: it was said that the rotted remains of the piglets sacrificed on day one guaranteed a good harvest, but the principal fertility at stake was human. The piglets, the products of multiple birth, could stand for fecundity in general, the mourning of the women was for the loss of Kore; the vitex could correct hormonal imbalance, and hence make the women fertile once more.[37] Obscene speech and actions were characteristic of the festival and the celebration on day three was surely of human Good Birth. The festival may have been read differently by women and men.[38] For women, the plant symbolism suggested the possibility of (female) control of human fertility. For men the emphasis was on human fertility, the reproduction of citizens, for the

---

[33] *LSAM* 61.5 = *Inschriften von Mylasa* 303. Mylasa, fourth century BC.
[34] *IG* 2² 1184 = *LSCG Supp.* 124.3, Athens, fourth century BC (trans. Appendix no. 2).
[35] Above, p. 58; cf. Burkert 1985: 242–3.     [36] Nixon 1995: 87–8.
[37] On pennyroyal, see below, p. 106. See now Lowe 1998, who discusses and translates the key texts.
[38] Nixon 1995.

benefit of the state. On this view, the festival asserted the importance of the wives of citizens for the continuity and prosperity of the community, and supported the belief that Demeter Thesmophoros was the bringer of order and civilisation. Women, excluded from the political structures of the state, were nonetheless, in this para-political context, seen as central.

### DEATH AND BURIAL

The ending of life is another time at which we expect to find a religious ceremony, and the expression of hope about the afterlife. In general neither occurred. Of course, funerals took place according to customary rites: the corpse was laid out by the next of kin, lamented over by the women, carried in procession to the grave for either cremation or inhumation.[39] There several formalised duties awaited the son of the deceased; their proper performance or non-performance mattered in the public estimation: it was held against the claimant to a man's estate that 'he neither took up the body of his [allegedly] adoptive father, nor committed it to the flames, nor collected the bones, but left all these duties to be done by complete strangers' (Isaeus 4.19). Conversely, the claimant to another estate argued that 'I buried him in a manner befitting both him and myself, and I erected a fine monument to him, and celebrated the commemorative ceremony on the ninth day and the other funerary rites in the best possible manner, to the acclamation of all the demesmen' (Isaeus 2.36).[40]

The types of funeral monument erected over graves varied at different periods.[41] In the sixth century BC, *kouroi* or (occasionally) *korai* sometimes stood there[42] and there were often large gravestones with carved decoration, but at Athens in the later sixth century there was a ban on extravagant tombs as part of a continuing curb on aristocratic display. Lavish gravestones reappear in the 420s, only to be banned again in the later fourth century. They depict both men and women, though in rather different ways. Women are often shown seated, beside household objects. Younger men appear as athletes or warriors, while older men (like women) are seated; the men generally are associated with life

---

[39] Cf. Appendix no. 6.
[40] For religious sanctions against excessive mourning see Appendix no. 14.
[41] Monuments and imagery: Kurtz and Boardman 1971; Garland 1985: 104–20; Shapiro 1991; Lissarrague 1992: 163–70; Morris 1992: 128–55.
[42] Above, p. 62, for these statues in sanctuaries.

outside the home. After the burial, rites were performed annually at the grave: chthonic sacrifices and libations were offered by the next of kin (Isaeus 6.65). Subsequently, women and children went in mourning to decorate the graves. A specific type of vase, the oil vessels (*lekythoi*) painted with a white background, which is the most common offering at classical Athenian burials, has two main subjects, a woman and servant at home preparing to visit the tomb, and the actual visit to the tomb. In all these customary rites there is nothing linking the gods with the dead, and no hope about the afterlife. Grief was depicted at the annual visit to the grave, the sacrifices were chthonic,[43] and the souls of the dead were generally believed to have been taken down to the underworld by Hermes, where they had some shadowy and unpleasant existence with Hades and Persephone. Death did not mean complete oblivion for the individual, but the conventional notions of the afterlife offered little comfort for the dying or the bereaved.[44]

CURSES

This lack of belief in a pleasant afterlife accounts for the use of lead curse tablets. Over 300 from Attica and another 800 from the rest of the Greek world have come to light, dating from the early fifth century BC onwards.[45] They were placed in chthonic sanctuaries, in underground sources of water and in graves, all locations which offered contact with the powers under the earth; in the case of graves there may have been a preference for the graves of the untimely dead, whose unsettled souls might more readily carry the message down to the underworld. The curse tablets sought action from the chthonic powers (especially Hecate and Hermes) on a wide range of issues: legal and political disputes, commercial rivalry, and sexual matters (for example, attracting a lover or cursing rivals). A nice example is a fourth-century BC spell cast by a man worried about the outcome of a lawsuit with one Pherenicus. The original location of the tablet is not known, but its outside was inscribed to Hermes Chthonios and Hecate Chthonia. Inside is the following message:

Let Pherenicus be bound before Hermes Chthonios and Hecate Chthonia. And I bind before Hermes Chthonios and Hecate Chthonia Galene [the name of a prostitute], who associated with Pherenicus. And just as the lead is held in no

---

[43] Above, p. 12, on 'chthonic'.     [44] Burkert 1985: 194–9.
[45] Faraone 1991; Gager 1992; Habicht 1993; Graf 1994.

esteem and is cold, so may Pherenicus and his things be held in no esteem and be cold, and so for the things which Pherenicus' collaborators say and plot concerning me.

Let Thersilochus, Oenophilos, Philotios and any other legal advocate of Pherenicus be bound before Hermes Chthonios and Hecate Chthonia. And I bind the soul and mind and tongue and plans of Pherenicus, whatever he does and plots concerning me, let all things be contrary for him and for those who plot and act with him.[46]

The employment of such curse tablets was not an index of the breakdown of classical rationality: the earliest examples, from Sicily, Olbia in the Crimea and Attica, date to the fifth century BC. Nor are they to be assigned to the 'superstitious' lower orders: fourth-century Attic curse tablets, for judicial and other purposes, mention the names of famous orators and politicians (including Demosthenes and Lycurgus); one even curses the Macedonian king (Cassander) and members of his family and entourage that occupied Athens at the end of the fourth century. Indeed the distinction between 'magical' curses and 'religious' rituals implied in many modern evaluations of the curse tablets is very problematic: the curse tablets simply employed forceful language to urge chthonic gods to act against one's enemies.[47]

### THE ELEUSINIAN MYSTERIES

The Eleusinian Mysteries, however, suggest that the bleak view of the afterlife implied in funerary rituals was accompanied by an alternative, for those initiated there.[48] The Mysteries were open to all, women and men, slave and free, Athenians and other Greeks. That is, unlike normal festivals, at which men and women had different roles, or which were limited to just one gender, the Eleusinian Mysteries did not discriminate by gender, freedom or nationality: the only formal rule was that candidates for initiation should be pure and not of unintelligible speech.[49] Women seem to have been initiated on the same basis as men, though we cannot tell in what numbers.[50]

---

[46] *IG* 3 Appendix 107; Gager 1992: no. 40, from Attica.

[47] For problems with the modern category 'magic' see, for example, Segal 1981.

[48] Mylonas 1961; Burkert 1985: 285–90; Clinton 1993. Cf. Sourvinou-Inwood 1997a for crucial developments in the sixth century BC.

[49] I.e. murderers and non-Greek-speaking barbarians were excluded. Under Roman rule, Romans were not classified as 'barbarians', and they, including Augustus and other emperors, were initiated.

[50] *IG* I³ 6 c 20–3 (trans. Fornara 1983: no. 75) ordains a slightly lower fee for women than for men.

The Mysteries were an item in the official Athenian calendar, celebrated annually in the autumn (Boedromion). Athenian officials were in charge and a grand procession from Athens to Eleusis linked the two (above, pp. 53–4). When in 480 BC the Athenians evacuated Attica in the face of the Persian invasion, the festival could not be celebrated, but an Athenian exile with the Persians, it was said, saw a cloud of dust raised as if by the feet of thirty thousand people, and heard a cry like that sung on the way to Eleusis. The exile, tellingly called Dikaios, 'Just', explained that this must be a miraculous enactment of the festival: 'It is kept each year by the Athenians in honour of the mother [Demeter] and daughter [Kore], and whatever Greek wishes, whether Athenian or not, is there initiated; and the cry which you hear is the "Iacchus" which is uttered at this festival.' The dramatic event was taken as a sign of divine favour for the Athenians in their struggles versus the Persians (Herodotos 8.65). In normal circumstances the Athenians declared a truce for all seeking initiation, for the initiates returning to Eleusis (*epoptai*) and the attendants and possessions of all strangers and Athenians, that is, the truce applied both to Athenians and to all other cities that made use of the sanctuary.[51] The sanctuary, though under Athenian control, was of Panhellenic standing.

The sanctuary itself was heavily fortified, perhaps at the end of the sixth century BC, because of its location on the western edge of Athenian territory and the need to protect the town there; the walls were rebuilt in the mid-fifth century and extended in the fourth century BC. The principal building, the *telesterion*, was quite unlike ordinary temples, which were designed to hold cult images and which faced the ritual on the altar outside at the front (above, pp. 56–8). It by contrast was a large, almost square building, with an unimpressive exterior. It increased in size from the sixth century BC onwards: the early-sixth-century building was 19 by 14 metres; the later-sixth-century one 30 by 27 metres; the preparation for rebuilding on twice the scale (49 by 27 metres) began 490–480 BC, but the project was interrupted by the Persian sack of the sanctuary in 480; however, in the 430s it was almost doubled in size again to a square with sides circa 51 metres long internally (Fig. 5.4).[52] This was the largest

---

Aristophanes, *Frogs* 409–12; pseudo-Demosthenes 59.135 (*Against Neaira*); Aelius Aristides, *Eleusinian Oration* 22.3 (Keil).

[51] *IG* I³ 6, trans. Fornara 1983: no. 75 (before 460 BC); cf. above, p. 80, for Athens' imperialist extension of the rules for the giving of first fruits to Eleusis.

[52] Shear 1982; Clinton 1987. The restoration in Roman times increased its length by some two metres. In the fourth century it was surpassed in size by the Assembly Hall at Megalopolis in the Peloponnese.

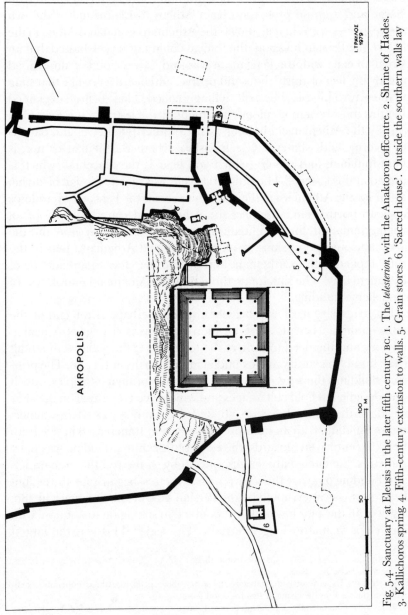

Fig. 5.4. Sanctuary at Eleusis in the later fifth century BC. 1. The *telesterion*, with the Anaktoron off-centre. 2. Shrine of Hades. 3. Kallichoros spring. 4. Fifth-century extension to walls. 5. Grain stores. 6. 'Sacred house'. Outside the southern walls lay a stadium.

roofed building of its period. A series of columns was necessary to support the roof, and around the sides were banks of seats. This was a congregational building where the initiates assembled.[53]

The ritual that occurred inside the building is largely concealed from us by the fact that the initiates did not break their vows of secrecy. When Pausanias was set to describe the architecture of the Eleusinion at Athens, he was warned off in a dream (1.14.3), and for the same reason he gives no description of the things within the walls of the sanctuary at Eleusis.[54] Archaeologically it is clear that a rectangular room inside the *telesterion*, the Anaktoron, was of fundamental importance: the successive rebuildings of the sanctuary preserved its size and location. Within it was preserved an outcrop of bedrock, perhaps to commemorate a spot in the myth of Demeter and Kore. The hierophant, a Eumolpid, who was in charge of the mysteries, sat on a throne beside the entrance to the Anaktoron and he alone could enter the room where the sacred objects were preserved. Those seeking initiation purified themselves, performed the necessary sacrifices and were presented one by one (heavy fines were imposed on the officials if people were initiated together).[55] In the darkness of the building, illuminated by torches, the initiate was shown the sacred objects. Only Christian writers of the third century revealed what they were and their 'testimony' is highly tendentious. One extended claim is as follows:

The Athenians, when they conduct Eleusinian mysteries, reveal in silence to the initiates the great, wonderful, most perfect initial mystery, an ear of grain. This ear of grain is, for the Athenians, the great initiatory light-bringer from that which is unformed, just as the hierophant himself, not castrated like Attis, but made impotent with hemlock and detached from his whole material being, at night in Eleusis celebrating the great and unspeakable mysteries with much fire, cries aloud and says: 'The lady Brimo has brought forth a holy son, Brimos.'[56]

But even this account leaves us with more questions than answers.

The significance of the ritual is complex and elusive. The sanctuary itself was at the place where Persephone had been seized by Hades; a cave of Hades just inside the entrance symbolised the entrance to the underworld, and at its mouth was the Mirthless Rock on which Demeter sat weeping when she was searching for Persephone.[57] The *Homeric Hymn*

---

[53] Compare the Samothracian building modelled on Eleusis, below, p. 112.

[54] 1.38.7. For iconography on vases relating to Eleusis cf. Bérard 1989: 114–20.

[55] *IG* i³ 6 c. 26–30, trans. Fornara 1983: no. 75 (before 460 BC).

[56] Hippolytos, *Refutation of All Heresies* 5.8.39–40 (trans. F. Legge, London 1921). This quotation comes from a long section of Hippolytos taken over from a Gnostic 'Naassene' Christian treatise: Frickel 1984; below, p. 161.      [57] Clinton 1992: 14–27.

*to Demeter* set both the seizure and Demeter's subsequent mourning at Eleusis, but the hymn is a Panhellenic document, not a sacred text of the Mysteries themselves, and should not be pressed too hard for answers about the Mysteries (above, pp. 18–19). Demeter was obviously central to the Mysteries as she was to the Thesmophoria, both peculiar but also mainstream Greek festivals. In the case of the Thesmophoria women alone were involved, and the festival may have had different meanings for women and men. In the Eleusinian Mysteries, because women were initiated alongside men, a specifically female reading is likely to be less apparent. Fertility was an important component of the festival, but it seems to have been primarily agricultural and not human: Demeter had caused the plants to die while she mourned her daughter, and the Athenians claimed that she had subsequently taught them how to cultivate grain. In commemoration of this they offered her the first fruits of the grain and the initiate was shown the ear of grain. The birth of the mysterious Brimos proclaimed by the hierophant may also be related. He was taken by some to be Ploutos, Wealth, the son of Demeter, a symbol of her productivity. Female fertility, however, seems also to have been an issue. Initiates drank as part of the preliminary ritual a special drink, the *kukeon*, as Demeter herself had once done. The *kukeon* includes pennyroyal, a plant that was known to be effective in preventing or ending pregnancy. And other aspects of the myth told in the *Homeric Hymn to Demeter* concern both the rearing of children and the strong ties between mother and daughter. As in the Thesmophoria, these may be hints of a different (female) reading of the festival.[58]

In addition the initiates gained hope of blessing in this life and the underworld. As the *Homeric Hymn to Demeter* says:

Blessed is the earth-bound mortal who has beheld these things, but the uninitiate who is without a share in these rites has no claim ever on such blessings, even when departed to the utter darkness. (480–2)

And earlier the Hymn described how the mourning Demeter had nursed a child at Eleusis with ambrosia and had at night hidden him like a log in the fire: she would have made him immortal had not the proceedings been interrupted. As it was, she gave him everlasting honour (212–74). Writers of the classical period also insisted on the blessings that came from the mysteries. According to the fourth-century Athenian writer Isocrates, Demeter gave twin gifts to the Athenians: the grain which allowed them to live a life distinct from the animals (agriculture

---

[58] *Kukeon: Homeric Hymn to Demeter* 208–10. Nixon 1995.

being seen as the foundation of civilisation); and 'the initiation which gave its participants pleasant hopes about the consummation of life and eternity'.[59] But despite this claim for the Mysteries, the future of the initiate was merely an amelioration of conditions in Hades, not 'immortality' in the Christian sense, and the funeral epitaphs of Athenians did not allude to any such hopes.[60]

---

[59] *Panegyric* 28; cf. Aristophanes, *Frogs* 448–59. Aelius Aristides, *Panathenaic Oration* 339–41 made a similar point in the second century AD. See Dover 1974: 261–8.

[60] For expressions of some hopes, especially for the pious, on tombstones mainly from outside Attica and of post-classical date see Lattimore 1942: 48–54.

CHAPTER 6

## Elective cults

Religious involvement of women and men at various stages during the life cycle generally resulted not from individual choices but from social expectations. For example, ephebes had certain religious functions prescribed for them by the assembly, and at marriages brides and grooms (and their families) performed fixed traditional rituals. Households were expected to have their cults of Zeus Ktesios. Participation by individuals in the regular cycle of civic festivals was also a matter of social expectation. Citizens were supposed to be present at the major festivals; women were appointed to perform the Thesmophoria.

Choices, however, did also exist within the framework of civic cults. Parents must have chosen to put forward their children to serve in particular cults. Individuals also chose to make dedications in civic sanctuaries, or to consult oracles. And women and men could decide to seek initiation at the Eleusinian Mysteries. Such choices may have been the result of greater or lesser levels of interest in the cults of one's own or other cities. Some no doubt had a fairly distant relationship to ordinary cults, like the bad-tempered man in Menander's play who (according to the prologue, spoken by Pan) has never opened a conversation with anyone. 'Except that, being my neighbour, he will speak in passing to me, Pan, because he's obliged to; but I'm sure that a moment later he wishes he hadn't.'[1] At the other extreme some individuals had a particularly close relationship to the cults of their own or other cities. Some people received visions from the gods in their dreams, and made dedications in their sanctuaries. For example, on the island of Patmos in the eastern Aegean 'Zois made a dedication to Artemis of Patmos in accordance with her dreams.'[2] Others, like Lampon in classical Athens (above, p. 73), were self-proclaimed religious experts. At a higher level, Hellenistic kings

[1] *Dyscolus* 11–13.
[2] *Syll.*³ 1152. This type of dream was important: Artemidorus, *Dream Book* 2.33–9; Price 1986: 19–20.

expressed their favour for and solicited the support of Greek cities by expressing their support of the sanctuaries of those cities.[3]

One personal choice stands out here: in case of illness, many Greeks turned to a sanctuary of Asclepius where they sought guidance in dreams by spending the night in the sanctuary. As there were other ways of obtaining diagnoses and cures (self-help, independent doctors), people must have had particular reasons for turning to Asclepius. The cult of Asclepius, a development of the fifth century, became very wide-spread in mainland Greece. The most prestigious sanctuary was at Epidauros, where the cult is first found about 500 BC and whose build-ings were transformed in the fourth century (above, pp. 63–4), but other major centres were at Kos and, in the imperial period, at Pergamon in north west Asia Minor. The cult was brought from Epidauros to Athens in 420 BC on the initiative of an Athenian citizen, Telemachos.[4] The cult was installed, perhaps after some initial opposition from the priestly lineage (*genos*) of the Kerykes, on the south slope of the Akropolis (above, Fig. 2.14 no. 29).[5]

The sick person would pray to the god, promising to make a gift to the deity when cured. If all went well, the god would appear to the sick person in a dream and miraculously cure the disease or suggest how it could be cured.[6] The records of the Athenian Asclepieion include details of such successful cures: for example, a temple warden put up an inscrip-tion detailing his problem of walking to the sanctuary, his prayer for a cure, and his gratitude: 'thrice blest Paean Asclepius, by your skill Diophantos was cured from his painful incurable ailment. No longer does he appear crab-footed, nor as if walking on sharp thorns, but sound of foot just as you promised.'[7] To judge by the dedications made in the sanctuary, men and women were equally likely to turn for help to Asclepius; those making dedications also came from a wide social range of the citizen body.[8] Athenians and others sometimes travelled to the

---

[3] E.g. *Syll.*[3] 672, trans. Austin 1981: no. 206 (Delphi); *Didyma* 2 (1958) 493, trans. Austin 1981: no. 186 (Miletos and Didyma); Samothrace, Fig. 6.2.

[4] Late sources and the iconography of a contemporary monument combine to make it likely that the tragedian Sophocles was the temporary host of the god, and was heroised after death as Dexion, 'Receiver': van Straten 1995: 70–1; Parker 1996: 184–5.

[5] Aleshire 1989: 7–36; Garland 1992: 116–35; Clinton 1994a; Parker 1996: 175–85, who argues, on weak grounds, that Telemachos was a citizen of Epidauros. There was another sanctuary of Asclepius in the Peiraeus.

[6] Burlesque account of procedure at one of the Athenian sanctuaries (? in the Peiraeus) in Aristophanes, *Wealth* 619–770 (Aleshire 1989: 13 on location).

[7] *IG* 2[2] 4514, mid second century AD, trans. Edelstein 1945: 1.242.

[8] Aleshire 1989: 45–6, and 1992; above, p. 63, on such dedications.

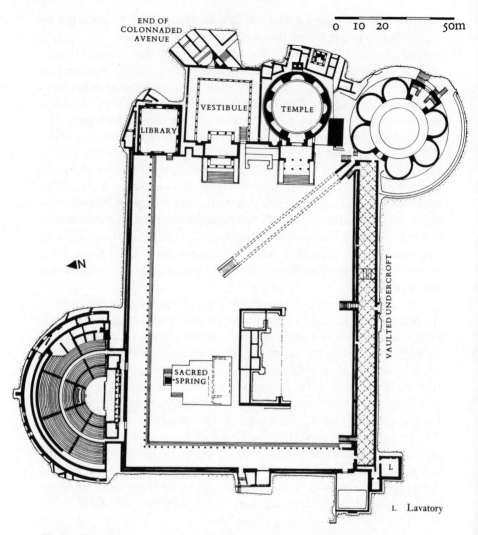

END OF COLONNADED AVENUE

VESTIBULE

TEMPLE

LIBRARY

N

VAULTED UNDERCROFT

SACRED SPRING

L

L Lavatory

Fig. 6.1. Plan of sanctuary of Asclepius, Pergamon, c. AD 140–175.

major sanctuary at Epidauros. Inscriptions of the second half of the fourth century BC collected a long sequence of successful cures; they were part of the promotion of the sanctuary to Panhellenic importance.[9]

The most vivid picture of a healing sanctuary can be given for the sanctuary of Asclepius at Pergamon (Fig. 6.1).[10] The sanctuary, founded

[9] *IG* 4² 121, 33–41, trans. Edelstein 1945: 1.221–37; Li Donnici 1995.
[10] Habicht 1969: 1–20; Radt 1988: 250–71.

in the first half of the fourth century BC as a private sanctuary, received official standing in the late third century BC and went through numerous building phases, but was substantially rebuilt in the early second century AD. It was so spectacular that it features in one of the ancient lists of wonders of the world. The second century AD phase includes a round temple of Zeus Asclepius modelled on a contemporary temple at Rome (the Pantheon), a library, a theatre seating 3,500, and a two-storey round building connected with the precinct by an underground passage. In the courtyard was the old temple of Asclepius and a building where those seeking cures slept. The complex is brought to life for us by the diary kept by Aelius Aristides on the instruction of Asclepius in a dream in the mid-second century AD.[11] Aristides, who had been in poor health for some time, records that he was summoned by the god to Pergamon, where he spent the next two years (AD 145–147). He lived with a temple warden, Asclepiacus, seeking cures from the god in dreams, at first in the sanctuary and then in Asclepiacus' house. For example, one night Asclepius appeared in a dream offering a cure for an ear-ache:

He said that there was a royal ointment. It was necessary to get it from the woman. And somehow after this, there appeared a servant of the imperial palace [in Pergamon], clad in white and girdled, at the temple and the statue of Telesphorus, and summoned by a herald, he went out by the doors where the statue of Artemis is, and bore the remainder of the ointment to the emperor. This more or less was the dream, at least in its outlines. When I entered the sanctuary and was walking about in the direction of the statue of Telesphorus, the temple warden Asclepiacus came up to me and, while he happened to stand by the statue, I told him the vision which I had, and I asked him what the ointment was or who should use it, but when he had listened and marvelled, as usual, he said, 'The search is not long, nor need there be much travelling, but I shall bring it to you from right here, for it lies by the feet of Hygieia, since Tuche herself has just put it there, as soon as the temple was open.' Tuche was one of the noble ladies. And, going to the temple of Hygieia, he brought the ointment and I anointed myself where I happened to stand. The ointment had a wonderful smell, and its power was immediately manifest, for faster than I have said it, the pressure [in my ear] relaxed.[12]

As a result of these and similar cures by the god, Aristides recovered his skill at oratory and made, at various times, speeches in the theatre at the sanctuary in honour of Asclepius and in praise of the sanctuary (*Orations*

[11] Behr 1968; cf. Remus 1996 on Aristides' contacts at the sanctuary.
[12] *Sacred Tales* 3.21–2. The statue of Telesphorus, a minor healing god, was in the temple of Hygieia ('Health'): *Sacred Tales* 4.16. Trans. of *Sacred Tales* in Behr 1968; trans. of all of Aelius Aristides' works by Behr (Leiden 1981–6).

39, 42). The speech in honour of Asclepius specified what he himself owed to the power of the god and a speech *To Plato: In Defence of Oratory* written during his stay at Pergamon noted that,

Truly just as the seers, initiated into the service of the gods who have given their name to their speciality, I have knowledge from the gods themselves. Through their aid, contrary to the likelihood of the circumstances, I am alive, having escaped at different times through various kinds of consolation and advice on the part of the god [Asclepius] from things which no doctor knew what to call, to say nothing of cure, nor had seen befall human nature. (2.67)

The intensity of his commitment to Asclepius is most striking, but similar feelings lie behind the drier epigraphic record of other sanctuaries of Asclepius, and only the unique literary output of Aristides makes him seem peculiar.

Some individuals chose to seek initiation into cults which might be far from home. In the case of the Eleusinian Mysteries the Athenians encouraged these by sending sacred heralds out all over Greece to proclaim the time for initiations (above, p. 26). Another mystery cult which also attracted initiates from far away was that of the Cabiri or Great Gods on the island of Samothrace in the north Aegean. Herodotos, who had visited the island, and had presumably been initiated himself, claims that the Athenian custom of making images of Hermes with an erect phallus was derived from Samothrace. The original inhabitants of the island, the Pelasgians, passed on this practice both to the Samothracians and to the Athenians, 'explaining it by a certain religious doctrine, the nature of which is made clear in the Samothracian mysteries'.[13] Though this allusion remains obscure to us (as Herodotos intended), we are quite well informed on other aspects of the Samothracian sanctuary and its prestigious annual festival (Fig. 6.2).

Candidates for initiation in the first degree (*muesis*) were predominantly male, but of very different statuses, citizens, ex-slaves and slaves. They assembled, both at the annual festival and at other times, in a large rectangular hall (the so-called Anaktoron. No. 23 on the plan). The larger chamber includes a 'pit' and viewing benches along two walls; initiates and initiands then went up through internal doors to a smaller room, at whose entrance was an inscription (in Latin and Greek) of the first or second century AD, 'Non-initiates may not enter.' Those seeking initiation in the second degree (*epopteia*) met in a different building (the 'Hieron'), a rectangular building lined with benches (No. 15 on

---

[13] 2.51. On herms see above, p. 82.

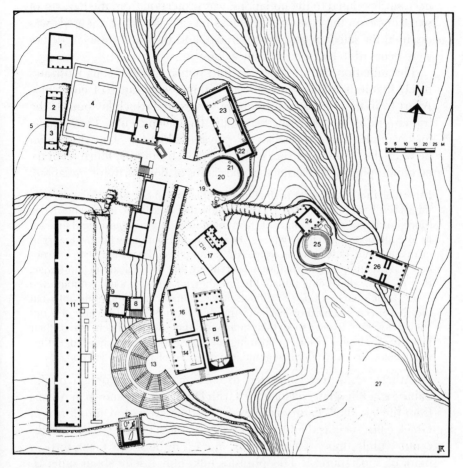

Fig. 6.2. Plan of sanctuary of the Great Gods, Samothrace. 1–3. Late Hellenistic
treasuries. 4. Uncompleted late Hellenistic building. 5. Byzantine fortification.
6. Milesian dedication. 7. Dining rooms. 8. Priests' house? 9. Entrance to heroic grave.
10. Priests' house? 11. Portico. 12. Nike fountain. 13. Theatre. 14. Altar courtyard.
15. 'Hieron'. 16. Dining room? 17. Temenos with entry way. 18. Hekate altar. 19. Stone
altar. 20. Arsinoeion. 21. Double area. 22. Sacristy. 23. Anaktoron. 24. Gift of
Macedonian king. 25. Circular cult place. 26. Ptolemaion. 27. South cemetery.

plan). At the entrance was a lustral drain, a chthonic hearth in the centre
and a raised apse at the far end: here also, an inscribed plaque warned
that 'non-initiates may not enter the sacred building'. The purpose of
the nocturnal initiation was to gain both cosmological revelation and the
protection of the Great Gods. One aspect of this protection, though not

necessarily related to the initiations, was protection from the hazards of seafaring.[14] As the case of Andocides reveals, favour of the gods was essential for safety at sea (above, p. 84), and the Samothracian deities were believed to be especially efficacious.[15]

The initiation or non-initiation into public mystery cults illustrates nicely that individuals made choices within a wide range of civic cults. Apart from these choices, further options existed which lay outside the framework of the established civic and Panhellenic cults. These came, for example, from specialists in private initiation. The distinction between the two sorts of rites is clearly drawn by an early fourth-century BC philosopher (who is critical of the claims of both forms of initiation):

[About all those who] after performing a public rite in cities have seen the holy things [i.e. have been initiated], I wonder less that they fail to attain knowledge (since it is impossible simultaneously to listen to what is being said and to learn it). But all those [i.e. who have received initiation] from one who makes a craft of the holy rites deserve to be wondered at and pitied. They deserve to be wondered at because, thinking before the ceremony that they will attain knowledge, they go away after being initiated before they have understood, without even asking additional questions, as though they had understood something of what they have seen or heard or learned. And they must be pitied because it is not enough for them to have spent their money, but they also go off deprived of their judgement. Hoping before performing the holy rites to gain knowledge, they nevertheless go away after being initiated deprived of their expectation.[16]

In Athens some were attracted to cults of explicitly foreign origin: Sabazios, a Phrygian god identified with Dionysos, was known in Athens from the late fifth century BC onwards. Others were drawn to forms of Greek cults, such as the Orphic mysteries. But according to the fourth-century philosopher Theophrastos, interest in both was taken to be a mark of superstition.[17] Theophrastos talks only briefly about superstition, 'fear of the divine', but 400 years later Plutarch developed his concept. For him a true piety which allows the worshipper a position of dignity in relation to the gods is the mean between two extremes: atheism, which denies existence of the gods, and superstition which assumes that the gods cause pain and injury. The superstitious man is fearful on what ought to be joyous occasions, the festivals of the ordinary gods. He also engages in debased and demeaning behaviour, 'magic charms and spells, rushing about and beating of drums, impure purifica-

---

[14] On religious responses to seafaring see Wachsmuth 1967; below, p. 136.
[15] Cole 1984b; Erhardt 1985; Cole 1989; Burkert 1993.
[16] *ZPE* 47 (1982), following p. 300, column 16 (now col. 20). On this text see below, p. 117.
[17] Theophrastos, *Characters* 16.4, 16.12.

tions and unclean sanctifications, barbarous and outlandish penances and mortifications at the shrines' (*Moralia* 171B).

Such critiques reveal that the choices which lay outside the range of civic cults did not just add additional options to the civic menu, but that they sometimes incorporated critiques of the civic cults and Panhellenic myths or were genuine alternatives to them.[18] In the Roman empire the complex religious choices were somewhat like a United Nations buffet. One could help oneself to dishes or whole meals which claimed to come from different culinary traditions (Egypt, Persia, Syria, Judaea). In the archaic and classical periods the principal options were variants on a Greek (or Hellenised) menu.

The figure of Dionysos had a critical role both within and outside the conventional choices.[19] He did receive official civic cults, as at Athens, he did play an important role at Delphi, but he was hardly ever the principal deity of a city, and some of his official rites did involve bizarre and abnormal behaviour.[20] On Mount Parnassos above Delphi women did act as maenads in the nocturnal festival of Dionysos and were believed to tear wild animals apart in a shocking version of animal sacrifice. Maenadic cults occurred however only sporadically in Greece and are not found, for example, in Attica itself (though Attic women went to Mount Parnassos to join the maenadic festival there).[21]

Initiations of individuals into the rites of Dionysos involved the temporary abandonment of reason. Herodotos as part of his ethnographic excursus on Scythia (north of the Black Sea) recounts a tale which stresses both the Greek nature of Dionysos and the madness of the cult. A Scythian king, Skyles, would live for a month as a Greek in the Greek city of Borysthenes (Olbia), a colony of Miletos on the north shore of the Black Sea; he worshipped the gods in the Greek manner and was even initiated into the rites of Dionysos Bakkheios. The Scythians were then told of his initiation: 'You Scythians mock us [Greeks] for revelling and being possessed by the god, but now this deity has taken possession of your own king so that he is revelling and is maddened by the god.' On

---

[18] Sabbatucci 1965; Detienne 1979. For an introduction see Burkert 1987a.

[19] His alleged origin on the margins of the Greek world (Thrace or Phrygia) made him a usefully ambivalent god.

[20] Athens: above, pp. 52–3; Delphi: above, p. 56. Principal deity at Thebes in central Greece, with Apollo Ismenios, and at Teos in western Asia Minor.

[21] On actual maenads see Henrichs 1978; *IG* 9.1² 670, trans. in Beard, North and Price 1998: II no. 12.1c. Below, p. 158, for the mythical killing of Pentheus. The role of the women need not be interpreted in terms of deprivation theory; for a critique see Wilson 1982: 115–18.

secretly seeing him revelling in the streets with a band of initiates (*thiasos*) the Scythians instigated the overthrow and murder of Skyles.[22] Herodotos is ambivalent towards this cult: it is represented as characteristically Greek, but anomalous in creating divine possession. The anomalous aspects of the cult were sometimes seized on explicitly by critics. Plato's staid ideal city of the *Laws* bans as unfitting for citizens 'all bacchic dances and those of a similar nature in which the dancers, calling themselves Nymphs, Pans, Sileni and Satyrs, imitate drunken people, while celebrating certain rites of expiation and initiation'.[23] Similarly the Athenian politician Demosthenes abuses his political opponent Aeschines for his participation in ecstatic rites. The passage is worth quoting in full as a vivid if hostile picture of what might be seen on the streets of fourth-century Athens:

On arriving at manhood you assisted your mother in her initiations, reading out the books while she performed the ritual and helping generally with the paraphernalia. At night it was your duty to clothe the initiands in fawn-skins, to mix the libations, to wash their bodies, to scour them with the loam and the bran and, when the lustrations were duly performed, to set them on their legs and give out the line: 'I have abjured evil and found a better way' and it was your pride that no one ever emitted the holy ululation so powerfully as yourself. I can well believe it! When you hear the loud tones of the orator, can you doubt that his ululations were simply magnificent? In daytime you marshalled your fine band of initiates through the streets, their heads garlanded with fennel and white poplar and as you went you squeezed the fat cheeked snakes, and brandished them above your head, now shouting your *euoi saboi*!, now dancing to the measure of *Hues attes, attes hues*, saluted by all the old women with such pious titles as Master of the Ceremonies (*exarkhos*), Instructor (*prohegemon*), Ivy Bearer (*kittophoros*) and Winnowing Fan Carrier (*liknophoros*), and receiving your recompense of cakes, rolls and buns.[24]

Although the cult described by Demosthenes was a private cult, it possessed very public manifestations. The noisy and intrusive Dionysiac *thiasos* created for the initiates a form of religious identity unbounded by normal conventions.[25] The Eleusinian Mysteries, which also admitted both men and women, offered some sort of precedent, but the mysteries involved words and visions, not possession. Dionysiac societies varied

---

[22] 4.78–80. Cf. Hartog 1988: 61–84.
[23] 815c; cf. Morrow 1960: 362–5, who argues that maenadic possession, not mentioned here, was accepted by Plato.
[24] 18.259–60. Though the cry '*saboi*' evokes the Thracian god Sabazios, the ceremony overall draws on Dionysiac and Orphic themes. Cf. Parker 1996: 159.
[25] It may also be relevant for understanding the role of Aeschines' mother that her brother was a noted seer (*mantis*): *SEG* 16.193; above, p. 73.

greatly, from maenadic cults involving nocturnal rites in the mountains to more domesticated groups. An association of worshippers of Dionysos in Athens in this case consisting only of men (mainly well-to-do) was much concerned about the maintenance of decorous behaviour at its monthly dinners, held in a special building, probably in the sanctuary of Dionysos in the Marshes.[26]

The figure of Dionysos also played a prominent role in revisionist theogonies from the archaic period onwards. They are illuminated by the discovery of a group of six tombs dating to the later fourth century BC at Derveni (circa twelve kilometres north-west of Thessaloniki in northern Greece).[27] In the funeral pyre beside one of the tombs there survived the charred remains of a papyrus roll. The text, perhaps composed in the early fourth century BC, is an allegorical interpretation of various texts including a cosmological poem, the *Theogony*. The poem, of which about nineteen individual lines are quoted, plus a few phrases, probably dates to the late sixth or early fifth century BC and offers our firmest early evidence for a cosmological poem that deviated from the Hesiodic view.[28] The Derveni cosmology presents a succession of sovereign gods: Ouranos, son of Night, Kronos, Zeus, who on the prophetic advice of Night swallows Protogonos the first-born who preceded Ouranos. The structure of the myth is the same as Hesiod's, and Protogonos may have been identified with Metis whom Hesiod's Zeus swallows (above, p. 17), but Protogonos is identified with the universe and Zeus is said to have swallowed all the immortals, the rivers and springs and everything else that existed. Zeus then 'brought them forth from his holy heart' (a more dignified recreation than Kronos' vomiting up of his children) and produced Aphrodite from his semen. Subsequently Zeus began to lust after others and mated with his mother, who gave birth probably to Persephone. Here the Derveni roll ends, but the commentary and poem must have continued onto another roll, which perished in the pyre, dealing with the creation of the Titans and of humans and probably ascribing the central role here to Dionysos.

The *Rhapsodies*, a poem perhaps of late Hellenistic date, circulated widely in the imperial period and is reasonably well known to us through quotations and discussions by philosophers and others down to

---

[26] *IG* 2² 1368 = *LSCG* no. 51 (c. AD 175) (trans. in Tod 1932: 86–91); Moretti 1986. Findspot: Dörpfeld 1894: 147; above, p. 28.

[27] On Orphism see West 1983; Burkert 1985: 290–304; Parker 1995.

[28] *ZPE* 47 (1982), following p. 300; Laks and Most 1997: 9–22 translate the text. West 1983; cf. Calame 1991b; Parker 1995.

the sixth century AD. The *Rhapsodies* overlaps with and prolongs the Derveni cosmology, and it is very likely that it is drawing on and systematising versions of the myth that go back to the Derveni poem.[29] However, after the procreation of Persephone the myth continued as follows. Zeus mated with Persephone in turn, who gave birth to Dionysos, and they become the central figures. After giving birth to the Eumenides, fathered by Apollo, Persephone probably reigns in the underworld, while Dionysos aided mortals in the upper world. The souls of the dead spend 300 years in the underworld and are then reborn, but they desire to escape from the round of death and rebirth. Dionysos and Persephone assist the human race to find release through purification ceremonies and sacrifices. Their role in the cyclical rebirth of the human race, which may have been taken over from the near east, is strikingly untraditional.

The story of Dionysos as told in the *Rhapsodies* includes further novel features, which probably also go back to the fifth century BC. Dionysos, born in Crete, was guarded by the dancing Kouretes, as Zeus had been, and after probably five years was installed by Zeus on his throne as king of the gods. In a gruesome way, parodic of normal sacrifice, the Titans then killed, cooked and ate Dionysos.[30] The story also distances the Dionysos of this myth from the Dionysos believed to foster the rending of animals and eating the warm flesh. This Dionysos stands for purity and so can aid the release of humans from rebirth.

Apart from other sources, the Derveni text ascribes its cosmogony focusing on Dionysos to Orpheus,[31] a musician from Thrace, who was believed to enchant birds and animals, rivers, rocks and trees, and who persuaded the infernal powers to allow his wife to leave Hades. He had no place in the Hesiodic genealogies of the Heroic age but was believed to have taken part in the expedition of the Argonauts to get the golden fleece. He was thus an authoritative figure of considerable antiquity who was conveniently independent of mainstream mythology. Under his authorship also goes a collection of eighty-seven hymns to a variety of gods (the so-called 'Orphic hymns'). They were probably composed by a single author in the second or third century AD somewhere in western Asia Minor, presumably for a religious society meeting at night by the light of torches and for the offering of incense. Again, Dionysos, being the recipient of eight hymns, is very prominent, and the hymns do show

---

[29] For a critique of West 1983 see Brisson 1985.     [30] Cf. Detienne 1979: ch. 4.
[31] *ZPE* 47 (1982), following p. 300, column 3 (now col. 7) refers to his, surely Orpheus', allegorical interpretations.

awareness of the *Rhapsodies*, but there is little real overlap with the cosmology of Derveni or the *Rhapsodies*.[32]

Closely related to Orpheus, even to the extent of confusion among both the Greeks and modern scholars, is another authority figure: Pythagoras.[33] In contrast to Orpheus, he was a real person who left his native Samos, allegedly in 532–531 BC, for Greek towns in south Italy, Croton and then Metapontion, where he died (494 BC). This charismatic figure seems to have left no writings under his own name. The first book about his doctrines was composed in the latter half of the fifth century BC by one Philolaus of Croton, and the first book explaining his orally transmitted maxims (*Acusmata* or *Symbola*) was composed about 400 BC (by one Anaximander of Miletos).[34] Statements about 'Pythagoras' are parallel to statements about 'Orpheus'; in both cases we are dealing with ascriptions of texts or ordinances to shadowy authority figures. 'Orphic' poems and 'Pythagorean' teachings emerge (and interrelate) in the late archaic and early classical periods, but do not represent coherent movements so that we could talk of Pythagoreanism or Orphism.

There were, however, people who described themselves or were described as 'Orphics' and 'Pythagoreans'.[35] The opening of the Orphic *Theogony*, as discussed in the Derveni papyrus, entrusts the text merely to insiders, initiates: 'I shall sing to those who understand. Bar your ears, you uninitiated.'[36] The pattern of 'Orphic' religiosity that emerges from our evidence has many bacchic elements.[37] Excavations of Olbia have yielded numerous bone plaques five to seven centimetres long of which some are carved or inscribed. Three plaques, dating to the fifth century, are particularly illuminating. They read as follows:

(1) Life: Death: Life. Truth. A.Z. Dio<nysos>, Orphics.
(2) Peace: War. Truth: Falsehood. Dio<nysos> N.A (there are further signs and a symbol on the reverse).
(3) Dio<nysos> Z. [Falsehood:] Truth. Body: Soul A (there is a symbol on the reverse).[38]

---

[32] Text and translation by Athanassakis 1977; cf. Linforth 1941: 179–89; Rudhardt 1991; Morand 1997 on local gods. See below, pp. 160–1, for Jewish and Christian uses of Orpheus.

[33] For an ancient confusion see Herodotos 2.81 (the shorter version of this passage is probably an accidental abridgement: Linforth 1941: 38–50; West 1983: 8 n.10).

[34] Cf. Burkert 1972; Kirk, Raven and Schofield 1983: 213–38 (Pythagoras), 322–50 (Philolaus); Huffman 1993 (Philolaus).    [35] Burkert 1982.

[36] *ZPE* 47 (1982), following p. 300, col. 3 (now col. 7).

[37] M. Schmidt 1991. Cf. Appendix no. 13 on initiation and burial.

[38] *SEG* 28.659–61; West 1982; 1983: 17–19; Vinogradov 1991. The reading 'Orphics' in no. 1 is that supported by those who have studied the actual plaques.

The bone plaques are presumably membership tokens of those initiated into the cult of Dionysos. The legends hint at doctrines concerning the soul and life after death, the 'true' doctrines revealed on initiation; Dionysos is the central god for initiates who probably described themselves as 'Orphics'.

Pythagorean groups were more cohesive, though elusive for us. A group existed around Pythagoras at Croton and had some political prominence until the house where they met was burned down by their opponents, killing most of those present. After this disaster (sometime between 450 and 400 BC), Tarentum became the chief centre for Pythagoreans until its extinction in the late fourth century BC,[39] but mendicant 'Pythagoreans' were also familiar figures in Athenian comedies of the fourth century BC, and Plato (*Republic* 10.600B) attests the conspicuousness of the Pythagorean way of life. Influence of the Pythagoreans was not limited to south Italy nor did it end in the fourth century BC. In the Hellenistic and Roman periods people continued to write treatises on Pythagorean themes, and again in the first century BC there were people who took seriously the Pythagorean way of life.

There is a further set of evidence about religious groups which belongs to the same world as that of avowed Orphics and Pythagoreans – gold leaves inscribed with verses about the underworld, the so-called 'Orphic gold leaves'. A dozen such gold leaves have been found in tombs of both men and women dating mainly to the fourth century BC with some from the third century.[40] They come from seven places, Thurii, Petelia and Hipponion in south Italy; Pharsalos and Pelinna in Thessaly; Eleutherna in Crete; and (it seems) Lesbos in the north-east Aegean. This extremely localised if widespread distribution suggests strongly that the texts emanate from specific religious groups. The texts fall into three main groups. The first group, found at Petelia, Hipponion, Pharsalos and Eleutherna, consists of instructions to the dead about the route to be followed in the underworld. The longest text of this group from the grave of a woman at Hipponion and dating to circa 400 BC runs as follows:

This is the leaf of Recollection. When he is going to die, he will go to the broad house of Hades; there is a spring to the right, by it stands a white cypress, here the descending souls of the dead are cooled. Do not approach this spring.

---

[39] Von Fritz 1940.

[40] Zuntz 1971: 277–393; to which add *SEG* 40.824 (Hipponion), 37.497, 39.505 (Pelinna), 27.226 bis (Thessaly). Unpublished finds: *Archaeological Reports 1988–89* (1989), 93 (Lesbos); Bremmer 1994: 88 (Thessaly). Cf. Calame 1991b; Bottini 1992.

Further on you will find cool water flowing from the lake of Recollection. Guardians stand over it who will ask you in their sensible minds what you are searching for in the darkness of corrupt Hades. Answer: 'I am a son of the earth and of the starry sky but I am desiccated with thirst and am perishing: therefore give me quickly cool water flowing from the lake of Recollection.' And then the subjects of the chthonian king will have pity and will give you to drink from the lake of Recollection. And indeed after drinking you will go along a sacred way along which also other initiates and *bakkhoi* walk in glory. (*SEG* 26.1139, 43.647)

The second group of texts come mainly from two grave mounds at Thurii. They proclaim the purity of the dead, hope for favourable judgement by Persephone and promise apotheosis.

The third group of texts, from Pelinna, found in a marble sarcophagus on the chest of a woman, combine the language of the second group with the religious context of the first group.[41]

Now you died and now you were born, thrice-happy one, on this day.
Tell Persephone that Bakkhios himself has released you.
A bull, you rushed into the milk.
A goat, you rushed into the milk.
A ram, you fell into the milk.
You have wine as your fortunate honour.
And there await you beneath the earth the rewards that the other happy ones
   have. (*SEG* 37.497A)

The texts have been variously described as Orphic, Pythagorean, or Bacchic. The reference in the last line of the Hipponion text to initiates and *bakkhoi* and in the Pelinna texts to release by Bakkhios is insufficient grounds to classify the text simply as Bacchic. As we have seen, initiation into Bacchic rites is perfectly compatible with claims to the authority of Orpheus. Some of the Thurii texts seem to assume the migration of souls, and there was ancient uncertainty as to what was properly Orphic and what was Pythagorean. It is best not to attempt a simple classification of the thinking of these texts.

A special lifestyle was expected of Orphics and Pythagoreans, which involved abstinence from eating animals and further dietary restrictions on eating eggs and beans and drinking wine.[42] Two very different positions were adopted and fathered on Pythagoras.[43] The more radical, like that of the Orphics, rejected any form of meat in the diet, while the

---

[41] Cf. Graf 1991; Graf 1993b.     [42] Orphics: Euripides, *Hippolytos* 952–5; Plato, *Laws* 6.782c.
[43] Pythagorean diet: Plutarch, *Table-Talk* 48.727B–730F (trans. Loeb *Moralia* 9); Detienne 1970; Burkert 1972: 180–5.

more moderate held that traditional animal sacrifice was acceptable and that the meat of those animals could be eaten. The rationale for both positions was the doctrine of the common nature of all living creatures and the belief that the souls of the dead could be reincarnated in any animal species, a topic to which we shall return. Pythagoreans, like Orphics, also abstained from eating beans. This seemingly bizarre taboo is explicable in different ways: physiologically because of the difficulty of digesting beans, more plausibly because of the similarity of beans to parts of the human body. Abstinence from beans was a logical extension of vegetarianism and the assertion of the moral superiority of the initiate. According to Pausanias, Demeter in giving the human race the products of the earth excluded beans 'and whoever has witnessed the rites at Eleusis or read the so-called Orphic writings will know what I mean'.[44] Murder and a carnivorous diet were excluded from the foundations of civilisation.

The creation of a religiously sanctioned way of life was unique to these elective groups. Admittedly, initiates at Samothrace were formally described as pious,[45] and Eleusinian initiates were expected to live their lives piously in relation to foreigners and ordinary people,[46] but such piety towards gods and humans was merely what was conventionally expected, and neither set of initiates lived a distinctive way of life. The refusal to kill animals was particularly radical, as it cut Orphics and some Pythagoreans off from animal sacrifices, the essential religious ritual of the Greek states. Their beliefs about the fate of the soul after death were equally radical.

Orphics and Pythagoreans both held that the souls of the dead were later reborn in this world. According to the Orphic *Rhapsodies*, human souls after judgement spend 300 years in the underworld until they are reborn, but initiation into the rites of Persephone and Dionysos can aid humans to achieve release from the endless round. Pythagoreans developed their own form of this theory, which may go back to Pythagoras himself. According to the contemporary evidence of Xenophanes (fragment 7a West), Pythagoras, on seeing someone beating a puppy, said, 'Stop. That's the soul of a friend of mine; I recognise the voice.' This doctrine of the migration of souls between different species was unique (in Greece) to the Pythagoreans, though some later Pythagorean traditions draw back from the idea.[47] The Pythagorean goal was, like the

---

[44] 1.37.4; cf. 8.15.3–4, Porphyry, *Abstinence* 4.16.
[45] E.g. *Syll.*[3] 1052–3; Schol. Aristophanes, *Peace* 278 (trans. in Rice and Stambaugh 1979: 215) adds the reputation of justice.    [46] Aristophanes, *Frogs* 456–9.    [47] Burkert 1972: 120–4.

Orphic, release, but by a different route. Pythagoras himself was reputed to have brought back from the underworld a revelation about the lot of the soul,[48] and later Pythagoreans apparently practised a form of memory training, the recall of all the events of the previous day, which may have been designed to strengthen the powers of the soul, so that it could avoid oblivion in the underworld.[49] A related eschatology is attested in the first, widespread, group of gold leaves, in which the soul is instructed to avoid the water of Oblivion in favour of that of Memory. And the hope in one of the Thurii gold leaves was for escape from the grievous cycle, which presumably implies the cycle of birth and rebirth, with the hope of being turned from a mortal into a god. Dionysos, despite having been killed by the Titans, would now offer release to those born from the ashes of the Titans. Hence the injunction in one of the gold leaves: 'Tell Persephone that Bakkhios himself has released you.'[50] If the victim was now placated, surely his mother Persephone would aid the soul of the deceased.

Elective cults continued to be important through the Hellenistic and Roman periods.[51] Egyptian Isis, whose worship began in Greece as an ethnic cult of migrant Egyptians, soon became domesticated (Fig. 6.3).[52] Herodotos had already seen Isis as the ultimate model for Demeter and the Eleusinian Mysteries (2.58–9), and there was considerable respect for Egypt as the source of antique wisdom. This is epitomised in a votive dedication put up in the temple of Isis at Kyme in western Asia Minor. The dedicant claimed to have copied a hymn to Isis inscribed at Memphis in Egypt, in which the goddess ascribed to herself the origins of civilisation and religion.[53] The text refers to initiation into the cult; by the Roman period this was probably an important element enabling the worshipper to enter into a more formal relationship with the god.[54]

The fullest surviving evocation of the power of Isis is given in Apuleius' novel *Metamorphoses* (also known as *The Golden Ass*). This Latin novel of the second century AD is in its final stages explicitly based on the saving power of Isis. The hapless central figure of the story, Lucius, has

---

[48] Diogenes Laertius 8.41 from Hermippus; Ennius, *Annals* frags. 2–10 (Skutsch) claimed inspiration from the fact that the soul of Homer had passed into him.

[49] Zuntz 1971: 380; Burkert 1972: 213.    [50] *SEG* 37.497A, Pelinna.

[51] Beard, North and Price 1998: 1.245–312 on Rome; cf. texts in Beard, North and Price 1998: II ch. 12.

[52] Above, pp. 77, 78 n.38. for Athens in the fourth century BC. Pakkanen 1996 includes material on the Hellenistic cult of Isis at Athens.

[53] First century BC? *IG* 12 Supp. 14 = *Inschriften von Kyme* 41, trans. in Beard, North and Price 1998: II no. 12.4a.    [54] Cf. Plutarch, *Moralia* 361DE.

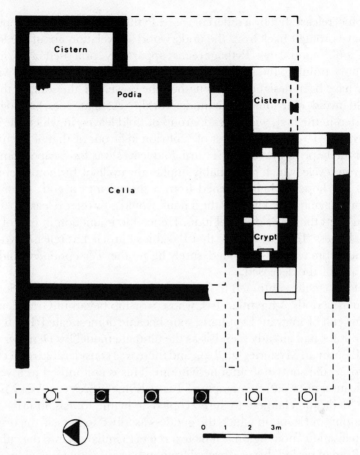

Fig. 6.3. Plan of sanctuary of Isis and Serapis, Gortyn (late first/second century AD, a rebuilding of a Hellenistic sanctuary). Inside stood a statue of Serapis, flanked by Isis and (probably) Hermes Anubis. 'Nile' water from the cisterns will have been used for initiations in the crypt.

been transformed into an ass, because of his improper curiosity about magic, a curiosity which is contrasted in the novel with proper interest in religious revelation. Isis appears to Lucius in a dream, using language of herself that is reminiscent of that used by Isis in the text from Kyme (11.5); she instructs Lucius as to how he is to be transformed back into a man, at a procession in her honour. Subsequently, Lucius in gratitude is initiated into her cult, and receives the promised revelation of the protection of Isis even in the underworld (11.6, 23). The extent to which a 'religious' reading of this and the other novels of the imperial period should be attempted is disputed. Some see them as *romans à clef*, whose deep meaning is an exposition of mystery cults; the opposite extreme is to doubt whether they have any particular religious significance. A more fruitful middling position is to treat the novels as explorations of themes also developed in the mysteries.[55] In the case of the *Metamorphoses* the reader is surely invited to reconsider some of the earlier scenes or stories in the light of the disclosure of Isis' significance. The novel ends on a strong note of religious commitment.[56] Lucius, like earlier Orphics and Pythagoreans, was devoted to his chosen deity, and now he was 'born again' and lived a new life at her command.

---

[55] *Romans à clef*: Chalk 1960; Merkelbach 1962; Henrichs 1972b. Just stories: Nock 1928. Themes in mysteries: Winkler 1980; Beck 1982, 1996.
[56] On religious commitment see below, pp. 140–1, and Beard, North and Price 1998: 1.307–12.

# CHAPTER 7

# *Greek thinkers*

The previous chapter considered cultic options, distinct from the official range, which offered new ideas about the creation of gods and mortals, and new forms of religious belonging. In this chapter the focus is on Greek thinkers, philosophers and others, who distanced themselves from mythology and theology in favour of their own articulate views of the world. In approaching these thinkers it is tempting to employ the model of the eighteenth-century French Enlightenment; self-styled philosophers rejected the teaching of the church and avowed the supremacy of 'rational thought', setting faith against atheism, belief against unbelief. As we shall see, it is profoundly misleading to talk of 'the fifth-century Enlightenment'; it is also quite misleading to treat Hellenistic philosophical schools as populated by crypto-sceptics, responding to an alleged decline in belief in civic gods.[1]

In the first place, there was no articulate body of belief for philosophers to reject. Greek religion was not like Christianity, which elevated belief in a central set of dogmas as a defining characteristic of the religion. There were commonly accepted ideas about the gods and about the appropriate ways of relating to them, but these remained generally inarticulate. The absence of an explicitly formulated and dynamic theology is due partly to the conservative influence of Homer and Hesiod, and partly to the absence of a professionally trained, vocational priesthood, which could have developed, internal to the religious system, an explicit 'creed'.[2] Only with the growth of explicit critiques of traditional ideas did there arise the issue of 'acknowledging the gods whom the city acknowledges' (above, p. 85). Secondly, it was very rare for people to declare themselves as 'atheists'.[3] None of the mainstream philosophers

---

[1] As does F.W. Walbank 1981: 218–19. Babut 1974 is a luminous study, to which this chapter owes much.
[2] For this theme see the sociologist Weber 1968: 1. 424–7 (also in his *Sociology of Religion*). See above, pp. 68–9, on priests.    [3] Drachmann 1922; Babut 1974: 5–9, 202.

did so, and those who did were seen as bizarre creatures: Diagoras of Melos was so notorious in fifth-century Athens for his atheism that Aristophanes' *Clouds* (830) can suggest that 'Socrates' was an atheist simply by calling him 'a Melian'. The issue of 'atheism' arises largely from the responses by defenders of traditional mythologies and theologies who accused philosophers of 'atheism'. Stories even developed, on the model of the trial of Socrates, about impiety accusations against other philosophers at Athens.[4]

The assumption of a conflict between belief and unbelief has often confounded efforts to understand the thought of individual philosophers. Pythagorean thought, whose 'religious' aspects were examined in the previous chapter, includes other elements (e.g. the theorem ascribed to Pythagoras), and one might be tempted to discover whether Pythagoras or his followers were mystics or scientists. Was their interest in numbers just an aspect of their cosmology, or were they also earnest enquirers after scientific truth? The issue is complicated by the evidential difficulties that bedevil the study of Pythagorean cosmology, but it is clear that the polarity is a false one. Though it is unclear how far Pythagoras himself developed the mathematical aspects of his thought, he seems to have held that 'attunement' (*harmonia*), which could be represented in music or numbers, had a cosmic significance.[5]

The common characteristic of the different philosophical schools was rejection of the mythology and theology of Homer and Hesiod. Alternatives to the received position are found in the fragments of work by Xenophanes, at the start of the Greek philosophical tradition in the sixth century. Xenophanes came from Kolophon in Ionia but left there when the Persians came in 546/5 BC, in favour of a wandering life, perhaps mainly in Sicily. Xenophanes' work was certainly later taken to constitute a radical critique of traditional views of the gods, but this may be a misreading of Xenophanes, and he may only have been raising alternative possibilities. At all events, those alternatives to the received position have two aspects, moral and physical. He claimed that

Homer and Hesiod have attributed to the gods everything that is a shame and reproach among mortals: stealing, committing adultery and deceiving each other. (fragment 11)

Secondly, he rejected the traditional anthropomorphism of the gods. He noted that different races attributed their own characteristics to the gods:

---

[4] Babut 1974: 107 on Aristotle; above, p. 85, for the problem of fifth-century trials.
[5] Burkert 1972: 401–82; Kirk, Raven and Schofield 1983: 232–5, 334–7.

The Ethiopians say that their gods are snub-nosed and black, the Thracians that theirs have light blue eyes and red hair. (fragment 16)

which implies that conventional Greek views of the gods are also cultur-ally relative. He also claimed as a *reductio ad absurdum* that, if they had the physical capabilities, horses would draw their gods like horses and cattle like cattle (fragment 15). The implication is that the anthropomorphic and demeaning view of the gods in Homer, 'according to whom all have learned from the beginning' (fragment 10), should be rejected.[6]

The moral issue raised by Xenophanes was greatly elaborated by Plato. In an early dialogue, Euthyphro and Socrates discuss the meaning of piety/impiety and holiness/unholiness. The dialogue, set just before Socrates' trial for impiety, forms part of Plato's defence of his master (above, p. 85). Euthyphro is prosecuting his father for murder of a servant (above, p. 70), and accuses those who criticise him for doing so of inconsistency: they attack him but revere Zeus who put his father in chains. Socrates comes in:

You believe that there really was a war between the gods and fearful enmities and battles and other things of the sort such as are told of by the poets and represented in varied degrees by the great artists in our sacred objects and espe-cially on the robe which is carried up to the Akropolis at the Great Panathenaia.[7]

Here criticism of mythology is incidental to the main purpose of the dia-logue, but in the *Republic* Plato offers a straightforward critique of the ancient tales. He makes Socrates prohibit all unsuitable tales to be told to children in his ideal state. The false stories that Hesiod, Homer and the other poets tell are to be banned, especially

the greatest lie about the things of greatest concern which was no pretty inven-tion of him who told how Ouranos did what Hesiod says he did to Kronos and how Kronos in turn took his revenge. The doings of Kronos and his sufferings at the hands of his son, even if they were true, certainly ought not to be told lightly to young and thoughtless persons.

Nor can Plato's Socrates accept that gods fight with gods and plot against each other: the stories are not true and also not conducive to harmony

---

[6] Kirk, Raven and Schofield 1983: 168–9. Edwards 1991 suggests that some 'fragments' of Xenophanes are Christian forgeries, but (as Myles Burnyeat has suggested to me) his case under-plays widespread problems with the 'fragments' of Xenophanes, and also rests on an unaccept-able reading of one fragment as an attack on *images* of the gods. Trans. of Xenophanes in Loeb *Elegy and Iambus* 1; trans. and commentary in Lesher 1992. On the sixth- and fifth-century philosophers see Vlastos 1952, Hussey 1972, Kerferd 1981: 163–72, and Taylor 1997.

[7] *Euthyphro* 5d–7c; above, p. 13, for these myths.

within the state and within individual families (*Republic* 2.377–8). While Orphic cosmogonies modified Hesiod's poem to express their novel views of the world, Plato rejects totally the tales told in his day by mothers and nurses to the young and represented in privileged positions in contemporary ritual.[8]

Aristotle, who was less interested than Plato in the philosophy of religion, picks up on Xenophanes' comments on anthropomorphism. As part of his exposition of his view of the divine, he claims that there was an early tradition that the heavenly bodies are gods and that the divine pervades the whole of nature and that the rest of the tradition has been added later in a mythological form to influence the masses and as a constitutional and utilitarian expedient.

They say that these gods are human in shape or are like certain other animals and make statements consequent upon and similar to that which we have mentioned.

Aristotle accepts that the early tradition was partially true, but rejects the anthropomorphic mythology out of hand (*Metaphysics* 12.8 1074b). However, he was less agitated than Plato on the whole issue. In his ideal state he was prepared to admit indecent sculpture and paintings in the temples of certain deities on grounds of convention (*Politics* 7.15 1336b), and in his treatise on poetry he held that poetry could represent matter that was not true.[9]

The rejection of traditional mythology had major implications for an understanding of natural phenomena, including the human race. Philosophers of the sixth and fifth century did not reject the notion of the divine, but rather argued that in a sense everything was divine. This meant that nature could become an object of enquiry in its own right, and that the questioning of religious explanations touched both natural phenomena and human actions in relation to the divine. In relation to both, philosophers held that their enquiries liberated humans from unnecessary fear, which was the origin of demeaning superstition.[10]

Once natural phenomena of all kinds became the object of enquiry, a polarity between religious and naturalistic explanations became an important issue. This is articulated most sharply in the story told by Plutarch about an encounter between the seer Lampon and Anaxagoras, the natural philosopher famous for his enquiries into

---

[8] Babut 1974: 78–82; above, p. 12.
[9] *Poetics* 25 1460b–1461a; Babut 1974: 168. For later critique of Greek myths see below, p. 135.
[10] Cf. p. 114; Plato, *Republic* 364b–365a; Lloyd 1987: 1–49.

nature.[11] Lampon and Anaxagoras each sought to account for a one-horned ram. Lampon took it to be a sign from the gods of the political ascendancy of Pericles, while Anaxagoras, who had the skull cut in two, showed that the horn resulted from a deformity in the growth of the brain. The story, like Aristophanes' *Clouds*, assumes that religious and naturalistic explanations were discrete alternatives, but Plutarch himself comments from his perspective 500 years later that both could be true, one relating to causation, the other to the purpose of the deformity, and he emphasises the value of disinterested enquiry into nature, which frees people who are ignorant about causation from fear of divine intervention and the superstitious beliefs that result from such fear. For Plutarch at least, natural philosophy promoted true piety.

Explanations and hence cures of human diseases were a particularly problematic area. Professional medical writers from the fifth century onwards emphasised that diseases had natural explanations and offered their own non-religious cures. The classic statement of this position appears in the fifth-century treatise *On the Sacred Disease* later ascribed to Hippocrates. The author argues firmly that this disease (a form of epilepsy) was in fact not sacred, or at least that it was no more and no less sacred than all other diseases and had a comprehensible natural cause, but

> while people continue to believe in its divine origin because they fail to understand the disease in fact they disprove its divinity by the facile method of healing which they adopt, consisting as it does of purifications and incantations. (1)

The text goes on to criticise at length the arbitrary prohibitions and purifications that these religious quacks allegedly devised to conceal their own ignorance. Not only are the 'cures' ineffective, but the diagnosis in terms of seizures by particular gods and purifications as if for pollution is impious. The author thus seeks to liberate people from unnecessary awe, much as Plutarch notes, but he should not therefore be seen as a modern white-coated doctor. He notes that, if the sacred disease was polluting, the appropriate response would be supplications in the sanctuaries of the gods, and his own explanation of the disease is as arbitrary as the religious one.[12] The development of professional doctors thus was compatible with the rise to importance of sanctuaries of Asclepius (cf. p. 109). There the sufferers were offered not religious explanations of their diseases, but diagnoses and cures of the sort which they might have obtained from doctors.

---

[11] *Pericles* 6. Cf. above, pp. 73, 86.    [12] Lloyd 1979: 10–58; 1987: 11–21.

The understanding of human behaviour was also profoundly affected by a rejection of traditional conceptions of the gods. The difference can be seen very clearly in the context of Greek historical writings. The starting point is Herodotos, who accepted divine interventions in battles, explicitly affirmed his belief in the validity of oracles (8.77) and implied his assent to the view that earthquakes were due to Poseidon (7.129). Thucydides, by contrast, excludes 'mythical' stories from his narrative,[13] and in general gives the divine no place in his general understanding of history, though he does note cases where his contemporaries thought otherwise.[14] The gods certainly do not intervene in Thucydides' battles, indeed he puts appeals in the names of the gods in the mouths of the losing side in conflicts (e.g. 3.58, 5.104–5, 7.77.3–4). He effectively denies the validity of oracles (2.54) while noting contemporary uses of them, and he offers naturalistic explanations of the storms, eclipses and diseases. His account of the great plague that struck Athens in 430 BC is particularly interesting (2.47–54). He notes that, to start with, people offered supplications to the gods, made enquiries of oracles, and so on, but that the religious options were abandoned when the disease was unabated. Thucydides also notes that there was discussion of two oracles, which were taken to predict the plague, but he makes clear that the interpretations of the oracles were entirely arbitrary.[15] Though he eschews any attempt at explanation of the plague, his own description is purely naturalistic and is related to, indeed improves on, contemporary medical writings.[16]

Later historians differed in their approaches to the role of the divine in human affairs. Their attitudes depended in part on whether they were handling recent or ancient periods. The diversity is summed up in a section of Diodorus Siculus' *Library*, a universal history which covered the whole period from the Trojan War down to 60 BC. Diodorus notes that earlier historians had excluded mythology on the grounds that it contained self-contradictions and confusions.[17] He himself, however, proposed to include the deeds of gods and heroes, such as Dionysos and

---

[13] 1.22. For this exclusion he was warmly commended by Dionysios of Halikarnassos (writing in the late first century BC), who contrasted the practice of local historians: *Thucydides* 6–7.

[14] Above, p. 4, for a debate on the religious rules of warfare.

[15] See 2.17 for similar distancing from contemporary discussion of another oracle.

[16] For rather different emphases on 'natural' phenomena as marking 'supernatural' disfavour see 1.23, 3.87, 4.52, with Hornblower ad loc. Hornblower 1992 redresses Thucydides' 'neglect of the religious factor in his narrative'.

[17] 1.3.2; 4 is devoted to this theme, citing, at 4.1.3, as excluders Ephorus, Callisthenes and Theopompus. Cf. Plutarch, *Theseus* 15–16 for different positions on the Minotaur.

Herakles, who were benefactors of the human race. Indeed it would be paradoxical, given that

our ancestors have unanimously accorded immortality to him [Herakles] because of his exceedingly great attainments, that we should nevertheless fail to cherish and maintain for the god the pious devotion which has been handed down to us from our fathers. (4.8.5)

Some, like Diodorus, thus regarded the stories of gods and heroes as a proper part of their 'true' history; others were agnostic, recommending that myths should be recorded if they arose, but that the author should distance himself from them; others dismissed them as simply 'fabulous'.[18]

With more recent history historians again differed, but perhaps not as greatly. Thucydides' general exclusion of the divine from human affairs had few followers. Later historians normally accepted that there was some divine role in the world, but disagreed on the extent and formulation of that role. Xenophon, for example, talks of divine intervention in his own life, and also states firmly the providential role of the gods:

Now one could mention many other incidents, both among Greeks and barbarians, to prove that the gods do not fail to take heed of the impious or of those who do unrighteous things; but at present I will speak of the case which is before me [concerning the punishment of the Spartans for breaking their oath that they would leave the other Greek states independent].[19]

Other historians had a more complex position. Polybius, writing in the second century BC his account of how Rome came to conquer the inhabited world in fewer than fifty-three years, ascribes Roman success both to human calculation and rational factors, and, at the same time, to the overarching figure of *tuche*, Fortune. *Tuche*, for Polybius, comes close to meaning 'divine providence', and may properly be invoked by the historian in default of other explanations.

In the case of things of which it is difficult or impossible for mortals to grasp the causes, one may justifiably refer them, in one's difficulty, to gods and to *tuche*.[20]

Such events might be storms, drought or plague, or they might be otherwise incomprehensible human actions which can only be termed 'divine punishment and vengeance from the gods'. The divine clearly

---

[18] 'True' history: Gabba 1981: 54. Distance: Lucian, *How History Should Be Written* 60.
[19] *Hellenica* 5.4.1; above, pp. 1–4, on Xenophon; above, p. 87, on oaths.
[20] 36.17. F.W. Walbank 1957: 16–26. Diodorus Siculus similarly invokes *tuche* and divine forces: Sacks 1990: 36–7.

had some role to play, but it was needed as an explanation only in default of other explanations. In this respect most historians were close to the thoughtworld of the majority of their contemporaries: though the gods obviously existed, only in exceptional circumstances would an individual be sure that one of them had intervened in his or her life.[21]

The naturalistic explanations of human behaviour were paralleled by doubts concerning the rationale for traditional forms of cult and piety. In Plato's dialogue *Euthyphro* 'Socrates' presses the conventional Euthyphro on the justification for bringing gifts to the gods. Do the gods in some way *need* the gifts, and are they actually benefited by them? Euthyphro's eventual response was to claim, in some anger, that of course the gods do not need them, it is simply an issue of 'honour and recognition and *charis*'.[22] Such unsettling questions were, however, not explicitly instigations to abandon the performance of conventional religious practices. In *The Laws* Plato prescribes elaborate ritual apparatus for the ideal state, which is modelled on that of contemporary Athens: civic sanctuaries and priesthoods for the Olympian gods, official interpreters (*exegetai*) of Delphic laws and diviners. His mouthpiece in that work argues for the fundamental importance of the performance of religious practices.

To engage in sacrifice and commune with the gods continually, by prayers and offerings and devotions of every kind, is a thing most noble and good and helpful towards the happy life, and superlatively fitting also for the good person. (4.716D)

Plato indeed is so committed to the role of the gods as the ultimate binding force in his ideal state that he went well beyond contemporary practice. One of the tasks of the supreme council of the *Laws* was to prove the existence of the gods, and only those who have worked at such studies were eligible for the office of guardian (12.966CD). Plato built on the Athenian impiety law (covering both actions and beliefs) to formulate his own far more extensive impiety law. Offences against the gods arose as a result of false beliefs about them:

No one who believes that there are gods as prescribed by law has ever knowingly done an impious act or uttered an unlawful word. But with offenders one

---

[21] Jewish and Christian historians had a much stronger view of divine providence. Eusebius, for example, in his history of the growth of the Christian church views the Roman empire as the result of divine providence, in that it offered the necessary framework for the dissemination of the faith.

[22] *Euthyphro* 12e-15b. Cf. above, p. 37, on reciprocity (*charis*). Athenian tragedies were much concerned with the issue of piety and its consequences: Yunis 1988; Mikalson 1991: 133–202.

of these things is true: either he denies that there are gods, or though he admits their existence he thinks that they give no attention to human affairs; or, thirdly, he thinks that they are easy to persuade and can be won over by sacrifices and prayers. (10.885B)

The consequential law against impiety makes Plato the first political thinker to argue that matters of belief can be criminal offences.[23]

Religious rites for Plato are not just a civic obligation; they are crucial to true wellbeing. Aristotle too in his ideal state prescribes the institution of priesthoods of the gods, though in a slightly grudging manner: he lists them fifth of the various institutions of the state 'though they are first in importance' (above, p. 67). In his treatise on reasoning he takes for granted that the gods should be worshipped:

It is not necessary to examine every problem and every theme but only ones about which doubt might be felt by the kind of person who requires to be argued with and does not need castigation or lack perception. For those who feel doubt whether or not the gods ought to be honoured and parents loved need castigation, while those who feel doubt whether or not snow is white lack perception. (*Topics* 1.11, 105A)

The assumption about divine worship, casually made, reveals how far Aristotle was from the position of a modern who takes the line of Xenophanes about the gods. Indeed, Aristotle's own will ended with the instruction to set up in his home town in fulfilment of a vow for the safe arrival of his adopted son stone statues to Zeus Saviour and Athena Saviour (Diogenes Laertius 5.16). The will, whose authenticity cannot seriously be doubted, reveals that Aristotle's critique of divine anthropomorphism was perfectly compatible with the performance of conventional religious practices.

An adherence to ancestral ways is found even on the part of two schools which appear very distant from the gods: the Sceptics and the Epicureans. Scepticism was a movement founded in the later fourth century BC by Pyrrho, and revived in the first century BC. Our fullest expression of its philosophy comes in the works of Sextus Empiricus (second century AD). Scepticism held that, as real knowledge of the world was unobtainable, one should suspend judgement on all philosophical matters; only then will the philosopher attain tranquillity of mind. One of the ten modes of suspending judgement was to point to conflict between or within myth, custom and dogmatic supposition:

---

[23] See above, p. 82; Dodds 1951: 207–35; Morrow 1960: 399–499; Saunders 1991: 301–23; Cohen 1991: 203–17.

We juxtapose belief in myth with belief in myth when we observe that in some myths the father of men and gods is Zeus, but in others it is Oceanus, quoting 'Oceanus who begat the gods and Tethys their mother'. [Homer, *Iliad* 14.201] . . . Custom is juxtaposed with belief in myth when the myths say that Kronos ate his own children, while our custom is to take care of children. And whereas it is conventional among us to revere the gods as good and impervious to harm, the poets presented gods who sustain wounds and bear grudges against each other. Custom is juxtaposed with dogmatic supposition: whereas our custom is to pray for blessings from the gods, Epicurus says that divinity pays no attention to us . . . It just remains for us to add that, since this mode too reveals such a great anomaly among things, we will not be able to say what each object is like in its nature, but just how it appears in respect of this particular way of life, or law, or custom and so on for each of the others. Therefore, this mode too makes it necessary for us to suspend judgement about the nature of external objects. (Sextus Empiricus, *Outlines of Pyrrhonism* 1.145–63)

The suspension of judgement thus includes any judgement about the nature of the gods, but Sceptics were not, therefore, atheists: they did not deny the existence of the gods. Indeed, that would have been a positive affirmation inconsistent with the principle of the suspension of the judgement. And Sextus Empiricus makes clear at the start of a section on the problem of the gods that Sceptics conform to conventional practices and beliefs: he admits, without claiming dogmatic certainty, that the gods exist, and that one should honour them and believe in their providence.[24]

Epicurus (341–270 BC) and his school were often seen in antiquity as atheistical: in the second century AD proponents of a new cult proclaimed on the first day of its mysteries, 'If any atheist or Christian or Epicurean has come to spy on these rites, let him be off', and began the ceremony by saying, 'Out with the Christians', to which the crowd chanted in response, 'Out with the Epicureans'.[25] The reason for the perception of Epicureans as atheists was the complex and somewhat ambivalent nature of Epicurus' theology. Epicurus himself seems to have held that the gods were mental images, extrapolated from the ideal for humans, characterised by blessedness and imperishability. This view on its own might have offered a philosophical justification of traditional beliefs about the Olympian gods. However, Epicurus combined it with the idea that neither was the world divinely created, nor did the gods intervene in it; as a consequence there was no divine providence governing human

---

[24] Sextus Empiricus, *Outlines of Pyrrhonism* 3.2. Annas and Barnes 1985: 156–71; Long and Sedley 1987: 1.13–24, 468–88; for Academics cf. below, p. 155.

[25] Lucian, *Alexander* 38. See Long and Sedley 1987: II.152 for philosophical texts.

affairs. Epicurus' position concerning the issue of the existence of mental images of the gods could be interpreted in different ways. It may be the case that Epicurus himself, like Plato, merely meant that if any object can be thought of, it must objectively exist, but followers of Epicurus in the first century BC certainly took the gods to be actual spatial beings, perhaps existing in the space between the worlds from which we receive our mental images of them.[26] This view articulated an important element of traditional religious belief. Moreover, the school was strongly committed to conventional religious practices. A treatise, perhaps by Epicurus himself, which is addressed to a non-Epicurean audience, argued in favour of religious observances:

[it is for you a thing both] salutary and agreeable, as suits the occasion, to observe this your own religious practice, while enjoying innate physical pleasures (which are fitting) and conforming besides to conventional social customs;[27]

and Philodemus (an Epicurean of the first century BC) wrote a treatise *On Piety* defending Epicurus against the charge of impiety: he claims that Epicurus himself took part in Athenian festivals and was even initiated into the Eleusinian Mysteries.[28]

The major exceptions to this conventionalism were the Cynics, followers of Diogenes of Sinope on the north-east coast of Asia Minor (c. 400 to c. 325 BC). They did not develop an elaborate philosophical system, but preached that happiness was the result of meeting only one's natural needs, and in the simplest manner. From this follows much caustic wit and invective directed at conventional practices including religion. It was said that, when someone expressed astonishment at the votive offerings in Samothrace, Diogenes replied, 'There would have been far more if those who were not saved had set up offerings.'[29] He was reputed never to take part in religious rituals and to hold that there was nothing wrong with stealing from temples or committing anything else conventionally seen as sacrilegious. Cynics, who had been prominent in the fourth and third centuries BC, became less so in the second and first centuries BC, but revived again under the Roman empire. In the early second century AD, one Oenomaus of Gadara (in Palestine)

---

[26] Long and Sedley 1987: 1.57–65, 139–49.

[27] *Oxyrhynchus Papyri* 215, column 2.1–8, with Obbink 1984; also in *Corpus dei Papiri Filosofici greci e latini* 1.2 (Florence 1992), 167–91 (partially trans. Long and Sedley 1987: 1.144).

[28] The charge was probably levelled by Stoic philosophers. Henrichs 1972a; Obbink 1996. Cf. also on Epicurus and religion: Babut 1974: 156–7; Festugière 1955 (2nd edn 1968); Parker 1996: 279.

[29] Diogenes Laertius 6.59; above, p. 114, on Samothrace. The anecdote was probably told originally of the 'atheist' Diagoras of Melos; cf. Burkert 1993: 183.

devoted a whole treatise, *Exposé of the Charlatans*, to attacking the validity of oracles. He criticised Delphic ambiguity, the banality of oracular advice and the stupidity of those who consulted oracles. He himself had originally believed in the power of oracles, and had consulted the oracle of Apollo at Claros, perhaps about how or when he should learn philosophy. His elation in receiving an encouraging if opaque response was destroyed when he discovered that a mere merchant had received an identical oracle, which he had interpreted in accordance with his own problems. Oenomaus came to reject not only the prestigious oracles, but even, it seems, all worship of the gods.[30]

The examples given so far have shown that the rejection of Homeric and Hesiodic conceptions of the gods could well go along with the general affirmation of ancestral religious practices; however, it is said sometimes that philosophers were frightened by the trial of Socrates and prudently offered a sop to public opinion. The situation was more complex. Their commitment to religious practices was accompanied by a reinterpretation of the significance of those practices, and their own constructions of philosophy were imbued with religious elements. So Aristotle may take it as obvious that the gods should be honoured, but his own developed notion of the divine was quite untraditional: the universe depended on a supreme being who was responsible for all movement in the universe while himself being immobile

We hold then that god is a living being, eternal, most good; and therefore life and a continuous eternal existence belong to god; for that is what god is. (*Metaphysics* 12.7, 1072B)

A very un-Homeric philosophy, but still profoundly religious in conception.[31] Aristotle's master, Plato, who was more concerned than Aristotle about religious issues, developed his own conception of religious piety. In the dialogue *Euthyphro* Plato sought to make true piety depend on the moral behaviour and intentions of the individual, that is it contained an element of justice. This was a crucial move which permitted real religious practices to be related to what was ultimately true. So cult images of the gods are lifeless objects, but when we worship them the living god beyond feels great goodwill and gratitude (*Laws* 11.931A). Prayers to the gods should not simply be for whatever the individual happens to desire.

---

[30] The work is known only through the use made of it by the Christian apologist Eusebius. On Claros, Eusebius, *Praeparatio Evangelica* 5.22, 214A (= Hammerstaedt 1988 frag. 14), trans. E.H. Gifford, Oxford 1903. Cf. Attridge 1978: 56–60; Parke 1985: 142–5.

[31] Hence the influence that Aristotle had on Christian philosophers, especially Aquinas, in the Middle Ages.

In the ideal state the prayers of a son who is still young and foolish should be countermanded by the prayers of his wiser father and conversely, if the father indulges in a violent prayer of passion,

what a man ought to pray and press for is not that everything should follow his own desires, if his desires in no way follow his reason, but it is the winning of reason that every one of us, states and individuals alike, ought to pray and strive for. (*Laws* 3.687E)

Because true piety depended on justice and offered at least a reflection of the true nature of the divine, Plato could, without inconsistency, develop his own very powerful myths about the nature of the soul and its fate after death (especially in the *Republic* and *Timaeus*).

The Stoic school of philosophy was also profoundly religious. Zeno (335–263 BC), the founder of the school, believed, like Socrates and Epicurus, that philosophy should offer a guide to moral conduct, on the basis of a coherent cosmology. His views were very influential for the next five hundred years. Stoics argued that there was only one natural god, which they identified with a rational principle immanent in the world: it had originally created everything from fire and would end the present in a great conflagration and then begin the cycle again. They were staunch defenders of the existence of god, they also argued that he was a benevolent deity who had a crucial providential role in human affairs.[32] Stoics rejected, like earlier philosophers, the impiety of traditional mythology and the irrationality of anthropomorphic representations of the gods and the idea that traditional cult practices offered any pleasure to the gods or influenced them in any way. But they also placed greater weight on the value of widespread general notions and defended traditional religious practices.[33] This seeming contradiction was solved by the Stoic interpretation of the traditional Olympian gods as aspects of the Stoic immanent deity. These Stoic themes are expressed most powerfully in a *Hymn to Zeus* by Cleanthes, head of the Stoic school from 263 to 232 BC.

Most majestic of immortals, many-titled, ever omnipotent Zeus, prime mover of nature, who with your law steer all things, hail to you. For it is proper for any mortal to address you: we are your offspring and alone of all mortal creatures

---

[32] The Stoics here pick up an argument going back to the fifth century BC, that the order of the world is itself an argument for the providential role of its creator god: Xenophon, *Memorabilia* 1.4, 4.3, with Parker 1992.

[33] On Stoic (and Epicurean) use of 'common conceptions', for example on the gods, see Obbink 1992 (who rejects the idea that Stoics offered 'allegorical' readings of myths). Cf. also Babut 1974: 172–201; Dragona-Monachou 1976; Long 1990 on the debate between Stoics and Sceptics.

who are alive and tread the earth we bear a likeness to god. Therefore I shall
hymn you and sing for ever of your might. All this cosmos, as it spins round the
earth, obeys you, whichever way you lead, and willingly submits to your sway.
Such is the double-edged, fiery, ever-living thunderbolt which you hold at the
ready in your unvanquished hands. For under its strokes all the works of nature
are accomplished. With it you direct the universal reason which runs through
all things and intermingles with the lights of heaven both great and small . . .
No deed is done on earth, god, without your offices, nor in the ethereal vaults
of heaven, nor at sea, save what bad men do in their folly . . .

Cleanthes uses the language and imagery of a traditional hymn to
express a novel view of the world. Zeus is re-interpreted as the supreme,
providential god, on whom the universe depends; his thunderbolt is no
longer the agent of doom for the wicked, but the creative force of fire in
the world; his reason and universal law underpin all of creation.[34]

The transformation of traditional ideas of piety is seen in a radical
form in Porphyry (AD 234–c.305), a polymathic philosopher, who wrote
very extensively on philosophical and religious matters. His *On Abstinence
from Animal Foods* was addressed to a pupil who had reverted from a
vegetarian to a carnivorous diet.[35] Book 1 rejects arguments against
abstinence mounted by various philosophical schools, Epicureans,
Stoics, Peripatetics (followers of Aristotle), and argues that abstinence
was necessary for the philosopher seeking to pursue the life of the intel-
lect. He then (in Book 2) faces the challenge that, if abstinence promoted
purity, why do Greeks sacrifice animals as pure and acceptable offerings
to the gods. Here, following a treatise *On Piety* by Theophrastos (c.
370–287 BC),[36] Porphyry presents a 'history' of sacrifice: primitive sacrifice involved only vegetables or incense, animal sacrifices were introduced out of ignorance, anger or fear. The origin of animal sacrifices
means that it is not pious to continue the practice and indeed the gods
prefer inexpensive (non-animal) offerings. Even if it is necessary to sacrifice an animal (in expiation or divination), it is necessary not to eat the
meat. But the philosopher should sacrifice only in a material way, in
contemplation, by offering the first fruits of his conception to the gods.
Next (Book 3) Porphyry rejects the point that killing animals is acceptable because of their differences from humans: in fact, all creatures that
share in sense perception and memory are rational, and therefore should

---

[34] Long and Sedley 1987: 1.326–7 (translation). For other Stoic arguments about the gods see Galen's
critique of the Stoic Chrysippus in *On the Doctrines of Hippocrates and Plato* (Corpus Medicorum
Graecorum 5.4.1.2, ed. and trans. P. de Lacy, Berlin 1978–84) 3.8, with Tieleman 1996: 220–33;
below, pp. 141–2, on Marcus Aurelius.    [35] Trans. by T. Taylor (London 1965).
[36] See Pötscher 1964; trans. Fortenbaugh et al. 1992: 2 nos. 531, 584. Cf. Obbink 1988.

be treated justly. And finally (Book 4) Porphyry presents the cases of nations that abstained totally or partially from meat, from those who lived during the Greek golden age to the Egyptians, Jews, Syrians and Persians. The book breaks off part way through the exceptions of individual Greeks who abstained from animal foods.

*On Abstinence*, often quarried for information about the views of earlier philosophers, especially Theophrastos, is itself an impressive treatise, whose arguments are, given its premises, compelling.[37] The argument is supported by vivid 'factual' examples: for example, a rich man accustomed to offering lavish animal sacrifices once visited Delphi, and having honoured Apollo in his usual manner asked who was the man who made the best sacrifices. He received an unexpected answer. The best sacrificer was not himself, as he had expected, but one Clearchus of Methydrium in Arcadia. The rich man immediately visited Methydrium, only to discover that Clearchus diligently honoured the gods only with offerings of first fruits.[38] Scholars have sometimes taken this vivid story to sum up real Greek ideas about piety, but in fact it is a fantasy embedded in a philosophical argument deliberately distancing itself from conventional ideas of piety. Porphyry's own position and perhaps Theophrastos' are the extreme form of philosophical spiritualisation of conventional piety. Theopompus, from whom Porphyry took the story of Clearchus, was arguing that inexpensive sacrifices were at least as pious as lavish ones and Theophrastos, from whom Porphyry takes much of his material on sacrifices, argued, contrary to normal Greek views, that animal sacrifice was inappropriate because of the natural kinship between humans and animals, and that its introduction marked a degeneration of the human condition. He followed Plato in asserting the importance of the disposition of the sacrificer and adapted Aristotle in arguing that god would appreciate the purity not of the body but of that part which is the most divine in us and related to him. It is Porphyry who, like some Pythagoreans before him, argued that the true sacrifice was contemplation of god.

The force and coherence of the individual systems of Greek philosophy have implications for our understanding of 'conversion' in the ancient world. A standard view holds that, in the Greek world before the rise of Christianity, conversion was a philosophical and not a religious phenomenon: people were converted to particular philosophical schools

---

[37] Babut 1974: 131–3; Sorabji 1993: 180–4.
[38] 2.16, from Theopompus, historian of the fourth century BC, *FGH* 115 F 344.

and not to new religions.[39] The problem with this view is that it assumes a sharp distinction between religion and philosophy, between mere ritual piety on the one hand and articulate programmes for life on the other. This assumption is unhelpful in its characterisation both of religion and of philosophy, and implicitly devalues Greek religion in comparison to Christianity. In fact, the particular ways of life associated with Orphics and Pythagoreans, who are not philosophical schools in the normal sense, certainly imply a type of conversion: a follower had to give up normal Greek practices to withdraw from the city as part of his adherence to the new cosmological system. Similarly, the adherence of 'Lucius' (in Apuleius' *Metamorphoses*) to the worship of Isis also obviously counts as conversion. After Lucius' initiation into the cult of Isis at Corinth, he ends his speech of gratitude to Isis by saying, 'I shall make sure I do the things a religious but poor person can: I shall for ever guard your sacred appearance and most holy divine power in the depth of my heart and gaze upon it.'[40] And subsequently he was told by the deity to go to Rome, where he obtained a series of extra initiations into the Egyptian cults. It is a circular (and desperate) argument to claim that the importance of the notion of conversion in the cult of Isis was itself a response to the rise of Christianity. Religious groups, from Orphics onwards, with their demands of personal commitment, offered a new sort of identity: religion was not just one of a bundle of characteristics defining ethnic or civic identity, it was the principal defining characteristic. These cults offered, in short, religious identity to their members.

The alleged distinction between religion and philosophy is misleading also in relation to philosophy. Adherence to a philosophical sect was not simply a matter for the mind, or the result of mere intellectual fashion. Those who took their philosophy seriously attempted to live that philosophy from day to day. And they did so not in opposition to religion, but in the light of their understanding of the role of the gods. This is seen most clearly and movingly in the *Meditations* of the Roman emperor Marcus Aurelius. In this work, which he wrote in Greek, Marcus, a convinced Stoic, attempted to think through his philosophy in relation to his life as emperor.[41] For example,

'Live with the gods.' He is living with the gods who continuously displays his soul to them, as content with what they have apportioned, and as doing what is willed by the spirit, the portion of himself which Zeus has given to each

---

[39] Nock 1933. Cf. Parente 1987.
[40] 11.25 (trans. Beard, North and Price 1998: II no. 12.4b). Cf. above, p. 123.
[41] Beard, North and Price 1998: II no. 13.5. Cf. Rutherford 1989.

person to lead and guide him. And this spirit is each person's mind and reason. (5.27)

The work consisted of a series of musings on the role of fate and the gods, and the transience of human affairs in relation to the divine. Philosophy remained in constant dialogue with traditional practices and traditional piety, and should not be deemed to be hostile to or more meaningful than Greek religions.

# CHAPTER 8

# *Reactions to Greek religions*

Reactions from outside came from the Romans, as well as from other groups with their own religious systems, namely Jews and Christians. Greek philosophers and other intellectuals engaged in debates about Greek religions, but from within Greek culture. Outsiders on the other hand were naturally convinced of the superiority of their own religious systems. Indeed in the fourth and fifth centuries the combination of Roman power and Christian belief was responsible for the official suppression of Greek cults. The responses of outsiders often focused on the issue of the antiquity of cults and religious practices, both Greek and other. This was a crucial issue because antiquity tends to be the principal guarantee of authority in institutionalised religious systems. Even in the case of Christianity, whose merits we often see as novelty, the antiquity of the Christian revelation was a pressing issue.

## ROMANS

From the earliest times Rome was in contact with her neighbours, both the Etruscans and, more remotely, the Greeks. The early phase of Roman interaction with Greek religion is attested most neatly in excavations of what is probably the sanctuary of Vulcan in the Roman Forum. A sixth-century votive deposit from here includes an Attic vase representing the return of Hephaistos to Olympos (Fig. 8.1).[1] It is likely that the Greek Hephaistos already at this time is identified with the Roman Vulcan. By the first century BC it was normal for Romans to assume correspondences between Greek and Roman gods: Zeus–Jupiter, Hera–Juno, Athena–Minerva, Artemis–Diana, Aphrodite–Venus, Demeter–Ceres, Ares–Mars.

Rome came into contact with the cults of Greek cities in south Italy

[1] Beard, North and Price 1998: II no. 1.7c.

Fig. 8.1. Drawing of fragment of Attic mixing bowl from Rome (c. 570–560 BC).
It shows Hephaistos seated on a donkey, returning to Olympos.

and Sicily, first as one among equals and then gradually as suzerain,
when Roman power expanded in the fourth and third centuries BC
(Sicily became Rome's first overseas province in 241 BC). A more Greek
appearance of the cult of Ceres, that is attested in the earliest calendar
of Rome already for the sixth century BC, can be observed in the early
fifth century BC.[2] A temple of Ceres, Liber and Libera was dedicated and
adorned with the works of Greek artists from south Italy or Sicily.[3] The
new triad of gods was probably also the result of borrowing from the
same region, and the additional gods were certainly taken later to correspond to Greek gods, Liber–Dionysos, Libera–Persephone. At least
from the third century BC, and possibly earlier, there was also a more
explicitly Greek element: Greek female priests, again from the south,
were responsible for new rituals that focused, in a Greek manner, on
Ceres–Demeter and Libera–Persephone. Though officially established
at Rome, the rituals were recognised as being specifically 'Greek rites'.
    Rome was also in contact with Greek communities further afield, both

[2] Calendar: Beard, North and Price 1998: II no. 3.3a, 19 April. Ceres: Le Bonniec 1958: 213–311,
    379–455.
[3] Beard, North and Price 1998: II Map 1 no. 18, 2 no. 3.3a. Steinby 1993– : 1.260–1.

western and eastern. From an early date Romans had dealings with Massilia (modern Marseilles), a Greek settlement founded c. 600 BC by Phocaeans from the west coast of Asia Minor. According to later legend, the Phocaean colonists, in accordance with an oracle, took with them an Ephesian woman Aristarche and a reproduction of the cult statue of Artemis of Ephesos. In the new city Aristarche was appointed female priest of the cult of Artemis Ephesia, whose rites were identical to those at Ephesos down to the imperial period.[4] In the sixth century BC at Rome there was founded a sanctuary to Diana on the Aventine. The original rules for the cult were written in Greek (and were still legible in the time of Augustus), and the cult image of the god was modelled on that worshipped at Massilia.[5] The original sixth-century statue was itself featured on a Roman coin of the first century BC.[6]

In other respects too Rome turned to and imitated Greek models; according to tradition, when the Romans were engaged in a lengthy siege of her northern neighbour Veii in the early fourth century BC, a prodigy occurred, which the Romans expiated on the advice of an oracle from Delphi.[7] Though much of the story of the siege of Veii is legendary, the Romans may indeed have consulted Delphi. Certainly after their victory over Veii in 396 BC, they sent a golden bowl to Delphi, which was placed in the treasury of the people of Massilia.[8] Following established Greek practice, the Romans imported the cult of Asclepius from Epidauros.[9] Healing cults, with a chief female deity, were already common in central Italy, but this is the first such cult known to have been backed by the authority of Greek antiquity. In 293 BC, because of a serious epidemic affecting the city, the Romans were advised to bring the god of medicine from Epidauros. According to Roman tradition, the ambassadors brought back a snake, symbolising the god, which jumped ship at Rome and made for an island in the river Tiber. Here the Romans built a temple to Aesculapius.[10] As at Epidauros, visitors to the sanctuary practised incubation, and recorded (in Latin) their thanks in votives for the god's help 'in a vision' (Fig. 8.2). The god gave detailed

---

[4] Strabo 4.1.4, 179c. Fleischer 1973: 137–9.
[5] Dionysios of Halikarnassos, *Roman Antiquities* 4.26; Strabo 4.1.5, 180c; Livy 1.45, trans. Beard, North and Price 1998: II no. 1.5d. The cult also spread to dependencies of Massilia in Gaul and Spain: Strabo 3.4.6, 159c; 3.4.8, 160c; 4.1.5, 180c; 4.1.8, 184A.      [6] Crawford 1974: no. 448, 3.
[7] Livy 5.15–17.
[8] Livy 5.25.7–10, 5.28.1–5; Appian, *Italica* frag.8.3. Above, p. 60, on treasuries at Delphi. For an alleged earlier consultation of Delphi see Livy 1.56.5.
[9] For imports to Athens and Pergamon in the fifth and fourth centuries see above, p. 109.
[10] Beard, North and Price 1998: 1.69–70, Map 1 no. 27; Steinby 1993– : 1.21–2.

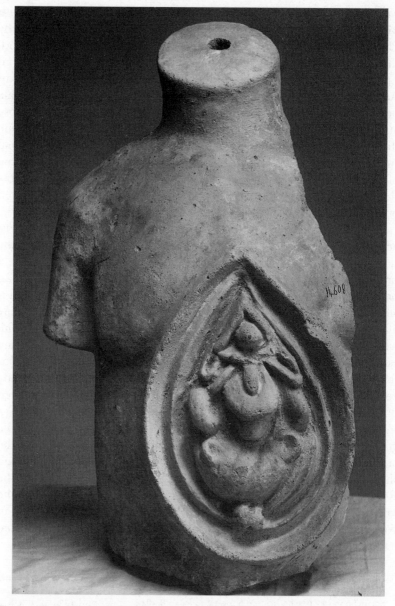

Fig. 8.2. Terracotta votive from sanctuary of Aesculapius, Rome (height 0.42m). The torso has been opened to reveal the internal organs. Anatomical votives were dedicated in healing sanctuaries also in Greece, and elsewhere in Italy.

instructions how the sick should be cured, as at Pergamon; this differed from the practice at Epidauros, where he sometimes himself cured the visitors. And late in the second or early third century AD an inscription in Greek itemised a list of recent cures.[11] The use of the Greek language refers to the origins of the god and the tone is self-consciously proud that the ancient rituals continue to be effective. For at least 500 years Aesculapius was a foreign presence in Rome.[12]

The Romans long believed that the ultimate origins of their city lay in the east. This belief certainly extended to the religious sphere. In Rome's neighbouring city of Lavinium, which had allegedly been founded by refugees from Troy, Aeneas was treated as a hero from early times. His monument, visible in the Augustan period, may have been discovered in excavations: there was a circular monument of the fourth century BC, which incorporated a tomb of the seventh century BC.[13] According to local tradition of the third century BC, Aeneas brought with him sacred objects from Troy.[14] These were the Penates of the Roman people, to whom Roman magistrates were obliged to sacrifice at Lavinium at the beginning of their year of office. In Rome itself two public cults of the Penates were practised; the one based on that at Lavinium was sited in the temple of Vesta. The cults were taken to stand for the durability of the city of Rome.

The prestige of the Penates allegedly brought to Italy by Aeneas can be linked to an exceptional Roman interest in the mysteries of the Great Gods on Samothrace.[15] Romans came in considerable numbers to Samothrace from the second century BC to the second century AD; about a third of the names of *mustai* inscribed there are Roman. Indeed, so common were they that the inscription regulating the entry of non-initiates to a building had to be bilingual Greek–Latin, which is unique in a Greek sanctuary. Governors of the adjacent province of Macedonia were often initiated, though only in the first degree, along with their entourage; military personnel and private citizens living in the east (as traders or tax-collectors) were also initiated. These initiations are hardly paralleled in any other Greek sanctuary, at least in the first centuries BC,

---

[11] *Syll.*[3] 1173 = *IGUR* 148 (trans. Edelstein 1945: 1.250–1). Greek was used at Rome sporadically also in the cults of other Greek gods.

[12] There were also sanctuaries of Aesculapius in towns dependent on Rome: Antium – Livy 43.4.6–7; Fregellae – Coarelli 1986.

[13] Dionysios of Halikarnassos, *Roman Antiquities* 1.64; Beard, North and Price 1998: ɪɪ no. 1.5b(ii). Cornell 1995: 68 counsels caution.

[14] Timaeus, *FGH* 566 F 59, in Dionysios of Halikarnassos, *Roman Antiquities* 1.67.4. Cf. Dubourdieu 1989.    [15] Cole 1989: 1588–96; Dubourdieu 1989: 125–50.

and indicate that the Romans accepted and adapted the Greek tradition that the ancestors of Priam and Hektor of Troy came from Samothrace, bringing with them the sacred objects, which were later brought to Italy by Aeneas and known as the Penates. For Romans initiation at Samothrace offered an entry to the ultimate origins of Rome itself.

Roman interest in Troy was consolidated with the introduction of the cult of Mater Magna, sometimes known as Cybele. The cult was introduced to Rome in 204 BC and its temple and associated games were in operation from 194 BC. The cult was initially very exotic: the symbol of the deity, a black stone, was anomalous in that it was not anthropomorphic. Apparently, there was a ban on actual Romans participating in the rites: 'no native-born Roman walks through the city dressed in bright clothes, begging for alms or accompanied by flute-players, nor worships the goddess with wild Phrygian ceremonies'.[16] Gradually, however, the deity became domesticated at Rome. There is no doubt that her homeland of Phrygia was associated with Troy and the origins of Rome.

Though the import of Greek cults and the establishment of correspondences between Roman and Greek gods might give the impression that Roman religion was much the same as Greek religion, in fact the two systems were profoundly different. The problems of mediating between Roman and foreign cults are illustrated by the Sibylline Books, written in Greek and an import from the Greek city of Cumae in south Italy. These books, which were the responsibility of a special college of priests, the *quindecimviri* ('Board of Fifteen'), were consulted at times of crisis, and sometimes advised the introduction of a foreign cult. Such consultations occurred before the building of the temple to Ceres, Liber and Libera, before the sending of an embassy to fetch the god from Epidaurus, and before the import of Mater Magna to Rome. And cults once imported were sometimes themselves under the supervision of the *quindecimviri*.

The distinction between Roman and foreign cults seen in these institutional arrangements is also reflected in a distinction between Roman and Greek rites.[17] This is why we find Dionysios of Halikarnassos, a Greek historian of Rome writing under Augustus, commenting on the existence of Greek rites in his own day, which he interprets as continuations of cults of extreme antiquity. For example,

---

[16] Dionysios of Halikarnassos, *Roman Antiquities* ii.19 (trans. Beard, North and Price 1998: ii no. 8.7a). See further Beard, North and Price 1998: 1.96–8.

[17] Wissowa 1912: 420–32; Scheid 1995 stresses the instability of the distinction.

according to Dionysios, at the Ara Maxima in Rome, dedicated to Herakles, there was an annual sacrifice of a calf performed according to Greek rites, a sacrifice which Herakles himself had instituted.[18] Various matters constituted a rite as 'Greek'. The sacrificial animals might differ from normal Roman practice: cocks were offered to Aesculapius, as in Greece.[19] The form of sacrifice might differ: at the 'Saecular Games', introduced as a result of consultation of the Sibylline Books, the whole animal was burnt 'in the Greek rite' for the Moerae (Fates) and Terra Mater (Earth Mother), who had 'chthonic' associations.[20] And, most characteristic of all, the manner of sacrifice of ordinary victims also differed: at 'Roman' rites the presiding figure had his toga pulled over his head, while at 'Greek' rites he had his head bare.[21]

The cult of Ceres illustrates a number of Greek ritual features, which would have been perceived as 'un-Roman'.[22] The Greek female priests were anomalous, not only in that they performed the rites in Greek, but also in their gender. Roman religious officials were almost exclusively male. Cult practice reflected that of the Greek Demeter: the annual festival for Ceres in June/July (distinct from the ancient Cerealia on 19 April) involved temporary sexual abstinence on the part of the participating women, and the ritual focused on the discovery of Proserpina by Ceres. The festival was even described as a 'mystery' into which the participating women were initiated: it was indeed unique at Rome as an official festival involving female initiation.[23] Finally, an additional, Greek rite was added in the second century BC, again as a result of consultation of the Sibylline Books: fasting in honour of Ceres, which was initially to occur every five years, but which became an annual occurrence, at a different time (4 October) from the other rites for Ceres. These rites combine elements from both the Thesmophoria and the Eleusinian Mysteries to constitute a new ritual complex that was nonetheless seen by the Romans as distinctively Greek.

Further differences between the Greek and Roman religious systems can be observed. Roman gods, though they might be given equivalences to Greek gods, had different resonances. They did not have stories associated with them in the Greek manner. There was no Roman equivalent

---

[18] *Roman Antiquities* 1.40.3. See Beard, North and Price 1998: I. 68, 173–4 on the Ara Maxima.
[19] Festus 98 Lindsay.
[20] Latte 1960: 392 n.I. See above, p. 12, on 'chthonic', and Beard, North and Price 1998: I.201–6 and II no. 5.7b on Saecular Games.
[21] For images of 'Roman' rites see Beard, North and Price 1998: II nos. 6.1b, 7.4d.
[22] Le Bonniec 1958: 379–455.
[23] Cicero, *Laws* 2.21.35–7 is minded to permit only such initiation 'by Greek ritual'.

of Hesiod's *Theogony*, offering a Panhellenic religious cosmology, nor were there many Roman equivalents to Greek stories relating gods to particular cities, like the Athenian myth of the contest between Athena and Poseidon (above, p. 19) or the Ephesian myth of the birth of Artemis (above, p. 23). For the Romans, Jupiter Optimus Maximus just was the most important god of Rome, the ultimate protector of the city, whose favour was responsible for the growth and might of Rome. In contrast, the role of the myth of Ceres and Proserpina in one of the festivals of Ceres is an index of the Greekness of that festival. Roman myths there certainly were, but they relate rather to divine favours shown at various stages in the growth of Rome: the establishment of rites by Hercules at the Ara Maxima, or Aeneas' bringing of the Penates to Italy.[24]

Roman religious places were different from Greek ones. The Romans did construct buildings to shelter cult images, but these buildings (*aedes*) had a rather different architecture: whereas a Greek temple (*naos*) was designed to be seen from all sides, the Roman *aedes* often had a much more frontal emphasis. It was raised on a high platform, with full columns sometimes only at the front, and sometimes set against a rear wall.[25] The Romans also took over from the Etruscans a non-Greek system of seeking divine favour. Observations of the heavens had to be made from within a special space ritually defined. This space, called a *templum*, might in fact include an *aedes* (or temple in our sense), but it might also include quite different sorts of buildings (such as the Roman senate house).[26] Indeed the senate had to hold its meetings in a *templum*, often the senate house, but also at various *aedes* in the city.

Religious authority was also quite different at Rome.[27] For public cults of Greek cities there were both priesthoods running in particular families and annual priests appointed by the city, and priests might be male or female, depending on the cult. At Rome, on the other hand, lineage priesthoods were almost non-existent, and the priests of the principal civic cults were men, appointed for life, and drawn not from the whole citizen body but only from the senatorial order.[28] There were the important exceptions of the female priests of Ceres, and the Vestal Virgins (the latter drawn, however, again only from senatorial families), but the

---

[24] Beard, North and Price 1998: I.171–81.
[25] Contrast above Fig. 2.14 no. 4 with Beard, North and Price 1998: II no. 4.1.
[26] Varro, *On the Latin Language* 7.8–10, trans. Beard, North and Price 1998: II no. 4.4.
[27] Beard and North 1990; Beard, North and Price 1998: II ch. 8.
[28] Control of the cult of Hercules at the Ara Maxima was removed in 312 BC from a lineage, the Potitii, to the state. Livy 9.29.9–11, trans. Beard, North and Price 1998: II no. 1.6c.

typical Roman priests were men like Cicero or the younger Pliny, both appointed to the college of *augures*, and in the imperial period inscriptions recording the careers of senators normally listed their priesthoods not only among the most prestigious public offices they obtained, but even first, out of chronological order. This monopolisation of key offices by members of the political elite meant that religion, even more clearly than in Greece, supported the political order. The different colleges of priests were each answerable to the senate, which itself took decisions on major matters of religious policy. With the occasional exception of Delphi, the principal sources of religious authority (even the Sibylline Books) were all within the city and under the ultimate control of the political elite.

Comparing Greece and Rome in general, one is not surprised also to notice differences in their religious systems. Rome was from very early times an expansionist state. It began by incorporating in a series of alliances the neighbouring states of central Italy, so that by the third century BC it held sway over most of the Italian peninsula. In the third and second centuries BC Rome also went on to conquer territories overseas, both western and eastern. One internal factor which generated this seemingly inexorable growth of Roman power was the value system of the Roman elite: competition among the senatorial order was played out partly through military conquests, which guaranteed political prestige at Rome. This competition was also fuelled by the near monopolisation by the same elite of religious offices: the gods had an essential role in the preservation and growth of Roman power. As the empire grew, so too did the city: Rome by the first and second centuries AD had a population at times approaching one million people. In the early empire over 300,000 of this vast number were (male) Roman citizens, the rest their families, and slaves, ex-slaves, and free-born migrants from cities all round the empire.

In particular, the different notion of imperial political integration entailed a different sort of religious integration. The Athenians in the fifth century BC, for example, had sought simply to dominate their allies: the model of religious participation that was imposed was that of colonies participating in the rites of their mother city and of the imposition of cults of 'Athena Ruler of the Athenians' on recalcitrant allies (above, p. 65). The Romans, on the other hand, from the outset extended Roman citizenship not just to ex-slaves but also to her allies. The corollary of this close political incorporation was the extension of religious authority over the whole Italian peninsula, and the adoption of Roman religious practices by individuals and communities, who were proud to be Roman. The most striking example of this is the *coloniae* of Roman citizens created in Italy and the empire, including the Greek world (below, pp. 157–8). Such close adaptation of religious institutions has no parallel among Greek empires and alliances.

Not surprisingly, differences were also perceived when Greeks looked at the Roman religious system. Polybius' history of Rome's conquests included a section analysing the peculiarities of the Roman constitution. This concluded with some remarks on religion:

The respect in which the Roman constitution is most markedly superior is in their behaviour towards the gods. It is, I think, the very thing that brings reproach amongst other peoples that binds the Roman state together: I mean their superstitiousness. For nothing could exceed the extent to which this aspect both of their private lives and of their public occasions is dramatised and elaborated. Many would find this astonishing.[29]

Polybius goes on to assert that this religion was in fact an opiate for the masses, a view that perhaps casts some light back on the religious assumptions of members of Greek elites at this period, but his actual example of the effectiveness of religion related to members of the Roman elite. Whereas Greeks will peculate public moneys entrusted to them, Roman magistrates and ambassadors operate honestly just because they have pledged their faith by oath. That is, the religious sanctions of the oath were as important for the Romans as they had been in classical Athens (above, pp. 95–6). For Polybius religiosity was the final peculiarity of the Romans, which underpinned their world domination.

In the first century BC Dionysios of Halikarnassos, in his history of Rome, contrasted Greek and Roman religion and observed that the Romans chose some but rejected other elements of Greek religious practice. He claims that in establishing temples, festivals, sacrifices and days of rest Romulus 'followed the best customs in use among the Greeks' (2.18.2). For example,

all the rites that are performed in the Greek ceremonies by the maidens whom they call *kanephoroi* and *arrhephoroi* are performed by those whom the Romans call *tutulatae*, who wear on their heads the same kind of crowns with which the statues of the Ephesian Artemis are adorned among the Greeks.[30]

But Dionysios also stressed the rejection of some Greek practices by the Romans. According to Dionysios, Romulus

---

[29] Polybius 6.56.6–8, trans. Beard, North and Price 1998: II no. 13.1b.
[30] 2.22.2. Like Polybius, he also notes the importance of Roman respect for obligations: 2.75.

rejected all the traditional myths concerning the gods that contain blasphemies or calumnies against them, looking upon them as wicked, useless and indecent, and unworthy, not only of the gods, but even of good men; and he accustomed people both to think and to speak the best of the gods and to attribute to them no conduct unworthy of their blessed nature.[31]

The Romans thus had no Hesiodic-style myths of Ouranos being castrated by his own sons or of Kronos devouring his own offspring to secure himself from their attacks, or of Zeus dethroning Kronos and confining his own father in Tartarus. Dionysios, following the long-standing Greek tradition of criticism of such myths, commends Romulus, and by implication the Romans of his own day, for eschewing such stories. In addition, the Romans are commended for their lack of correspondingly unseemly religious practices: they have no festivals at which women beat their breasts and lament the disappearance of deities, like the Greek ritual commemorating the disappearance of Persephone;[32] they indulge in no ecstatic behaviour, no frenzies, no begging, no secret bacchic mysteries, no all-night vigils in sanctuaries with men and women together (2.19.2). Finally, Dionysios drew particular attention to the way that the Romans had not officially adopted the rites of foreigners who had come to Rome, and that any new rites that were duly introduced in accordance with the Sibylline Books were purged of any fabulous nonsense. For example, Mater Magna retained her own Phrygian male and female priests, but by senatorial decree no native Roman could take part in the procession, with its unseemly dress, and the begging for alms. 'So careful are the Romans to guard against religious practices that are not part of their own traditions; and they abominate all empty pomp that falls below proper standards of decency.'[33]

There was indeed in the second century BC a real anxiety on the part of the senatorial elite about inappropriate Greek practices at Rome. The most dramatic incident is the repression in 186 BC by the senate of the cult of Bacchus.[34] The cult of Bacchus had become established in Rome and Italy well before the 180s BC; it was found in communities of all statuses, and ignored the usual distinctions of social ranks: initiates were drawn from men and women, rich and poor, slave and free, country-folk and town-dwellers. A scandal affecting a good family in Rome was the pretext for a repression of the cult of unprecedented scope. The senate

---

[31] 2.18.3. Cf. Borgeaud 1993.    [32] See above, p. 149, for the 'discovery' of Persephone at Rome.
[33] 2.19.5, trans. Beard, North and Price 1998: II no. 8.7a.
[34] Beard, North and Price 1998: I.91–6; II no. 12.1.

decided to intervene both in cities under her control and (very anom-
alously) in allied cities over which she had no jurisdiction. It passed a
decree that instituted tight control over the cult: it was to be of small
scale, not permitting the mingling of the sexes, and it should not possess
a strong internal organisation (with its own leadership, oaths and
common funds). The threat allegedly posed by the cult was perceived by
the senate to lie in its underground organisation, linking all parts of Italy
in a common conspiracy, and in its threat to the Roman family. The
repression of the cult was not a gesture against general Greek influences
at Rome: it was a response to a cult of Greek origin which was genuinely
seen as threatening to traditional authority.

Anxieties about Greek ideas surfaced again at Rome a few years later.
There is a curious story that in 181 BC a coffin was discovered contain-
ing the body of king Numa and wonderfully preserved books of his with
the philosophical doctrines of Pythagoras. The books came to the attention of a Roman magistrate, who decided that they were destructive of
Roman religion. On his recommendation, the senate decreed that the
books should be burnt.[35] There is a chronological absurdity in the story,
realised by some ancient writers: Numa, according to conventional
chronologies, would have died 140 years before Pythagoras even came
to Italy. But the alleged links between Pythagoras and the mild king who
created many of Rome's religious institutions and laws were probably
long established by 181 BC. Some have seen this incident as evidence for
a real Pythagorean movement at Rome, aiming to reform Roman religion on Greek philosophic principles, but the story reads as if the 'discovery' of the books was itself engineered by those who then sought to
express their repugnance at the nature of Greek philosophic influence
on Rome's wisest king. The startling decision to burn the books epitomised a feeling that Roman religion should be independent of foreign
influence.

An intellectual response to Greek philosophy emerges most clearly in
the mid-first century BC in the works of Cicero. Some Romans had long
been interested in the teachings of contemporary Greek philosophers,
but Cicero was among the first to domesticate Greek philosophy by
developing its arguments in Latin. In so doing he faced explicitly the
problem of relating Roman religious practices and Greek philosophic
theory. The problem is most evident in his dialogue *On Divination* composed in 44 BC.[36] The first half of the treatise, in the mouth of Cicero's

[35] Pliny, *Natural History* 13.84–7, trans. Beard, North and Price 1998: II no. 11.1; Livy 40.29.3–14.
Gruen 1990: 158–70.    [36] Beard 1986; Beard, North and Price 1998: 1.150–1.

brother, expounded Stoic arguments in favour of the validity of divination, drawing many of its examples from the actual workings of Roman
divination. The second half, in the mouth of Cicero himself, explored
the sceptical arguments of the Academic school of philosophy. This
school, which originated in the teachings of Plato, had taken a sceptical
turn in the third century BC. Cicero's own teacher, Philo, held a moderate form of scepticism: there was no certain knowledge, but one should
accept on a provisional basis the arguments that seemed the most per-
suasive. In this dialogue the character of Cicero adopts the characteristic Academic position of attacking the positive Stoic arguments of the
first speaker. The implication of this critique should not be that Cicero
himself was sceptical about the validity of divination (indeed the
Academic critique of Stoics is philosophically unconvincing). Rather,
the unresolved conflict between assertions that Roman divination does
work in practice and the concluding argument that it cannot work
exposed the problems of forming a Roman intellectual language about
Roman religion.[37]

In the first century AD the authorities were still capable of expelling
from Rome and Italy the adherents of cults that were undesirably
foreign.[38] The official religious ideology of the state was overtly
Roman: emperors or members of the senatorial elite who deviated
from it publicly received opprobrium. For example, the senator and
philosopher Seneca was tempted by Pythagorean arguments in his
youth and gave up eating meat, but was instructed by his father to
return to a normal carnivorous diet.[39] Marcus Aurelius kept private *To
Himself*, his record, in Greek, of his attempts to live out the Stoic philosophic code, although Stoicism was compatible with and to some
extent a justification of traditional Roman practices. For Marcus there
was no problem about being represented on a victory arch performing
a sacrifice in the traditional Roman manner.[40] However, Rome under
the emperors no longer displayed the extreme reaction to things Greek
that it did in the second century BC. As for the religious position of
emperors, there is nothing to be said for the old view that the so-called
imperial cult at Rome was based on earlier Greek ruler cults. The religious articulation of imperial power at Rome itself paraded its roots in
Roman practices (for example, the apotheosis of Romulus) and was

---

[37] Epicureanism was also attractive to some Romans in the first century BC. See most obviously
Lucretius' *On the Nature of Things*. For political implications see Fowler 1989.
[38] Beard, North and Price 1998: I. 160–1, 230–2. 'Foreign' now no longer includes 'Greek'.
[39] Seneca, *Letters* 108.17–22.    [40] Trans. Beard, North and Price 1998: II no. 6.1b.

distinguished from whatever religious honours the Greek subjects saw fit to offer the Roman emperor.[41]

As the different parts of the Greek world came under Rome, their cults too were subject to Roman control. Though there was no attempt to make Roman religious law apply outside Rome and Italy, it was one of the jobs of Roman governors to ensure that religious property was not expropriated by individuals or communities and to ensure that temple finances were in good order. The essentially conservative role of the Roman authorities operated on the assumption that Greek civic cults were appropriate, for the Greeks, because of their antiquity. This tacit assumption came to the fore on occasions when the Romans decided that there was a problem with some aspect of Greek cults. In AD 22 the emperor Tiberius was disquieted by accounts that there was widespread abuse in Greece of asylum rights at sanctuaries: bankrupts and murder suspects were taking refuge there, resulting in possible civic disturbances.[42] The senate, to which Tiberius referred the affair, then heard deputations from numerous sanctuaries in the Greek world, each claiming the defence of antiquity for their particular right of asylum. For example, the Ephesians claimed that Artemis and Apollo had been born not at Delos but at Ephesos; Apollo himself had avoided there the wrath of Zeus for the murder of the Cyclops; Dionysos had pardoned some Amazons who were suppliants at the altar there; Herakles had further extended the sanctity of the temple, privileges which had been respected by the Persians, the Macedonians and the Romans. These arguments presented to the Roman senate drew on common Ephesian beliefs about the relationship of the gods to the city (above, pp. 22–3), and served to convince the Romans that these and other asylum rights of genuine antiquity should, though circumscribed, be preserved. Greek mythology and the long tradition of important Greek religious practices might be the subject of public debate, and might determine public policy.

Control was only one aspect of the contacts between Roman emperors and Greek cults. The cults were, after all, perceived as admirable for their antiquity. Emperors who visited the Greek world were happy to take part in local sacrifices and festivals, and even to be initiated into the Eleusinian Mysteries. When problems arose for cities and sanctuaries, emperors received embassies and petitions, adjudicated in favour of sanctuaries, and emphasised their own piety towards the gods. The

---

[41] Price 1987; Beard, North and Price 1998: I.206–10.
[42] Tacitus, *Annals* 3.60–3, 4.14. Cf. above, p. 23; Beard, North and Price 1998: I.224.

concern of emperor and Roman governor is well illustrated in an edict issued in the first century AD by a governor of the province of Asia in favour of the temple of Artemis at Ephesos:

For many temples of the gods have been destroyed by fire or lie collapsed in ruins, and the temple of Artemis herself, which is the ornament of the whole province because of the greatness of the work, the antiquity of the reverence of the god and because of the abundance of the revenues restored to the god by the deified Augustus, is being deprived of its own money, which used to suffice for its upkeep and the adornment of the votive offerings.[43]

Emperors also helped to repair temples damaged in earthquakes, and also paid for the building of some new temples, alongside secular public buildings such as baths, theatres and aqueducts.[44] The emperor Hadrian spent lavishly in the Greek provinces on a whole range of new buildings, particularly temples, especially to Zeus. At Athens he completed the vast temple to Zeus Olympios, begun in the sixth century BC; work had progressed in the second century BC thanks to the generosity of a Hellenistic king, Antiochus IV Epiphanes of Syria, but the project was too vast to be completed with Athenian resources.[45] Hadrian also built a temple to Hera and Zeus Panhellenios, with a new sanctuary of all the gods.[46] These two projects were connected with Hadrian's attempt to promote Athens as the central focus for a revived Panhellenic movement. But Hadrian also paid at least part of the costs of huge temples in Asia Minor: a temple to Zeus Akraios ('On the Peak') at Smyrna, and a temple perhaps also to Zeus at Cyzikos.[47] Roman rule thus supported Greek religious practices; the Romans did not generally seek to export the cults of the city of Rome. There were indeed almost no specifically Roman cults in Greek cities. The one exception is the Roman *coloniae* in the Greek world. These towns, dating mainly to the late first century BC and early first century AD and populated in part by retired legionaries, were in principle clones of Rome, from their seven hills to the use of the Latin language and Roman religious institutions.[48] Corinth, for example, which had been sacked by Rome in 146 BC, was refounded as a *colonia* in 44 BC and largely rebuilt in the Roman period. The largest

---

[43] *Inschriften von Ephesos* 1a, 18b, 1–8, 19b, 0–7; trans. in D.C. Braund, *Augustus to Nero* (London and Sydney 1985) 213–15. Cf. Appendix no. 15 for the intervention of later governors. Emperors: Millar 1977: 447–56.   [44] Mitchell 1987; Winter 1996: 168–77.

[45] Pausanias 1.18.6–8. Travlos 1971: 402–11.

[46] Pausanias 1.18.9. Travlos 1971: 429–31; Spawforth and Walker 1985.

[47] Smyrna: Philostratus, *Lives of the Sophists* 1.25.2, 9; Cyzikos: Price 1984a: 153–5, 251–2. See above, p. 75, for his completion of the temple at Claros.

[48] Beard, North and Price 1998: 1.313–63.

temple flanking the main square was now almost certainly a temple of the Capitoline triad, Jupiter, Juno and Minerva.[49] But even at Corinth Greek traditions were remembered or reinvented by the second century AD, and Pausanias was able to describe Greek religious monuments such as the gilded wooden image of Dionysos which the Corinthians created, on the advice of the Pythia, from the tree in which Pentheus tried to hide when spying on the maenads.[50]

Greek cities also used old language and ancient forms of honouring the gods in relation to Rome. Cults which had reference to Rome (cults of emperors and empresses, and of 'Roma' herself) were not Roman but Greek cults. Cities from the Hellenistic period onwards had established cults of their new rulers, and, though there was little continuity in the actual cults, similar responses were made when Greek cities fell under the sway of Rome. Indeed as late as the end of the second century AD the Athenians established a cult of Julia Domna, wife of the emperor Septimius Severus, which was modelled quite closely on their ancestral cult of Athena Polias.[51] The Greeks employed traditional forms to articulate their position in a new world.

## JEWS AND CHRISTIANS

The antiquity, status and value of Greek cults were an issue also for Jews and Christians. From the Hellenistic period onwards Jewish communities existed in Asia Minor and mainland Greece. Christian communities also developed in the Greek world from the first century AD onwards. We are used to the idea of opposition between Judaism and Christianity on the one hand and 'paganism' on the other, but that opposition is problematic. We expect Jews and Christians to have engaged only in polemic against the cults, and to have asserted the novel truths of their own faiths, but in fact both Jews and Christians also claimed the authority of antiquity, and sometimes enlisted the Greeks on their side. We also expect Jews and Christians each to be unified bodies of people with their own distinct doctrines and practices, but this expectation is the result of the development of orthodoxies from the third century (for Jews) and fourth

---

[49] Mary Walbank 1989; Williams 1989 on architectural issues.

[50] Pausanias 2.2.6–7; above, p. 115, on maenads. Dio, *Oration* 37.26 asserts that Corinth has become Hellenised; from the early second century AD Greek inscriptions outnumber Latin: *Corinth* 8.3.18–19.

[51] Oliver 1940, trans. Beard, North and Price 1998: II no. 10.5c. For a small temple of Rome and Augustus on the Athenian Akropolis, whose decoration echoes that of the Erechtheion, see above, Fig. 2.14 no. 3; Price 1984a: 147 n.40. Hellenistic: above, p. 7. Roman: Price 1984a.

century (for Christians). In the earlier centuries there was no orthodoxy in either Judaism or Christianity, though some people did claim that others were 'heretics': each contained a variety of practices and ideas.[52]

Greek charges against both Jews and Christians were that their practices were novel, and hence worthless. By the first century AD Jews were criticised by some Greeks for their modernity in comparison with the antiquity of the Greeks, and for being in origin undesirables expelled from Egypt, and for having bizarre and immoral practices. The charge of novelty was also levelled against Christians. In the 170s AD a Greek writer named Celsus wrote the first known tract *Against the Christians*. He asserted that the Christians were doubly at fault: they had fallen away from the faith of the Jews, who were themselves little more than renegade Egyptians. Such charges were disturbing to Jews and Christians, who sought to refute them. Josephus wrote a wide-ranging treatise defending the antiquity of the Jews;[53] Origen composed a refutation of Celsus, preserving for us lengthy quotations from the original.[54] Both authors also used the opportunity to offer a positive account of Jewish and Christian beliefs and practices.

One response on the part of Jews and Christians to Greek criticisms was to criticise Greek myths and rituals. One might wonder if they were simply 'tilting at windmills', but the importance of Greek myths in the first and second centuries AD is abundantly clear, and Jews and Christians were obviously attacking real targets of their own day, though their selection of the specific target accorded with the rhetorical needs of the treatise. Josephus expressed distaste at the need for polemic against Greek religion, but claimed that he was forced into it by the fact that others derided Judaism in comparison with other religions. Indeed Greek writers themselves had already criticised Greek poets and lawgivers for propagating absurd and immoral ideas about the gods (above, ch. 7). For example, the gods are endless in number, born in all sorts of ways, living like animals in all sorts of locations (Hades underground, Poseidon in the sea, Titans chained in Tartarus). The gods have all sorts of ages and professions; they quarrel, and even engage in adultery.[55] As Josephus said, this critique was developed from the internal Greek debate about the propriety of Greek mythology (above, p. 153). Though of long standing, this debate was still lively in the first centuries AD.

---

[52] Beard, North and Price 1998: 1.248–9.
[53] *Against Apion*, late first century AD. Cf. Goodman 1999.
[54] *Against Celsus*, trans. H. Chadwick (Cambridge 1953), late 240s AD. Cf. Chadwick 1966: 22–30, 66–94.   [55] *Against Apion* 2.236–49.

Greek Christian writers of the second century AD also started to
defend Christianity against alleged calumnies, in part by attacking contemporary Greek cults. Justin, for example, writing in the 150s AD, noted
that 'we' (i.e. Greek Christians) used to worship Dionysos, Apollo,
Persephone, Aphrodite, Asclepius; now 'although we are threatened
with death, through Jesus Christ we have come to depise these immoral
deities, and have given ourselves to the unbegotten and impassive god'.
'Our' god could not be driven wild by sexual passion, would not need to
be rescued, nor would he plan the death of many Greeks for the sake of
a concubine. 'We pity those who believe such stories and we recognise
that demons are responsible for them.'[56] Athenagoras, writing in the
170s, extended the line that attack was the best form of defence. His treatise begins by pointing out that the other (non-Christian) inhabitants of
the empire are entitled to follow their ancestral religious customs, no
matter how absurd they are: for example, the Athenians sacrifice to
Poseidon Erechtheus, and celebrate rites and mysteries for Aglauros and
Pandrosos, despite the fact that they were considered impious for
opening the chest entrusted to them.[57] His targets are those cults in
which humans were absurdly worshipped as gods – cults lovingly
described by his contemporary Pausanias. Later the treatise turns to the
alleged absurdity of myths about the major Olympian deities: it cites
Orpheus, who is taken to have preceded Homer and Hesiod in defining
the nature of the gods, for the 'absurd' idea that the gods have come into
being and indeed have their substance from water; with reference to
Homer, it also goes on to criticise the idea that the gods could be corpo-
real, with blood, semen, and the passions of anger and lust.[58]
Athenagoras and the other second-century Greek apologists for
Christianity attack both Panhellenic ideas and local practices.

The other strand to the case of the Jewish and Christian apologists is
that in certain respects Greek ideas prefigure, and thus support by their
antiquity, their own doctrines. The religious authority of Orpheus was
subpoenaed by some Jews and then Christians. By the mid-second
century BC there existed two Jewish versions of a set of verses modelled
on 'traditional' Orphic revelation. In them Orpheus was made to proclaim to his son Musaios the power of the one true god; the longer
version says that only a figure who may be identified with Abraham has

---

[56] *First Apology* 25, trans. Beard, North and Price 1998: II no. 12.7a(i). Cf. Chadwick 1966: 9–23;
Pagels 1988: 32–56.
[57] *Legatio* 1, trans. W.R. Schoedel (Oxford 1972). Cf. above, p. 94, for these cults.
[58] *Legatio* 18–19, 21. Cf. above, p. 118, for Orpheus.

ever seen him (Fig. 8.3). This Jewish Orpheus was then adapted and exploited by Christian writers up until the fifth century AD. By the early fourth century, a Christian could claim that Orpheus' poems implied that he recanted his original proclamation of the existence of 360 gods.[59] The Greek Orpheus thus guaranteed the truth of first the Jewish and then the Christian faith.

Support for Jewish and Christian doctrine was in fact sought in a wide range of Greek authors. The same Jewish author of the mid-second century BC, Aristoboulos, who quotes one version of the *Sacred Text* of Orpheus, goes on to cite the beginning of a Hellenistic poem by Aratus as evidence for the power of god.[60] A line from this passage of Aratus was also cited approvingly in Acts of the Apostles (17.28), and it seems to have formed part of a collection of (contradictory) extracts from Greek poets on the issue of the power of god. Some of the 'extracts' in such collections were genuine, though sometimes misleading in being torn from their original contexts, others were specially composed to prove a point.[61]

Some Christians even sought support for their ideas in Greek rituals. This was a controversial position, condemned by self-styled defenders of 'orthodoxy', but one which may have been more common than is suggested by our surviving Christian evidence, which has been through the filter of later orthodoxy. In the first and second centuries some Christians felt that it was acceptable to partake in Greek sacrifices, either because it was a matter of religious indifference or because of some positive sense of the importance of ancestral traditions.[62] In the second century a group known as the Naassenes expressed a very positive attitude to the wisdom embedded in Greek mysteries. They were attracted to the Eleusinian Mysteries, some of whose ritual they alone describe for us (above, p. 105); they were also attracted to rituals of Mater Magna, describing the public performances in the theatre and quoting the sacred songs recited there. According to their 'orthodox' critic, they interpret

---

[59] Translation: M. Lafargue in Charlesworth 1983–5: II.795–801. 360 gods: Pseudo-Justin, *On Monarchy* 2 (trans. T.B. Falls, *Fathers of the Church* 6, New York 1948); above, p. 11, for 365 gods. Cf. Schürer 1973–87: III.1, 656–67; Riedweg 1993. Cf. C. Murray 1981: 37–63, 114–21 on images of Orpheus in Christian traditions. In the early fourth century the Christian Lactantius enlisted the revelations of the Egyptian Hermes as prophetic of Christianity, but other Christians rejected them: Fowden 1986: 196–212.

[60] Introduction and translation: A. Yarbro Collins in Charlesworth 1983–5: II.831–42, and Holladay 1995. Cf. Schürer 1973–87: 3.1, 579–87.

[61] On such collections see H. Chadwick in *Reallexikon für Antike und Christentum* 7 (1968): 1131–60.

[62] I. Corinthians 8.10; Revelation 2.14–15, 20; Irenaeus, *Against Heresies* 1.6.2–4, trans. Beard, North and Price 1998: II no. 12.7e(ii).

Fig. 8.3. King David, shown as Orpheus, on a mosaic from a synagogue in Gaza (AD 508–9). David, so labelled in Hebrew, is seated, apparently on a rock, with a halo, holding a lyre. To the right is a lioness, her head bowed to the music, and the traces of another animal.

everything said and done by anyone in the light of their own theory, saying that everything happens in accordance with the spirit. Hence they say that even the performers in theatres do not speak or act without providential guidance . . . They [therefore] attend the so-called mysteries of the Great Mother, considering that they can actually observe [their own] whole mystery in those rites.[63]

Jewish and Christian writers also found inspiration and support in the arguments of the Greek philosophers. Philo, a Jew writing in Greek in Alexandria in the mid-first century AD, was well grounded in Greek literature and philosophy, but was particularly impressed by Plato and the Stoics. For example, he adapted Platonic ideas concerning the dichotomy between the human soul, divine power, and the human body, a prison for the soul, and Stoic ideas concerning control of the sensuality that is innate in the human body. He also applied to the Torah or Pentateuch (the first five books of what Christians call the Old Testament) allegorical interpretations of a sort long applied by Greek philosophers to Greek myths. These borrowings make Philo sound more like a Hellene than a Jew, but for Philo there was no conflict. Most of his treatises are in fact interpretations of Jewish scripture (read at least primarily in Greek, i.e. the Septuagint), and the wisdom found in Plato and the Stoics was derived ultimately from Moses, the first law-giver and the earliest and greatest philosopher.[64] This claim of dependence of Greek wisdom on Moses, bizarre to our eyes, was not a peculiar type of argument in antiquity.

Though Philo had no discernible influence on later Jewish writers, his arguments were extremely attractive to Greek Christian writers. Justin, for example, agrees on the priority of Moses, and is particularly impressed by Plato, who he even argued adopted from Moses the metaphysical relationship between the son of god and the cross.[65] Justin took over Plato's ideas about the transcendence of god, and argued that Christ was the pre-existent divine Logos ('Word'). The god who appeared to Moses and other figures in the Old Testament must have been this Logos–Son, not the supreme god, who was too remote from this world to become incarnated in one part of it.[66] This argument, though later deemed to be unacceptable because of its denial of the

---

[63] Hippolytos, *Refutation of All Heresies* 5.6–9, partly trans. Beard, North and Price 1998: II no. 12.7e(iv). Cf. Frickel 1984; Beard, North and Price 1998: 1.311. The name 'Naassenes' refers to their respect for the wisdom of the serpent, *naas* in Hebrew.

[64] Schürer 1973–87: III.2, 809–89. Aristoboulos had earlier taken the same line on allegory and on the priority of Moses; Josephus also asserts the primacy of Moses.

[65] *First Apology* 59–60 (trans. T.B. Falls, *Fathers of the Church* 6, New York 1948).

[66] *Dialogue with Trypho* 55–60. Cf. Chadwick 1966: 1–22.

humanity of Christ, is a striking example of the impact of Greek philosophy on a central tenet of Christian theology.[67] Justin claims that he himself went through various philosophies, Stoic, Peripatetic, Pythagorean and finally Platonic before his conversion to the true 'Christian philosophy'.[68] He then avowed his Christian faith, because the philosophers had a share, but only a share, of the word of god disseminated in the world.[69] Greek philosophy could then be an entirely legitimate inspiration to Greek Christian theologians.[70]

### CHRISTIAN EMPERORS AND GREEK RELIGION

The conversion of the emperor Constantine to Christianity in AD 312 began a process of profound changes for the Greek world, as for the rest of the Roman empire.[71] It did *not* mean that from now on the empire was Christian, nor even that Constantine began to suppress paganism. It did mean that he ended the series of persecutions of the Christians, and it also meant that he began almost immediately to shift imperial resources and favour towards Catholic/Orthodox Christianity: he made grants of money to the Christian church, and started to build churches in Rome, the Holy Land and elsewhere. It became increasingly clear that the future lay with Christianity: only the brief reign of the non-Christian emperor Julian (AD 361–3) interrupted the flow, and his support for traditional Greek cults was unable to achieve very much.

Constantine legislated against aspects of traditional cults; only at the end of the fourth century did such actions amount to an attack on paganism. Constantine, like his non-Christian predecessors, acted against potentially dangerous forms of divination which might threaten the stability of private families or even of the emperor himself. Nocturnal sacrifices were deemed to be particularly noxious as potentially magical acts.[72] The question arose as to whether the Eleusinian Mysteries fell under the ban on nocturnal sacrifices, but in AD 364 the governor of Achaia (i.e. Greece) persuaded the emperor not to enforce the ban in Greece. However, as imperial legislation became more inclusive in scope, all traditional sacrifices were assimilated to dangerous divinatory sacrifices and in AD 391–2 were banned. The most severe

---

[67] Analogies were also drawn between Socrates and Christ: e.g. Justin, *Second Apology* 10. Cf. Döring 1979: 143–61.    [68] *Dialogue with Trypho* 2.    [69] *Second Apology* 13.

[70] Daniélou 1973 and Stead 1994 explore the borrowings.

[71] For sketches see Brown 1992; Fowden 1993; Brown 1995; Beard, North and Price 1998: 1.364–88.

[72] Beard, North and Price 1998: 1.372.

penalties were prescribed for individuals and for complaisant officials.[73] Sanctuaries too came under imperial scrutiny from the 380s onwards: as the location of public sacrifices, they too were potentially dangerous places. Though Greeks were afraid that they might be closed permanently,[74] in the east they remained accessible, if under a cloud.

The local response to these imperial rulings varied. In some places civic sanctuaries had fallen on hard times already in the turmoil of the third century, and in the fourth century, though sanctuaries retained their traditional income from estates, local elites generally ceased to spend their money on civic amenities, including traditional sanctuaries. For example, the temple of Artemis at Ephesos had been badly damaged in a barbarian attack of AD 262, and was only partially rebuilt. The *cella* of the temple was repaired at the turn of the third and fourth centuries, but only by reusing material from other ruined parts of the building.[75] The existence of local Christian communities in many Greek cities by the fourth century exacerbated the problems of Greek sanctuaries. At Cyzikos in north-west Asia Minor by the time of Julian the local bishop had already destroyed some temples and converted many of the local population to Christianity; Julian's response to an embassy from Cyzikos was to expel the bishop.[76] And at Aegeae in Cilicia on the south coast of Asia Minor local Christians had removed columns from the temple of Asclepius. The local bishop was ordered by Julian to restore the temple at his own expense, but shortly afterwards he removed the columns again.[77] Local Christian actions against pagan sanctuaries increased again in the 380s and 390s. In AD 386 the temple of Zeus at Apamea in Syria was destroyed by the local bishop, with the help of troops provided by the imperial official in charge of the east. In AD 392 the great sanctuary of Serapis in Alexandria in Egypt was stormed and sacked, following provocative actions taken by the bishop of Alexandria. This was a spectacular success for hard-line Christians, as the sanctuary had considerable importance as a cultural centre.[78]

---

[73] *Theodosian Code* 16.10.10, trans. C. Pharr (Princeton 1952) (AD 391); 16.10.12, trans. Beard, North and Price 1998: II no. 11.14 (AD 392).

[74] Libanius, *Oration* 30 (? AD 386) is a plea on behalf of temples and their estates.

[75] Foss 1979: 86–7. For the oracles at Didyma and Delphi in the third and fourth centuries see Athanassiadi 1989–90.

[76] Sozomen, *Church History* 5.15.4–10 (trans. *Nicene and Post-Nicene Fathers* 2, 2nd series, Oxford and New York 1891, repr. Grand Rapids Michigan 1957).

[77] Zonaras, *Epitome of Histories* 13.12, p. 212.9–27 Dindorf. Cf. Robert 1973; Fowden 1978 on the role of bishops.

[78] Chuvin 1990: 57–72. For AD 392 (rather than 391) see G.W. Bowersock, *JRS* 80 (1990) 246.

In the fifth century Christians became even more active in their destruction of traditional religious monuments, especially following an imperial ruling of AD 435.[79] At Delphi the *aduton* of the temple of Apollo was systematically destroyed, and crosses were scratched onto at least some of the monuments of the sanctuary (the 'Altar of the Chians', the treasuries of Cyrene and Siphnos), in accordance with the imperial ruling. The temple of Apollo itself was left standing, but towards the end of the fifth century a substantial Christian church was built, probably in the last third of the fifth century, on the terrace above the temple.[80] But from the fifth century if temples had survived in good enough condition they could also be converted into churches. At Aphrodisias in western Asia Minor in the mid- to late fifth century the temple of Aphrodite had its cult images destroyed, and was extended to form a great new church.[81] At Athens at an uncertain date between the mid-fifth and the early seventh centuries the Parthenon, the Erechtheion and the Hephaisteion were all converted into churches.[82] The plan of the Hephaisteion shows how suitable the pagan shell was for the standard basilica-style Christian church (Fig. 8.4). Such adaptations, which asserted the superiority of the new religion over the old, were however rare: reuse of earlier secular buildings was more common, and temples were either used just for secular purposes, or abandoned as places where demons lived.[83]

The process of actions against traditional cults from Constantine onwards did not mean that traditional cults died out rapidly in the fourth century. Indeed in many places there was a natural desire to preserve and perpetuate at least some elements of the traditional cults, which had for so long helped to define the identities of individual communities.[84] In the fifth century though sacrifices (the key rite) were now illegal, the rest of the traditional rites could continue as before. So at Athens in the early fifth century one Plutarch, a sophist and philosopher, was honoured by the Athenian people with a statue for having personally paid for the Panathenaic procession on three occasions:

---

[79]  *Theodosian Code* 16.10.25, trans. C. Pharr (Princeton 1952).

[80]  Deroche 1989. At Ephesos the church of Saint John was built partially out of material from the temple of Artemis.

[81]  Cormack 1990a; cf. generally 1990b. Dating: Smith and Ratté 1995: 43–6.

[82]  Frantz 1965 argues for the late fifth/early sixth century, but Mango 1995 gives good reason for accepting the second half of the fifth century.

[83]  Spieser 1976; Vaes 1984–6: 326–38.

[84]  Harl 1990; Bowersock 1990; Trombley 1993; MacMullen 1997. Cf. Beard, North and Price 1998: 1.381–8 for this phenomenon at Rome.

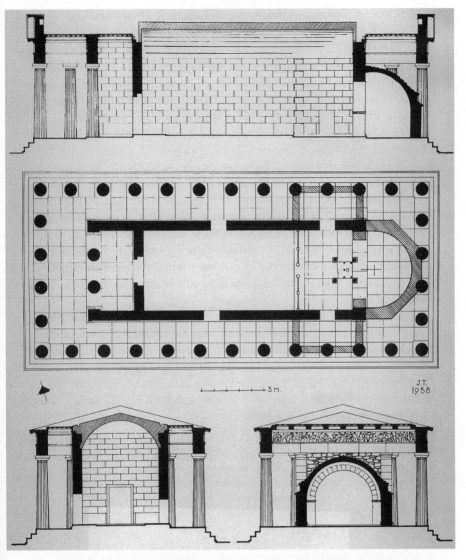

Fig. 8.4. Plan of the temple of Hephaistos, Athens. The conversion into a Christian church, of S. George, included the demolition of the east wall of the cella to allow the building of an apse, and the creation of doors in the sidewalls of the cella as entrances to two small transepts.

The people of Erechtheus have set up [a statue of] Plutarchos, king of discourses, a foundation of steady wisdom, who thrice sailed the sacred ship and moored it at the temple of Athena, having poured out great wealth.[85]

The great procession along the Sacred Way up to the Parthenon thus continued, so long as it could be funded. Games also continued in some places. Though the Olympic games at Olympia seem to have ceased in the late fourth century, other Olympic games are found elsewhere. Indeed at Antioch in Syria they were celebrated until AD 520, when they were terminated apparently on grounds of public order.[86] In 435–6 Leontius, Prefect of Constantinople, actually decided to reinstate Olympic games at the theatre in Chalcedon just over the straits from Constantinople. Though the attempt failed because of the intervention of a monk Hypatius, it does not follow that Leontius was anti-Christian. The local bishop of Chalcedon was initially not opposed to the games; and Leontius himself later founded a church in Thessalonica to S. Demetrius. There was room for disagreement about the distinction between religion and traditional ceremonial and entertainment.[87]

Traditional healing cults also continued to be popular in some places into the fifth century. Though the sanctuary at Epidaurus seems to have gone out of use in the fourth century,[88] that on the slopes of the Athenian Akropolis remained accessible into the second half of the fifth century.[89] The biography of the philosopher Proclus recounts a visit by Proclus to the shrine on behalf of a friend's daughter, herself significantly named Asclepigeneia, 'Born of Asclepius':

Taking along the great Pericles of Lydia, who was a great friend of wisdom, [Proclus] went up to the Asclepieion to pray to the god on behalf of the suffering girl. For the city at that time had the good fortune of this [the god's presence], and the temple of the Saviour [Asclepius] was still unpillaged. While he prayed in the ancient manner, a sudden change appeared in the girl, and she was immediately relieved. For the Saviour healed her easily, as befits a god.[90]

---

[85] _IG_ 2² 3818, with Trombley 1993: 1.18–20, 322, 325. Cf. above, pp. 32–3, on this procession.

[86] Olympia: list of victors running from first century BC to late fourth century AD, _Archaeological Reports for 1994–1995_ (London 1995): 22; on closure the only explicit testimony is a slightly confused passage in a twelfth-century historian, Cedrenus 1.573 (_Patrologia Graeca_ 121.622). Antioch: Malalas, _Chronicle_, trans. E.M. Jeffreys et al. (Sydney NSW 1986) 17, 417.5–8; cf. Downey 1961: 439–43, 455–6, 482–3, 504–7, 518.

[87] Callinicus, _Life of Hypatius_ (ed. G.J.M. Bartelink, _Sources Chrétiennes_ 177, Paris 1971) ch. 33, with Trombley 1993: II.83–5.    [88] Trombley 1993: 1.119.

[89] Trombley 1993: 1.294, 308–9, 323. Cf. above, p. 109, on this sanctuary.

[90] Marinus, _Life of Proclus_ 29 (trans. Edelstein 1945: 1.323–4).

As late as the 480s the philosopher Plutarch (not the same one who paid for the Panathenaic procession) also visited the sanctuary and practised the ancient rite of incubation:

Asclepius at Athens delivered the same oracular cure to Plutarch the Athenian and Domninus the Syrian, the latter after frequently spitting blood . . . the former, I do not know what ailed him. The cure entailed being sated with pork. Plutarch however could not stand medicine of this kind, even though it did not contravene his ancestral customs. Upon being awakened from sleep and then leaning upon his elbow on the bedding, he gazed at the statue of Asclepius (for he happened to be sleeping in the forecourt of the sanctuary) and said: 'O master, what would you command to a Jew who was ailing with the same sickness? You would not order him too to consume pork, would you?' He said this, and Asclepius immediately sent forth out of the statue a very harmonious voice and presented another treatment for the malady.[91]

Though there is no mention of temple personnel or of sacrifices at this date and the cult may have become a purely private matter, these anecdotes reveal the possibility of enduring attachment to the god. However, as is shown by the passage from the biography of Proclus (written c. 486), the temple itself was to be pillaged, perhaps in the early 480s, and the votive reliefs systematically mutilated. Subsequently a church was built on the site, perhaps towards the end of the fifth century. The church may have been dedicated to St Andrew, patron of healing, and included an extra aisle, perhaps for incubation, which suggests that the ancient functions of Asclepius may have been incorporated into the new Christian structures.[92]

In the sixth century some intellectuals continued to express their commitment to the traditional gods. Zosimus, writing his history in the early sixth century, argues that Rome's fall to the barbarians in 410 was due to her abandonment of ancient cults, while Athens remained under divine protection. The great earthquake of AD 375 which had afflicted much of mainland Greece had, according to Zosimus following earlier sources, spared Athens because of the piety of the hierophant of Eleusis.[93] More dramatically, Zosimus recounts how in 396 the barbarian Alaric was warned off sacking Athens by a divine epiphany:

Upon approaching Athens with his whole army, Alaric saw Athena Promachos inspecting the walls, just as she is to be seen in statues, armed as a hoplite and

[91] Damascius, *Life of Isidore* fr. 218 Zintzen, from the Suda.
[92] Frantz 1965: 194–5; Gregory 1986: 237–40; Karivieri 1995.
[93] Zosimus 4.18.2–4, from Eunapios, trans. R.T. Ridley (Sydney NSW, 1982). Cf. Paschoud 1971–89: II.2.367–9; Trombley 1993: 1.304–6.

about to resist attackers. He also saw Achilles the hero standing in front of the walls, just as Homer shows him before Troy when he fought in his wrath to avenge the death of Patroclus.

Alaric was so shaken that he sent heralds and entered the city peacefully.[94] The historicity of the story is dubious for various reasons: Alaric was a pious Christian, several earlier writers are ignorant of the alleged epiphanies, and there is some archaeological evidence for destruction in Athens at this period. But Zosimus' telling of the story is significant of his personal attitudes to the traditional gods.

Despite the fact that in 529 the emperor Justinian gave orders that 'those remaining in the impious and accursed error of the Greeks' be baptised as Christians, on penalty of being excluded from holding public office or receiving any bequest,[95] some non-Christian cults continued until the forcible intervention of Christian missionaries. The actions of John, bishop of Ephesos, may serve to illustrate the scope of the 'problem'. According to his own account, in the 540s John began at Justinian's request the process of converting pagans in the area inland from Ephesos. For example, he visited a sanctuary, probably of the Mother of the Gods, in the mountains above Tralles (modern Aydin), where the old men told him that at one time 1,500 smaller temples had been under its jurisdiction and that its priests had instructed the people in law.[96] John ordered the temple to be destroyed and supervised the building on the site of a monastery which had jurisdiction over the fourteen churches and seven monasteries also built in that region. The monastery seems to have replaced the ancient shrine as the new focus for the region (though the shrine is not known in earlier sources and the claim of the old men about the 1,500 temples is wishful thinking). John claimed in the course of thirty years to have baptised in Asia 80,000 people and to have built ninety-six churches and twelve monasteries. The numbers are impressive, but are probably evidence only for patchy rather than pervasive rural paganism. John's actions are nonetheless emblematic of more intensive imperial and ecclesiastical actions against traditional beliefs and practices. The sixth century seems to mark a sign-

---

[94] Zosimus 5.5.8–5.6.3, perhaps from fifth-century philosopher Syrianus. Cf. Paschoud 1971–89: III.1.94–8; Fowden 1988: 53, 1995: 556–8.

[95] *Codex Justinianus* 1.11.10, undated, but AD 528/9; cf. Honoré 1978: 14–16, 46–7. AD 529 is also when Justinian forbad the teaching of (pagan) philosophy at Athens. See in general Athanassiadi 1993.

[96] John of Ephesos, *Church History* 3.36, preserved only in Syriac (trans. R. Payne Smith, Oxford 1860). See also the cult of Apollo near Magnesia, known from the sixth century BC to the sixth century AD: Robert 1977: 77–88. Cf. Trombley 1985; Mitchell 1993: 2.118–19.

ficant stage in the creation of a fully Christian empire, but in some areas of Greece mass conversions were necessary into the ninth century.[97] Thereafter, some traditional practices may have continued, not as an independent system in opposition to Christianity, but as individual elements within the Greek Orthodox system.[98] The old ways had been either suppressed or incorporated within the new.

[97] Whitby 1991.
[98] Danforth 1984, arguing against the folklorist search for fossilised lumps of paganism in modern Greece (for example, the modern Greek firewalking as a survival of pagan, Dionysiac rites). See Danforth 1989 for his positive study of firewalking.

# Appendix of Greek inscriptions in translation

I have used square brackets for words that are no longer preserved in the surviving text; round brackets for parentheses in the original; and curly brackets for places where I have translated or explained technical terms. Readers might like to be reminded here of the monetary units that occur in these texts:

6 obols = 1 drachma
2 drachmas = 1 stater
6000 drachmas = 1 talent.

In the fifth century BC 1 drachma was the daily wage for a skilled labourer.

## 1 Sacrificial Calendar from the Attic Deme of Thorikos (430s BC?)

*While the state of Athens had its sacrificial calendar, the constituent demes of Attica each had their own, interlocking calendars (above, pp. 28–30). There follows the calendar of Thorikos, which lies at the south-east of Attica. The sacrifices are organised under the twelve Attic months (see above, Fig. 2.9). The sacrifices here have both central and local interest. The layout of the translation indicates the (hypothetical) grouping of sacrifices.*

[These sacrifices are made by the Thorikians?]

Hekatombaion. . . . for Hekate . . . a full-grown victim, to be sold.

[Metageitnion.] For Zeus Kataibates {Who Comes Down} in the enclosure beside the [Delphinion] a full-grown victim, to be sold.

An oath-victim is to be provided for the scrutinies.

Boedromion. The Proerosia: For Zeus Polieus a selected sheep (and?) a selected piglet. {For Zeus?} to Automenai a bought piglet, to be burnt whole. The priest is to provide lunch for the attendant.

For Kephalos a selected sheep, for Prokris an offering-table. For Thorikos a selected sheep, for the Heroines of Thorikos an offering-table.

To Sunium, for Poseidon, a selected lamb. For Apollo a selected kid.

For Korotrophos a selected piglet, for Demeter a full-grown victim, for Zeus Herkeios a full-grown victim.

For Korotrophos a piglet, for Athena a sheep, to be sold. For Poseidon, at the salt-works, a full-grown victim. For Apollo a piglet.

Pyanopsion. For Zeus Kataibates, on the property of the Philomelidai (?), a full-grown victim, to be sold on the 16th.

For Neanias, a full-grown victim at the Pyanopsia [to be sold?].

172

Maimakterion. For Thorikos a cow costing not less than 40 and up to 50 drachmas. For the Heroines of Thorikos an offering-table.

Posideion. The Dionysia.

Gamelion. For Hera, at the Sacred Marriage . . .

Anthesterion. For Dionysos, on the 12th (?), a tawny or [black] kid that lacks first teeth.

At the Diasia, for Zeus Meilichios, a sheep, to be sold.

Elaphebolion. For the Childen of Herakles [a full-grown victim], for Alkmene a full-grown victim. For the two Anakes a full-grown victim, for Helen (?) a full-grown victim.

For Demeter, as the Green Shoot offering, a selected pregnant ewe. For Zeus a selected lamb.

Mounuchion. For Artemis Mounuchia a full-grown victim.

To the temple of Pythian Apollo a triple-offering (?), (i.e.?) for Korotrophos a piglet, for Leto a goat, for Artemis a goat, for Apollo a goat that lacks first teeth.

For Demeter a pregnant sheep as the Flower offering (?). For Philonis an offering-table.

For Dionysos, to Mykenos, a tawny or black [billy-goat].

Thargelion. For Zeus to Automenai a selected lamb.

For Hyperpedios a sheep, for the Heroines of Hyperpedios an offering-table. For Nisos a sheep. For Thras[. . .] a sheep. For Sosineos a sheep. For Rhogios a sheep. For Pylochos {Gate-Holder} a piglet, for the Gate-Holding Heroines an offering-table.

Skirophorion. An oath-victim is to be provided.

At the Plynteria for Athena a selected sheep, for Aglauros a sheep.

For Kephalos a cow costing not less than 40 and up to 50 drachmas. For [Prokris?] a sheep [costing 20 drachmas?]

The scrutineer and his assessors shall swear: 'I will discharge the office of scrutineer for which I have been designated by lot in accordance with the decrees establishing (?) the office.' He shall swear by Zeus, Apollo and Demeter, invoking complete destruction on himself; and his assessors shall swear likewise. The oath shall be inscribed on a stele and positioned beside the [Delphinion]. All offices to which appointments are made shall be subject to scrutiny.

*SEG* 33.147; Parker 1987a (whose translation is used here)

### 2 Celebration of the Thesmophoria (Fourth Century BC)

*The following text is the ending of a decree passed by an Attic deme (Cholargos) on the arrangements for representation of the deme by two local women (the female officials) at the celebration of the Thesmophoria in Athens (above, p. 98).*

. . . the *hieromnemones* {religious registrars}. The *archousai* {female officials} shall each together present in the name of the female priest for the festival and the provision of the Thesmophoria a *hemihekteus* {c.4.3 litres} of barley, a *hemihekteus* of wheat, a *hemihekteus* of groats, a *hemihekteus* of meal, a *hemihekteus* of dried figs, a flagon {c.3.12 litres} of wine, a half-flagon of oil, two cups {c. 0.52 litres} of honey, a *choinix* {1.09 litres} of white sesame and another of black, a *choinix* of poppy-seeds, two rounds of cheese each weighing not less than a stater, two staters of garlic, and a torch worth not less than 2 obols and 4 silver drachmas: those shall be presented by the female officials. So that this shall take place according to the laws for all time on behalf of the people of Cholargos, the officials in charge during the the the archonship of Ktesikles {334/3 BC} shall set up a stele and shall inscribe this decree on the stone stele in the sanctuary of {Apollo} Pythios {in the deme}; they shall bill their expenditure to the people of Cholargos.

*IG* 2² 1184; *LSCG Supp.* 124

C.J. Schwenk, *Athens in the Age of Alexander* (Chicago, 1986) no. 26

### 3 Civic Sacrifices at Magnesia on the Maeander (197–196 BC)

*This civic decree, inscribed on one side of the doorway into the temple of Zeus, establishes new civic sacrifices; this happened in difficult political circumstances, as is emphasised in the last line of the decree. The regulations illustrate ritual niceties (which deity is to get which animal), the organisation of public participation and the corresponding receipt of portions of the sacrificial animals. See above, pp. 33–6 (sacrifices), pp. 30–3 (processions).*

In the stephanephorate {chief magistracy} of Aristeas son of Demetrius son of [. . .]on {197–196 BC}, in the month of Smision {the third month?}, when the Attalid tribe was president, and Pythokleios son of Hegesippos was Secretary of the Council, four days from the end of the month, in a scheduled meeting of the assembly when Menestratos son of Artemidorus was chair of the presidents,

concerning the designation each year of a bull for Zeus at the start of the sowing and concerning the prayer and procession and sacrifice, and concerning the erection of a round structure in the agora and the laying-out of couches.

It was decided by the council and people, on the proposal of the people:

that the Financial Managers in office shall buy the best possible bull and that those who succeed them shall ever after buy the best possible bull in the month of Heraion {the last month} at the annual festival, and shall dedicate it to Zeus at the start of the sowing in the month of Kronion {the first month} at the new moon together with the male priest and the female priest of Artemis Leukophryene and the chief magistrate and the Sacred Herald and the one serving as sacrificer for the city.

that the *paidonomoi* {Supervisors of Boys} send nine boys, with both parents alive, and the *gunaikonomoi* {Supervisors of Women} likewise send nine girls, with both parents alive. At the designation of the bull, the Sacred Herald shall pray with the male priest and the female priest and the stephanephoros and the boys and the girls and the army commanders and the cavalry commanders and the Financial Managers and the Secretary of the council and the notary and the general for the wellbeing of the city and the territory and the citizens and women and children and the other inhabitants of the city and territory for peace and prosperity and the yield of grain and of all other crops and livestock.

that it was decided by council and people:

that the stephanephoros in office together with the male priest and the female priest of Artemis Leukophryene shall ever after lead the procession in the month of Artemision {the seventh month} on the twelfth day, and sacrifice the designated bull; that in the procession shall also be the council of elders, the priests, the magistrates (both elected and appointed by lot), the ephebes, the youths, the boys, the victors in the Leukophryene games, and the victors in the other crown-bearing games. The stephanephoros in leading the procession shall carry images (*xoana*) of all twelve gods attired as beautifully as possible, and shall erect a round structure in the agora by the altar of the twelve gods, and shall lay out three couches of the finest quality, and shall also provide music, a shawm-player, a pan-pipe-player and a lyre-player.

that also the Financial Managers shall provide in the month of Artemision on the twelfth day an additional three sacrificial victims, which they shall sacrifice to Zeus Sosipolis, to Artemis Leukophryene and to Apollo Pythios, to Zeus the finest ram, to Artemis a nanny-goat and to Apollo a billy-goat, sacrificing to Zeus on the altar of Zeus Sosipolis, to Artemis and Apollo on the altar of Artemis. The priests of these gods shall take their customary privileged portions.

that when they sacrifice the bull, they shall divide up the meat among the participants in the procession; they shall divide up the meat of the ram, the nanny-goat and the billy-goat among the stephanephoros, the female priest, the army commanders, the presidents, the Temple Clerks of Work, the Judges and those who have assisted in the rituals; the Financial Managers shall divide up the meat.

that once a bull has been dedicated, the Financial Managers shall make a contract so that the bull is maintained by the contractor; that the contractor bring the bull into the agora, and take a collection from the grain-dealers and from the other stall-holders for what he spends on the maintenance of the bull, and it is recommended that they make a donation.

that the Financial Managers inscribe this decree in the sanctuary of Zeus on the doorway; that the Financial Managers pay for the writing of all these things from the income which they have for the administration of the city.

that this decree is for the protection of the city.

*Inschriften von Magnesia* 98; *LSAM* 32

## 4 Temple and Priest of Athena Nike, Athens (c. 448 BC)

*The following text, inscribed on a marble stele set up on the Athenian Akropolis, records a civic decree providing (a) for the appointment of a female priest of Athena Nike, (b) for the building of a door for the (existing) sanctuary, (c) for the perquisites of the priest, and (d) for the building of a new temple; at the end is an emendment to ensure a more democratic procedure. On the other side of the stele is a decree of 424–3 BC on the payment of the priest (ML 71, trans Fornara 1983: no. 139). For the procedure see above, p. 69. For the tombstone of the first priest see below, no. 5.*

[It was decided by the council and the] people. [. . . was president,] Glaucus proposed: the female priest of [Athena Ni]ke who [takes office by lot] be appointed from all Athenian women; and a door be built for the sanctuary in accordance with the design of Callicrates (the Official Contractors shall let out the contract in the prytany of {the tribe} Leontis); the female priest to receive 50 drachmas, and to receive the legs and hides from public sacrifices; a temple in accordance with the design of Callicrates and a stone altar shall be built. Hestiaios proposed: three men are to be elected from the Council; they shall draw up the design with Callicrates and shall submit their proposals for the letting of the contract [to the Council] [. . .]

ML 44; *IG* I³ 35

### 5 Tombstone of Priest of Athena Nike (c. 430–400 BC?)

*The following verse texts were inscribed on a marble stele (0.98m high) found in the outskirts of Athens (above, p. 69). The first one plays upon the notion that divine providence ensured that the lot selected Myrrhina whose name ('Myrtle') alluded to the composition of her priestly crown. The second text overlaps with the sense of the first. For illustrations of tombstones of priests see Figs. 4.1 and 4.2.*

{This is} the far-shining memorial of the daughter of Callimachus, who was the first servant of the temple of Nike. She had a name that proved auspicious, as by divine dispensation she was truly called Myrrhina.
As the first there served the shrine of Athena Nike Myrrhina, chosen by lot from all, with good fortune.

*SEG* 12.80; *IG* I³ 1330;
P.A. Hansen, *Carmina Epigraphica Graeca* I (Berlin 1983) 93

### 6 Regulations for the Cult of Athena Nikephoros, Pergamum (after 133 BC)

*The following three texts relating to the cult of Athena were collected and published on a single stone by one Dionysius, in memory of his service as hieronomos (religious registrar). The first is a sacred law regulating ritual purity; the other two are civic decrees on taxes on sacrifices (above, pp. 66, 68). The stone was erected in the sanctuary of Athena at Pergamum.*

Dionysius son of Menophilus
former *hieronomos* for the people
Citizens and all other people who enter the temple of the female god shall be pure, having washed themselves clean from their own wife or their own husband for one day, or from another woman or another man for two days; similarly from a corpse or from a woman in labour for two days. But those who have cleansed themselves from a funeral and carrying out of the corpse and have passed back through the gate where the means of purification are placed shall be cleansed on the same day.
It was decided by the council and people, on the proposal of the chief magistrates: in general the arrangements for those sacrificing to Nikephoros Athena

shall continue in accordance with the law, but in addition to the existing portions set aside for the female god and to the money placed in the collection box, they shall also deposit the right leg and the skin of each sacrificial animal. They shall place in the collection box the posted four obols for pigs and two and a half obols for other sacrificial animals, as is prescribed in writing. The decree shall be valid in perpetuity, unless another decree supersedes it.

It was decided by the council and people, on the proposal of the chief magistrates: since it has been customary that those sacrificing to Nikephoros Athena should give, together with the prescribed portions for the female god, also to some others of those who deal with the sanctuary more than a triple portion, it was decided: that with immediate effect the annually appointed *hieronomoi* shall take the skins deposited by those offering sacrifices, sell them, and give to the temple warden two obols for a pig and a half obol for a sheep, and shall give the same jointly to the (female) shawm-player and the (female) lamenter. Of what is sacrificed on the akropolis the *hieronomoi* shall give also to the gatekeeper of the akropolis a drachma for an ox, and a drachma for a sheep. The rest of the profit shall be attributed to the sacred revenues. The decree shall be valid in perpetuity, unless another decree supersedes it.

*Inschriften von Pergamon* 255; *Syll.*³ 982; *LSAM* 12

## 7 Ancestral Sacrifices at Ephesos (Third Century AD)

*The following text was inscribed on a stone slab in front of the theatre. It illustrates the procedures of civic sacrifices (above, pp. 33–4), the responsibilities and perquisites of various officials (above, p. 68), and the continuing importance of ancestral customs in the Roman imperial period (above, pp. 8, 156).*

Good Fortune
Summary of Ancestral Law

That the prutanis {a magistrate} shall light a fire on all the altars and burn incense and sacred aromatic herbs, offering to the gods on the customary days sacrifices numbering 365 in all, of which 190 shall be with the heart taken out and the thighs removed, and 175 shall be entirely dedicated, all this from his own resources. The public hierophant {instructor of rites} shall guide and instruct him on each point as to what is customary for the gods.

That they shall sing the paean at the appropriate sacrifices, processions and nocturnal festivals in the ancestral fashion, and shall pray on behalf of the sacred Senate and People of the Romans and the People of the Ephesians.

Another portion:

That the prutanis shall give to the hierophant the customary portions of every sacrifice offered to the gods – the head, tongue and skin – for his experience and the importance of his assistance; to the Sacred Herald and shawm-player and trumpeter and second hierophant and diviner from entrails and the Seventh Koures {a member of an association attached to the prutaneion} baskets of food corresponding to their assistance.

But if the prutanis fails to do any of the individual points specified above, he shall pay for the adornment of (the statue of) Demeter Karpophoros {Harvest Bringer} standing in the prutaneion, to whom the temple belongs, and for the repair of that building 10 Daric staters. The kouretes and the hierophant shall take action in case each matter is not carried out as has been prescribed.

*LSCG Supp.* 121; *Inschriften von Ephesos* 10

## 8 Regulation of Votives (Third Century BC)

*Offerings to the gods by individuals and communities were prominent features of Greek sanctuaries (above, pp. 58–63). In some cases lengthy regulations were published on the display and care for votives (above, p. 59). This text, from Loryma in Caria, makes the points more briefly.*

It is not permitted to remove from the sanctuary any of the offerings, nor to damage anything, nor to rearrange the position of the plaques, nor to introduce any [plaque] [without permission of the priest].

*LSAM* 74

## 9 A Woman's Votive (Fourth–Third Century BC)

*This text, inscribed on a marble block on which once stood an image, was displayed in the sanctuary of Demeter and Kore at Knidus. Here practically all the dedications were made by women; for women's votives see above, pp. 24–5, 61, 95.*

To Demeter and Kore and the gods with Demeter and Kore Plathainis wife of Platon dedicated this as gratitude and reciprocation.

*Ancient Greek Inscriptions in the British Museum* 4.1.810; *Syll.*³ 1146

## 10 A Civic Votive (Fifth Century BC)

*This text was inscribed on a limestone block in Temple G at Selinus. See above, pp. 49, 51 on the cults of Selinus.*

Through the following gods the Selinuntians are victorious: through Zeus we are victorious and through Phobos {Panic} and through Herakles and through Apollo and through Poseidon and through the Tyndaridai {Castor and Polydeuces} and through Athena and through Malophoros {Demeter} and through Pasikrateia {Persephone} and through the other gods but especially through Zeus. As peace has come, we are to chase a gold plaque, prick in these names and then deposit it in the sanctuary of Apollo {i.e. Temple G?}, having inscribed it as the property of Zeus. The gold to be worth 60 talents.

*ML* 38; *SEG* 34.970

## 11 Delphic Oracle for Cyzikos (late Third/early Second Century BC)

*After the foundation of their Soteria festival for Kore Soteira, the Cyzikenes asked the oracle at Delphi how to add to the honours of the god. The reply was that they should seek Panhellenic recognition of the inviolability of the city and the games. The text is a good example of the creation of a new festival in the Hellenistic period (above, p. 7), its exploitation by the city to promote its international status, the involvement of Delphi in the process (above, pp. 73–6), the procedures of international diplomacy, and the procedures leading to the creation of inscriptions. The first text is a copy of the Delphic oracle, the second a decree of Delos. This inscription comes from Delos, but there survives another, slightly later, copy of the oracle from Delphi itself (Fouilles de Delphes 3.3.342).*

On the Cyzikenes. The god {Apollo} uttered the following prophecy: since [the Cyzikenes] [first of all people] have performed the Soteria to Soteira well, piously and fortunately, that it is much better that they proclaim to the human race that their city is sacred, in accordance with the oracles and the sacrifice to the female god.

It was decreed by the council and people {of Delos}. Charias son of Charistios spoke: Since the Cyzikenes, who are friends of the people of the Delians, have sent [. . .] as chief envoy and [ . . . ] and Theopompus son of Nikaios as envoys bringing a decree in which they ask the Delians, as friends of their city, to appoint a place in the sanctuary of Apollo in which a stele can be put up on which will be inscribed the oracle given to the Cyzikenes by Pythios Apollo in the same manner as it is also inscribed in the sanctuary at Delphi. As far as these very matters are concerned, the chief envoy and the envoys spoke accordingly.

Decree of the council and people: that the *hieropoioi* {officials responsible for rites} shall ensure with the council that an extremely prominent place be given in which the stele shall be put up, as the Cyzikenes asked, so that the matter concerning the gods and the people of the Cyzikenes be in good and pious order with regard to the people of the Delians; that they commend the envoys and invite them to dinner in the prutaneion tomorrow; the treasurer shall pay the statutory costs. Parmenion [. . . put it to the vote.]

*IG* 11.4.1298 + 1027; *Syll.*[3] 1158;
K.J. Rigsby, *Asylia* (Berkeley 1996) no. 165 (oracle only)

## 12 Oracle on Piracy (First Century BC)

*An oracle (probably that at Claros) was consulted by the small city of Syedra in Pamphylia (on the southern coast of Turkey) about how it should cope with raids from pirates (above, p. 75). The oracle, which the Syedrans inscribed, perhaps at a later date, advised, in hexameters and in epic language, the setting up of a special statue group which symbolised the victory of Justice over Violence; coins of Syedra of the second century AD depict this group. The oracle also advised strenuous actions by the Syedrans.*

Pamphylians of Syedra, you who in the common land inhabit a fertile territory of people of mixed race, set up a representation of Ares the blood-stained slayer of men in the middle of the city, and perform sacrifices beside it, holding him in the iron bonds of Hermes. On the other side let Justice giving sentence judge him, while he himself is like to one pleading. For thus he will be peaceful to you, having driven the hostile mob far from your native land, and will raise up much-prayed-for prosperity. But you too must grasp the hard task, either chasing them away or manacling them in unloosable bonds, and do not hesitate at all about exacting terrible vengeance on the plunderers. For thus you will escape every impairment.

*SEG* 41.1411

## 13 Initiation and Burial (Fifth Century BC)

*The following text, on a tufa block from Cumae in southern Italy, shows the importance of groupings based on initiation rites (above, pp. 112–25).*

It is not proper to bury here anyone who has not been initiated into the Bacchic rites.

*SEG* 4.92; *LSCG Supp.* 120

## 14 Law on Mourning (Third Century BC)

*This law from Gambreion (a small town c. 25 km south-east of Pergamon) specifies details of mourning, and sets temporal limits for that mourning (above, pp. 100–1 on burials). One might note the differences between the rules for men and women, and also the striking religious sanctions, perhaps aimed mostly at women, designed to enforce the law.*

Good Fortune.

When Demetrius was *hieronomos* {religious registrar}, on the second day of the month of Thargelion, Alexon son of Damon made the following proposal:

there shall be a law for the people of Gambreion that women in mourning shall have grey rather than soiled clothing. Men and boys in mourning shall also wear grey clothing, unless they prefer to wear white. They shall perform the customary rites for the departed within three months at the most, and in the fourth month men shall end their mourning, and women in the fifth month; and by way of fixed custom the women shall rise from the burial and perform the processions {of mourning} prescribed in the law. The *gunaikonomos* {Supervisor of Women} elected by the people shall pray at the purification rituals before the Thesmophoria that for the men who abide by and the women who obey this law things will be well and that their existing goods will increase, and that for the men who do not obey and the women who do not abide by this law the opposite will occur. And it shall not be proper for those women, because of being impious, to sacrifice to any god for ten years. The treasurer elected after the stephanephorate {chief magistracy} of Demetrius shall inscribe this law on two stelai and set up one in front of the doors of the Thesmophorion and the other in front of the temple of Artemis Lochia {of Childbirth}. Let the treasurer report the cost of the stelai at the first meeting of the accountants.

*Syll.*³ 1219; *LSAM* 16

## 15 The prestige of the cult of Artemis of Ephesos (AD 162/3 or 163/4)

*The following texts, inscribed on a statue base at Ephesos, reveal how the identity of Ephesos was bound up with that of her major cult, rather as is suggested in a polemical fashion in the account in the Acts of the Apostles of the hostile response to Paul's preaching of Christianity there (19.23–41; above, p. 23). They also illustrate the importance of festivals and their effect on the internal or external business of the state (above, pp. 25–9), and the support of the Roman authorities for Greek cults (above, pp. 156–7). The first text is an edict of the governor of the Roman province of Asia; the second an Ephesian decree, extending to a month the festival of Artemis and the period for which public business was banned (Roman assent was obtained for this latter honour, which closed courts and prevented the exaction of money); in the third the city honours a local benefactor of the festival, who had helped obtain the governor's assent, and whose statue once stood on the base.*

Gaius Popillius Carus Pedo, proconsul, declares: I have learned from the decree sent to me by the most distinguished council of the Ephesians that the most excellent proconsuls before me had considered the days of the festival of the Artemisia to be sacred, and had so declared this by edict. Therefore, as I am myself mindful of the piety shown to the female god and of the honour of the most distinguished city of the Ephesians, I have considered it necessary to make clear by edict that these days will be sacred and that public business will not be held on them; the president of the general festival will be Titus Aelius Marcianus Priscus, son of Aelius Priscus, the provider of the games, a man most distinguished and worthy of every honour and welcome.

It was decided by the council and people of the First and Greatest Metropolis of Asia, the city of the Ephesians, twice Temple Warden of the Emperors and Devoted to the Emperors. Concerning the question brought forward by [. . .] Laberius Amoenus, Devoted to the Emperors, Secretary of the people, the generals of the city, Devoted to the Emperors, put the following to the vote: Since the god Artemis, patron of our city, is honoured not only in her native city, which she has made more famous than all other cities through her own divinity, but also by Greeks and barbarians, so that everywhere sanctuaries and precincts are consecrated for her, temples are dedicated and altars set up for her, on account of her manifest epiphanies. But this is the greatest testimony of the reverence for her that there is a month named after her, Artemision in our city, Artemisios among the Macedonians and other Greek tribes and their cities: in this month are held festivals and cessation of public business, especially in our city, the nurse of its own Ephesian god. The people of the Ephesians, considering it fitting that the whole month which bears the divine name should be sacred and dedicated to the female god, has resolved through this decree to regulate its religious observance. Therefore it was decided that the whole month of Artemision be sacred in all its days, that there be held during these days every year in this month the festivals, both the festival of the Artemisia and the cessation of public business throughout the whole month, since the whole month is dedicated to the god. In this way, with the god honoured more highly, our city will remain for all time more famous and more blessed.

His native city honours Titus Aelius Marcianus Priscus, son of Titus, of the Claudian tribe, the provider of the games and president of the festival of the Great Artemisia, the first to have himself held the festival in perfected form,

having obtained a cessation of public business for the whole month named after
the god, establisher of the Artemisian contest, increaser of the rewards for
contestants, and erector of statues for victors. Lucius Faenius Faustus, his
kinsman, erected this honour {i.e. the base and statue}.

*Syll.*³ 867; *LSAM* 31 (text 2 only); *Inschriften von Ephesos* 24

# Bibliographical essay

## APPROACHES

Questions of method and approaches have been touched on throughout this book. In current scholarship there are some very different emphases and interests. Burkert (e.g. 1966 and 1983) has tended to look for explanations in terms of origins (whether hypothetical prehistoric practices or closer near-eastern sources for Greek myths). In contrast, a strong French school has sought for meanings in terms of contemporary structures (e.g. Gordon 1981; Vernant 1991: 268–89; Bruit Zaidman and Schmitt Pantel 1992). Others have traced changes in religion, and looked for significance in terms of historical context (e.g. Parker 1996). Studies of the Hellenistic and Roman periods used to be dogged by a false assumption that Greek cities in those periods were in general decline, and in particular that their cults were in terminal decline, especially in the face of Christianity. For studies which reject those assumptions see Price 1984a and Lane Fox 1986. Assumptions about 'real' religion derived consciously or unconsciously from Judaism and Christianity need constantly to be guarded against: for a statement of some dangers see Price 1984a: 11–16. For methodological issues arising in the study of later Greek religion see Phillips 1986.

Much may be learned from anthropologists, who have long faced the problem of studying the rituals of inarticulate religions. R. Towler, *Homo Religiosus: Sociological Problems in the Study of Religion* (London 1974) is a useful introduction. E.E. Evans-Pritchard, *Theories of Primitive Religion* (Oxford 1965) discusses theoretical issues first outlined at the beginning of this century. *Anthropological Approaches to the Study of Religion*, ed. M. Banton (London 1966), includes interesting papers by M. Spiro and C. Geertz. Geertz's influential, essentialist definition of religion has been criticised by Asad 1983 as crypto-Christian, and by Saler 1993: 93–104 as Western. The category 'religion' is unavoidable, though we need to fight against ethnocentrism, but it now seems preferable to work with an implicit, 'open-textured' definition of religion: Poole 1986. Anthropologists have also come to stress the problematic nature both of the relationship between anthropologists and 'natives', and of the anthropologist's text. See Danforth 1989 for a model, modern account (of fire-walking).

## FURTHER BIBLIOGRAPHICAL GUIDANCE

Several good books and articles offer introductions to Greek religion of the archaic and classical periods: Burkert 1985 (basic modern handbook); Parker 1986 (a short article); Bruit Zaidman and Schmitt Pantel 1992 (an excellent synthesis of the French approach); Bremmer 1994. Sourvinou-Inwood 1988a and 1990 are fine syntheses on 'polis religion'. On the Hellenistic period see Gordon 1972, J.K. Davies in *CAH*, 2nd edn, vii.1 (Cambridge 1984) 314–20, Martin 1987 and Mikalson 1998. For Greek cults in the Roman empire see Price 1984a and Lane Fox 1986. Beard, North and Price 1998: vol. 1 is an introduction to the parallel, and sometimes interlocking, history of Roman religion.

For further bibliography on particular points, one can mine Nilsson 1955–67 (even if one lacks German); Burkert 1985; Bremmer 1994 (with more recent bibliography in the German edition, 1996). S. Settis (ed.), *I Greci* 2.1 (Turin 1996) includes a range of chapters (in Italian) which offer good starting points on various aspects of Greek religion. A bibliographical database of Greek religion can be found in Motte et al. 1992, which is now joined by a second volume of 1998. *L'Année philologique* and *Archäologische Bibliographie* list the year's publications on Greek religion (in recent years the latter has helpful subdivisions, and covers much more than pure archaeology); A. Chaniotis reports annually in *Kernos* on relevant new inscriptions. DYABOLA, the German Archaeological Institute's CD ROM, makes available their incomparable bibliographical files from 1956 onwards; in the UK there are copies in the Institute of Classical Studies, London, and the Ashmolean Library, Oxford.

## SOURCES

Sources on Greek religion are incredibly abundant, in contrast to the evidence for some standard topics of political history. For those who want to explore texts further, there are two possible routes. The first is to focus on some specific texts and to investigate their arguments and structures. I list here some suggestions for further reading:

Hesiod, *Theogony* (with introduction by J.P. Barron in P.E. Easterling and B.M.W. Knox (eds.), *The Cambridge History of Classical Literature* 1 (Cambridge 1985), 92–105, 724–6).

*Homeric Hymn to Demeter* (with Foley 1994).

Aristophanes, *Clouds* and Plato, *Apology*, on Socrates and the Sophists (with Hansen 1995; Burnyeat 1996).

Euripides, *Bacchae*, on Dionysos (with edn by E.R. Dodds (Oxford 1960); Yunis 1988).

Andocides 1 *On the Mysteries* and Lysias 6 *Against Andocides*, on threats to the civic system (the latter text ed. and trans. by C. Carey (Warminster 1992); Murray 1990; Furley 1996).

Plato, *Euthyphro*, with critique of conventional piety (with Vlastos 1991).

Plutarch, *The Obsolescence of Oracles* and *The Oracles at Delphi no longer given in verse*, on Delphi in the early empire (with Price 1985; Lane Fox 1986: 184–6).

Plutarch, *Isis and Osiris*, on the Greek incorporation of an Egyptian cult (with edn by J.G. Griffiths (Cardiff 1970); Hardie 1992).

Aelius Aristides, *Sacred Tales (Orations* 47–52), on Asclepius (with Behr 1968 and Lane Fox 1986: 160–3).

Lucian, *Alexander* and *Peregrinos*, on two alleged charlatans of the second century AD (with Lane Fox 1986: 243–50).

Pausanias, *Guide to Greece* (with Elsner 1992; Arafat 1996; Swain 1996: 330–56).

Sallustius, *Concerning the Gods and the Universe* (translated and commented on by A.D. Nock (Cambridge 1926)).

The other route is via sourcebooks, but there is no one good sourcebook on Greek religion, and all omit material evidence. Rice and Stambaugh 1979 include both literary texts and inscriptions, mainly of classical date; Grant 1953 consists of epigraphical and other texts of the Hellenistic and Roman periods; Ferguson 1980 has some Greek texts. For the Roman period see Kraemer 1988 (on women's religions); MacMullen and Lane 1992 (mixing Greek and Roman); Beard, North and Price 1998 vol. II, though focused on Rome, includes some Greek texts and images. Morford and Lenardon 1995 collect texts on myths, but in an inadequate framework and without due attention to the nature of individual texts.

Material evidence can be pursued through discussions of individual sites or topics in the preceding chapters. I also give here some further suggestions. On sanctuaries see Melas 1973; Schroder 1974; Nixon 1995 on Demeter sanctuaries. The following list of sites gives bibliography in English, which mostly leads on to further publications in English.

Athens, Akropolis: Herington 1955; Hooker 1963; Hopper 1971; Travlos 1971; Economakis 1994.

Athens, Agora: J.M. Camp, *Gods and Heroes in the Athenian Agora* (Princeton NJ 1980); Camp 1986; Travlos 1971.

Eleusis: Mylonas 1961; Travlos 1988.

Delphi: Price 1985; Morgan 1990.

Olympia: Finley and Pleket 1976; Morgan 1990.

Epidaurus: Burford 1969.

Corinth: M. Lang, *Cure and Cult in Ancient Corinth: A Guide to the Asklepieion* (Princeton NJ 1977); N. Bookidis and R.S. Stroud, *Demeter and Persephone in Ancient Corinth* (Princeton NJ 1987).

Samothrace: Lehmann 1975.

Cyrene: D. White (ed.), *The Extramural Sanctuary of Demeter and Persephone at Cyrene, Libya* V (Philadelphia 1993).

On iconography, see Bérard 1989; Carpenter 1991; *LIMC* (which presents a wealth of material; even articles not in English can be followed by the brave). On votives, Van Straten 1992. On sacrifices, Durand in Detienne and Vernant 1989; Van Straten 1995. On Athenian festivals, E. Simon 1983.

# Bibliography

ALCOCK, S.E. (1993) *Graecia Capta. The Landscapes of Roman Greece* (Cambridge)
  (1996) 'Landscapes of memory and the authority of Pausanias', in J. Bingen
  (ed.), *Pausanias historien (Entretiens Hardt 41)* (Vandoeuvres-Geneva), 241–61
ALCOCK, S.E. and R.G. OSBORNE (eds.) (1994) *Placing the Gods: Sanctuaries and
  Sacred Space in Ancient Greece* (Oxford)
ALDRICH, K. (1975) *Apollodorus. The Library of Greek Mythology* (Lawrence, Kansas)
ALESHIRE, S.B. (1989) *The Athenian Asclepieion. The People, their Dedications, and the
  Inventories* (Amsterdam)
  (1992) 'The economics of dedication at the Athenian Asklepieion', in Linders
  and Alroth (1992), 85–98
  (1994) 'The demos and the priests', in Osborne and Hornblower (1994),
  325–37
ALROTH, B. (1989) *Greek Gods and Figurines: Aspects of the Anthropomorphic Dedications*
  (Uppsala)
AMANDRY, P. (1939) 'Rapport préliminaire sur les statues chryséléphantines de
  Delphes', *BCH* 63: 86–119
  (1977) 'Statue de taureau en argent', *BCH* Supp. 4: 273–93
AMPOLO, C. (1989–90) 'Fra economia, religione e politica: tesori e offerte nei
  santuari greci', *Scienze dell'Antichità* 3–4: 271–9
  (1992) 'The economics of the sanctuaries in southern Italy and Sicily', in
  Linders and Alroth (1992), 25–8
ANNAS, J. and J. BARNES (1985) *The Modes of Scepticism* (Cambridge)
ARAFAT, K.W. (1996) *Pausanias' Greece: Ancient Artists and Roman Rulers*
  (Cambridge)
ASAD, T. (1983) 'Anthropological conceptions of religion: reflections on Geertz',
  *Man* 18: 237–59, revised in his *Genealogies of Religion: Disciplines and Reasons of
  Power in Christianity and Islam* (Baltimore and London, 1993), 27–54
ATHANASSAKIS, A.N. (1977) *The Homeric Hymns* (Baltimore)
ATHANASSIADI, P. (1989–90) 'The fate of oracles in late antiquity: Didyma and
  Delphi', *Deltion tis Christianikis Archaiologikis Etaireias* 15: 271–8
  (1993) 'Persecution and response in late paganism: the evidence of
  Damascius', *JHS* 113: 1–29
ATTRIDGE, H.W. (1978) 'The philosophical critique of religion under the early
  empire', *ANRW* 2.16.1: 45–78

AUBRIOT-SÉVIN, D. (1992) *Prière et conceptions religieuses en Grèce ancienne jusqu'à la fin du V<sup>e</sup> siècle av. J.-C.* (Lyons)

AUSTIN, M.M. (1981) *The Hellenistic World, from Alexander to the Roman Conquest* (Cambridge)

BABUT, D. (1974) *La religion des philosophes grecs* (Paris)

BAMMER, A. (1974) *Führer durch das archäologische Museum in Selçuk-Ephesos* (Vienna)
(1976) 'Amazonen und das Artemision von Ephesos', *RA* 1976: 91–102

BAMMER, A. and U. MUSS (1996) *Das Artemision von Ephesos* (*Antike Welt* Supp.) (Mainz am Rhein)

BARBER, E.J.W. (1991) *Prehistoric Textiles* (Princeton, NJ)
(1992) 'The peplos of Athena', in Neils (1992), 103–17, 208–10

BARRON, J.P. (1972) 'New light on old walls', *JHS* 92: 32–45

BEARD, M. (1986) 'Cicero and divination: the formation of a Latin discourse', *JRS* 76: 33–46

BEARD, M. and J. NORTH (eds.) (1990) *Pagan Priests. Religion and Power in the Ancient World* (London)

BEARD, M., J. NORTH and S. PRICE (1998) *Religions of Rome*, 2 vols. (Cambridge)

BEAZLEY, J.D. (1951) *The Development of Attic Black-Figure* (Berkeley) (rev. edn 1986)

BECK, R.L. (1982) 'Soteriology, the mysteries, and the ancient novel: Iamblichus' *Babyloniaca* as a test-case', in U. Bianchi and M.J. Vermaseren (eds.), *La soteriologia dei culti orientali nell' impero romano* (EPRO 92) (Leiden), 527–46
(1996) 'Mystery religions, aretalogy and the ancient novel', in G. Schmeling, *The Novel in the Ancient World* (*Mnemosyne* Supp. 159) (Leiden), 131–50

BEHR, C.A. (1968) *Aelius Aristides and the Sacred Tales* (Amsterdam)

BÉRARD, C. et al. (1989) *A City of Images. Iconography and Society in Ancient Greece* (Princeton, NJ) (French original 1984)

BERGQUIST, B. (1992) 'The archaic temenos in western Greece. A survey and two inquiries', in Schachter (1992), 109–52

BIRGE, D. (1994) 'Trees in the landscape of Pausanias' *Periegesis*', in Alcock and Osborne (1994), 231–45

BLOK, J.H. (1995) *The Early Amazons. Modern and Ancient Perspectives on a Persistent Myth* (Leiden)

BLUNDELL, S. and M. WILLIAMSON (eds.) (1998) *The Sacred and the Feminine in Ancient Greece* (London and New York)

BOARDMAN, J. (1974) *Athenian Black Figure Vases* (London and New York)

BONNECHERE, P. (1994) *Le sacrifice humain en Grèce ancienne* (*Kernos* Supp. 3) (Athens and Liège)

BORGEAUD, P. (1988) *The Cult of Pan in Ancient Greece* (Chicago and London) (French original 1979)
(ed.) (1991) *Orphisme et Orphée en l'honneur de Jean Rudhardt* (Geneva)
(1993) 'Quelques remarques sur la mythologie divine à Rome, à propos de Denys d'Halicarnasse (ant. Rom. 2,18–20)', in F. Graf (ed.), *Mythos in mythenloser Gesellschaft. Das Paradigma Roms* (Stuttgart and Leipzig), 175–87

BOTTINI, A. (1992) *Archeologia della salvezza* (Milan)

BOUSQUET, J. (1988) 'Etat des travaux sur les comptes du IV^e siècle: l'amende des Phocidiens', in Knoepfler (1988), 83–9

BOWERSOCK, G.W. (1990) *Hellenism in Late Antiquity* (Cambridge, MA)

BRELICH, A. (1969) *Paides e Parthenoi* I (Rome)

BREMER, J.M. (1981) 'Greek hymns', in Versnel (1981a), 193–215

BREMMER, J.N. (ed.) (1987) *Interpretations of Greek Mythology* (London and Sydney)

(1994) *Greek Religion* (Oxford) (revised as *Götter, Mythen und Heiligtümer im antiken Griechenland*, Darmstadt 1996)

(1996a) 'Modi di communicazione con il divino: la preghiera, la divinazione e il sacrificio nella civiltà greca', in S. Settis (ed.), *I Greci . . I. Noi e i Greci* (Turin), 239–83

(1996b) 'The status and symbolic capital of the seer', in R. Hägg (ed.), *The Role of Religion in the Early Greek Polis* (Stockholm), 97–109

BRILLANTE, C. (1990) 'History and the historical interpretation of myth', in Edmunds (1990), 93–138

BRISSON, L. (1985) 'Les théogonies orphiques et le papyrus de Derveni: notes critiques', *Rev. de l'Hist. de Rel.* 202: 389–420, repr. in his *Orphée et l'Orphisme dans l'Antiquité gréco-romaine* (Aldershot, Hampshire and Brookfield, VA, 1995)

BRONEER, O. (1942) 'The Thesmophorion in Athens', *Hesperia* II: 250–74

BROWN, P. (1992) *Power and Persuasion in Late Antiquity. Towards a Christian Empire* (Madison, WI and London)

(1995) *Authority and the Sacred. Aspects of the Christianisation of the Roman World* (Cambridge)

BRUIT ZAIDMAN, L. and P. SCHMITT PANTEL (1992) *Religion in the Ancient Greek City*, ed. P. Cartledge (Cambridge) (latest repr. with bibliographical addenda 1997)

BRULÉ, P. (1987) *La fille d'Athènes. La religion des filles à Athènes à l'époque classique* (Annales Litt. de l'Univ. de Besançon 363) (Paris)

BRUNAUX, J.L. (1988) *The Celtic Gauls: Gods, Rites and Sanctuaries* (London)

BURFORD, A. (1963) 'The builders of the Parthenon', in *Parthenos and Parthenon* (*Greece and Rome* Supp. to vol. 10) (Oxford), 23–35

(1969) *The Greek Temple Builders at Epidaurus* (Liverpool and Toronto)

BURKERT, W. (1966) 'Greek tragedy and sacrificial ritual', *GRBS* 7: 83–121

(1972) *Lore and Science in Ancient Pythagoreanism* (Cambridge, MA)

(1982) 'Craft versus sect: the problem of Orphics and Pythagoreans', in B.F. Meyer and E.P. Sanders (eds.), *Jewish and Christian Self-Definition* 3 (Philadelphia), 1–22

(1983) *Homo Necans* (Berkeley) (German original 1972)

(1985) *Greek Religion: Archaic and Classical* (Oxford) (German original 1977)

(1987a) *Ancient Mystery Cults* (Cambridge, MA and London)

(1987b) 'Oriental and Greek mythology: the meeting of parallels', in Bremmer (1987), 10–40

(1990) 'Herodot als Historiker fremder Religionen', in G. Nenci (ed.), *Hérodote et les peuples non grecs* (Entretiens Hardt 35) (Geneva), 1–32

(1991) 'Homer's anthropomorphism: narrative and ritual', in D. Buitron-Oliver (ed.), *New Perspectives in Early Greek Art* (Hanover, NH and London), 81–91

(1992a) *The Orientalizing Revolution* (Cambridge, MA and London) (German original 1984)

(1992b) 'The formation of Greek religion at the close of the Dark Ages', *Studi Italiani di Filologia Classica*, 3rd series, 10: 533–51

(1993) 'Concordia discors: the literary and the archaeological evidence on the sanctuary of Samothrace', in Marinatos and Hägg (1993), 178–91

(1995) 'Greek *poleis* and civic cults: some further thoughts', in M.H. Hansen and K. Raaflaub (eds.), *Studies in the Ancient Greek Polis* (*Historia* Supp. 95) (Stuttgart), 201–10

BURNYEAT, M. (1996) 'The impiety of Socrates', in A. Dykman and W. Godzich (eds.), *Platon et les poètes: hommages à George Steiner* (Geneva), 13–36; revised in *Ancient Philosophy* 17 (1997), 1–12

BUXTON R. (1994) *Imaginary Greece. The Contexts of Mythology* (Cambridge)

CALAME, C. (1990) 'Narrating the foundation of a city: the symbolic birth of Cyrene', in Edmunds (1990), 275–341

(1991a) '"Mythe" et "rite" en Grèce: des catégories indigènes?', *Kernos* 4: 179–204

(1991b) 'Eros initiatique et la cosmogonie orphique', in Borgeaud (1991), 227–47

(1995a) 'Pausanias le périégète en ethnographe ou comment décrire un culte grec', in J.-M. Adam et al., *Le discours anthropologique*, 2nd edn (Lausanne), 205–26

(1995b) 'Variations énonciatives, relations avec les dieux et fonctions poétiques dans les *Hymnes homériques*', *Museum Helveticum* 52: 1–19

(1996) *Mythe et histoire dans l'Antiquité grecque. La création symbolique d'une colonie* (Lausanne)

(1997) *Choruses of Young Women in Ancient Greece. Their Morphology, Religious Role, and Social Functions* (Lanham, MD and London) (French original 1977)

CAMP, J.M. (1986) *The Athenian Agora* (London)

CAREY, C. (1989) 'The performance of the victory ode', *AJPhil.* 110: 545–65

CARPENTER, T.H. (1991) *Art and Myth of Classical Greece: A Handbook* (London)

CARTER, J.C. (1983) *The Sculptors of the Sanctuary of Athena Polias at Priene* (London)

CARTLEDGE, P. and A.J. SPAWFORTH (1989) *Hellenistic and Roman Sparta* (London and New York)

CARTLEDGE, P. and F.D. HARVEY (eds.) (1985) *Crux. Essays in Greek History Presented to G. E. M. de Ste. Croix* (Exeter and London)

CASTRIOTA, D. (1992) *Myth, Ethos, and Actuality. Official Art in Fifth-century BC Athens* (Madison, WI and London)

CAVANAUGH, M.B. (1996) *Eleusis and Athens: Documents in Finance, Religion and Politics in the Fifth Century BC* (Atlanta, GA)

CHADWICK, H. (1966) *Early Christian Thought and the Classical Tradition* (Oxford)

CHALK, H.H.O. (1960) 'Eros and the Lesbian pastorals of Longus', *JHS* 80: 32–51

CHANIOTIS, A. (1995) 'Sich selbst feiern? Städtische Feste des Hellenismus im Spannungsfeld von Religion und Politik', in M. Wörrle and P. Zanker (eds.), *Stadtbild und Bürgerbild im Hellenismus* (*Vestigia* 47) (Munich), 147–72

CHARLESWORTH, J.H. (ed.) (1983–5) *The Old Testament Pseudepigrapha* 2 vols. (London)

CHUVIN, P. (1987) 'Observations sur les reliefs du théâtre de Hiérapolis', *Revue archéologique* 1987: 97–108

(1990) *A Chronicle of the Last Pagans* (Cambridge, MA and London) (French original 1990)

CLAIRMONT, C.W. (1993) *Classical Attic Tombstones* (Kilchberg)

CLINTON, K. (1974) *The Sacred Officials of the Eleusinian Mysteries* (Philadelphia)

(1987) 'The date of the classical Telesterion at Eleusis', in *Philia Epe eis Georgion E. Mylonan* 2 (Athens), 2.254–62

(1992) *Myth and Cult. The Iconography of the Eleusinian Mysteries* (Stockholm)

(1993) 'The sanctuary of Demeter and Kore at Eleusis', in Marinatos and Hägg (1993), 110–24

(1994a) 'The Epidauria and the arrival of Asclepius in Athens', in R. Hägg (ed.), *Ancient Greek Cult Practice from the Epigraphical Evidence* (Stockholm), 17–34

(1994b) 'The Eleusinian mysteries and panhellenism in democratic Athens', in W.D.E. Coulson et al. (eds.), *The Archaeology of Athens and Attica under the Democracy* (Oxbow Monographs 37) (Oxford), 161–72

(1996a) 'A new *lex sacra* from Selinus', *Classical Philology* 91: 159–79

(1996b) 'The Thesmophorion in central Athens and the celebration of the Thesmophoria in Attica', in Hägg (1996), 111–25

COARELLI, F. (ed.) (1986) *Fregellae. 2. Il santuario di Esculapio* (Rome)

COARELLI, F. and M. TORELLI (1984) *Sicilia* (Rome–Bari)

COHEN, D. (1991) *Law, Sexuality and Society. The Enforcement of Morals in Classical Athens* (Cambridge)

COLE, S.G. (1984a) 'The social function of rituals of maturation: the Koureion and the Arkteia', *ZPE* 55: 233–44

(1984b) *Theoi Megaloi: the Cult of the Great Gods at Samothrace* (EPRO 86) (Leiden)

(1989) 'The mysteries of Samothrace during the Roman period', *ANRW* 2.18.2: 1564–98

(1994) 'Demeter in the ancient Greek city and its countryside', in Alcock and Osborne (1994), 199–216

(1995) 'Civic cult and civic identity', in M.H. Hansen (ed.), *Sources for the Ancient Greek City-State* (Copenhagen), 292–325

CONNELLY, J.B. (1996) 'Parthenon and *Parthenoi*: a mythological interpretation of the Parthenon frieze', *AJA* 100: 53–80

CONNOR, W.R. (1987) 'Tribes, festivals and processions: civic ceremonial and political manipulation in archaic Greece', *JHS* 107: 40–50

(1988) '"Sacred" and "secular": *Hiera kai hosia* and the classical Athenian concept of the state', *Ancient Society* 19: 161–88

(1990) 'City Dionysia and Athenian democracy', in J.R. Fears (ed.), *Aspects of Athenian Democracy* (Copenhagen), 7–32

(1991) 'The other 399: religion and the trial of Socrates', in M.A. Flower and M. Toher (eds.), *Georgica. Greek Studies in Honour of George Cawkwell* (*BICS* Supp. 58) (London), 49–56

COOK, A.B. (1914–40) *Zeus. A Study in Greek Religion* (Cambridge)

CORBETT, P.E. (1970) 'Greek temples and Greek worshippers', *Bull. Inst. Class. Stud.* 17: 149–58

CORMACK, R. (1990a) 'The temple as the cathedral', in C. Roueché and K.T. Erim (eds.), *Aphrodisias Papers* (*JRA* Supp. 1) (Ann Arbor, MI), 75–88

(1990b) 'Byzantine Aphrodisias. Changing the symbolic map of a city', *PCPhS* N.S. 36: 26–41

CORNELL, T.J. (1995) *The Beginnings of Rome: Italy and Rome from the Bronze Age to the Punic Wars (c. 1000–264 BC)* (London and New York)

COULTON, J.J. (1977) *Greek Architects at Work* (London)

CRAWFORD, M.H. (1974) *Roman Republican Coinage* (Cambridge)

CULLEY, G.R. (1977) 'The restoration of sanctuaries in Attica', *Hesperia* 46: 282–98

CUNNINGHAM, I.C. (1966) 'Herodas 4', *CQ* 16: 113–25

DALLEY, S. (1989) *Myths of Mesopotamia* (Oxford and New York)

DANFORTH, L.M. (1984) 'The ideological context of the search for continuities in Greek culture', *Journal of Modern Greek Studies* 2: 53–85

(1989) *Firewalking and Religious Healing. The Anastenaria of Greece and the American Firewalking Movement* (Princeton, NJ)

DANIÉLOU, J. (1973) *Gospel Message and Hellenistic Culture* (London and Philadelphia)

DAVIES, J.K. (1967) 'Demosthenes on liturgies: a note', *JHS* 87: 33–40

(1971) *Athenian Propertied Families 600–300 BC* (Oxford)

(1988) 'Religion and the state', *CAH* 2nd edn 4: 368–88

DAVIES, M. (1990) '"Popular justice" and the end of Aristophanes' *Clouds*', *Hermes* 118: 237–42

DE CAZANOVE, O. and J. SCHEID (eds.) (1993) *Les bois sacrés* (Naples)

DEBORD, P. (1982) *Aspects sociaux et économiques de la vie religieuse dans l'Anatolie gréco-romaine* (EPRO 88) (Leiden)

DELEBECQUE, E. (1955) 'Le site de Scillonte', *Annales de la Faculté des Lettres d'Aix* 29: 5–18

DE POLIGNAC, F. (1994) 'Mediation, competition, and sovereignty: the evolution of rural sanctuaries', in Alcock and Osborne (1994), 3–18

(1995) *Cults, Territory, and the Origins of the Greek City-State* (Chicago and London) (French original 1984)

DEROCHE, V. (1989) 'Delphes: la christianisation d'un sanctuaire païen', in *Actes du XI^e Congrès International d'Archéologie Chrétienne* (Coll. Ecole franç. de Rome 123) (Rome and Paris), 3.2713–26

DETIENNE, M. (1970) 'La cuisine de Pythagore', *Archives de Sociologie des Religions* 29: 141–62

(1979) *Dionysus Slain* (Baltimore) (French original 1977)

(1986) *The Creation of Mythology* (Chicago) (French original 1981)

(1989) 'The violence of wellborn ladies: women in the Thesmophoria', in Detienne and Vernant (1989), 129–47

DETIENNE, M. and J.-P. VERNANT (1978) *Cunning Intelligence in Greek Culture and Society* (Hassocks and Atlantic Highlands, NJ) (French original 1974)

(1989) *The Cuisine of Sacrifice among the Greeks* (Chicago and London) (French original 1979)

DEUBNER, L. (1932) *Attische Feste* (Berlin)

DILLON, M. (1997) *Pilgrims and Pilgrimage in Ancient Greece* (London and New York)

DODDS, E.R. (1951) *The Greeks and the Irrational* (Berkeley)

DÖRING, K. (1979) *Exemplum Socratis. Studien zur Sokratesnachwirkung in der kynisch-stoischen Popularphilosophie der frühen Kaiserzeit und im frühen Christentum* (*Hermes* Supp. 42) (Wiesbaden)

DÖRPFELD, W. (1894) 'Die Ausgrabungen an der Enneakrunos. II', *Athenische Mitteilungen* 19: 143–51

DONOHUE, A.A. (1988) *Xoana and the Origins of Greek Sculpture* (Atlanta, GA)

DONTAS, G. (1983) 'The true Aglaurion', *Hesperia* 52: 48–63

DOUGHERTY, C. (1993) *The Poetics of Colonisation. From City to Text in Archaic Greece* (New York and Oxford)

DOVER, K.J. (1968) *Aristophanes' Clouds* (Oxford), xxxii-lvii (reprinted in G. Vlastos (ed.) (1971), *The Philosophy of Socrates* (New York), 50–77)

(1970) 'Mutilation of the Herms', in A.W. Gomme, A. Andrewes and K.J. Dover, *A Historical Commentary on Thucydides* (Oxford), 4.264–88

(1974) *Greek Popular Morality in the Time of Plato and Aristotle* (Oxford)

(1975) 'The freedom of the intellectual in Greek society', *Talanta* 7: 24–54 (reprinted with addendum in K.J. Dover (1988), *The Greeks and their Legacy* (Oxford), 135–58)

DOW, S. (1937) 'The Egyptian cults in Athens', *HThR* 30: 183–232

DOWDEN, K. (1989) *Death and the Maiden. Girls' Initiation Rites in Greek Mythology* (London and New York)

(1992) *The Uses of Greek Mythology* (London and New York)

DOWNEY, G. (1961) *A History of Antioch in Syria* (Princeton, NJ)

DRACHMANN, A.B. (1922) *Atheism in Pagan Antiquity* (London and Copenhagen)

DRAGONA-MONACHOU, M. (1976) *The Stoic Arguments for the Existence and the Providence of the Gods* (Athens)

DUBOIS, P. (1982) *Centaurs and Amazons: Women and the Prehistory of the Great Chain of Being* (Ann Arbor, MI)

DUBOURDIEU, A. (1989) *Les origines et le développement du culte des Pénates à Rome* (Coll. Ecole franç. de Rome 118) (Rome and Paris)

DUMÉZIL, G. (1968–73) *Mythe et épopée*, 3 vols. (Paris)

DUNAND, F. (1973) *Le culte d'Isis dans le bassin oriental de la Méditerranée* (3 vols.) (EPRO 26) (Leiden)

DURAND, J.-L. (1986) *Sacrifice et labour en Grèce ancienne* (Paris and Rome)

DURAND, J.-L. and A. SCHNAPP (1989) 'Sacrificial slaughter and initiatory hunt', in Bérard et al. (1989), 53–70

EASTERLING, P.E. and J.V. MUIR (eds.) (1985) *Greek Religion and Society* (Cambridge)

ECONOMAKIS, R. (ed.) (1994) *Acropolis Restoration: The CCAM Interventions* (London)

EDELSTEIN, E.J. and L. (1945) *Asclepius. A Collection and Interpretation of the Testimonies*, 2 vols. (Baltimore)

EDLUND, I.E.M. (1987) *The Gods and the Place. The Location and Function of Sanctuaries in the Countryside of Etruria and Magna Graecia (700–400 BC)* (Stockholm)

EDMUNDS, L. (ed.) (1990) *Approaches to Greek Myth* (Baltimore and London)

EDWARDS, M.J. (1991) 'Xenophanes Christianus?', *GRBS* 32: 219–28

ELSNER, J. (1992) 'Pausanias: a Greek pilgrim in the Roman world', *Past and Present* 135: 1–29, revised in Elsner (1995), *Art and the Roman Viewer* (Cambridge), 125–55

ERHARDT, H. (1985) *Samothrake. Heiligtümer in ihrer Landschaft und Geschichte als Zeugen antiken Geisteslebens* (Stuttgart)

FAHR, W. (1969) *Theous Nomizein. Zum Problem der Anfänge des Atheismus bei den Griechen* (Hildesheim and New York)

FARAGUNA, M. (1992) *Atene nell' età dei Alessandro. Problemi politici, economici, finanziari (Atti della Accad. Naz. dei Lincei*, Memorie, Ser. 9, 2.2) (Rome)

FARAONE, C.A. (1991) 'The agonistic context of early Greek binding spells', in C.A. Faraone and D. Obbink (eds.), *Magika Hiera. Ancient Greek Magic and Religion* (New York and Oxford), 3–32.

(1992) *Talisman and Trojan Horse: Guardian Statues in Ancient Greek Myth and Ritual* (New York and Oxford)

FEAVER, D.D. (1957) 'Historical development in the priesthoods of Athens', *Yale Classical Studies* 15: 123–58

FERGUSON, J. (1980) *Greek and Roman Religion. A Source Book* (Park Ridge, NJ)

FESTUGIÈRE, A.-J. (1954) *Personal Religion among the Greeks* (Berkeley)

(1955) *Epicurus and his Gods* (Oxford)

(1968) *Épicure et ses dieux*, 2nd edn (Paris)

FINLEY, M.I. and H.W. PLEKET (1976) *The Olympic Games. The First Thousand Years* (London)

FLEISCHER, R. (1973) *Artemis von Ephesos und verwandte Kultstatuen aus Anatolien und Syrien* (EPRO 35) (Leiden)

(1974) 'Fries vom Hadrianstempel', in Bammer (1974), 78–82

FOLEY, H.P. (ed.) (1994) *The Homeric Hymn to Demeter: Translation, Commentary and Interpretive Essays* (Princeton, NJ)

FORNARA, C.W. (1983) *Archaic Times to the End of the Peloponnesian War*, 2nd edn (Cambridge)

FORTENBAUGH, W.W. et al. (eds.) (1992) *Theophrastus of Eresus. Sources* (Leiden)

FOSS, C. (1979) *Ephesus after Antiquity: A Late Antique, Byzantine and Turkish City* (Cambridge)

FOWDEN, G. (1978) 'Bishops and temples in the eastern Roman empire AD 320–435', *Journal of Theological Studies* N.S. 29: 53–78

(1986) *The Egyptian Hermes. A Historical Approach to the Late Pagan Mind* (Cambridge)

(1988) 'City and mountain in late Roman Attica', *JHS* 108: 48–59

(1993) *Empire to Commonwealth. Consequences of Monotheism in Late Antiquity* (Princeton, NJ)

(1995) 'Late Roman Achaea: identity and defence', *JRA* 8: 549–67

FOWLER, D.P. (1989) 'Lucretius and politics', in M. Griffin and J. Barnes (eds.), *Philosophia Togata. Essays on Philosophy and Roman Society* (Oxford), 120–50

FRANTZ, A. (1965) 'From paganism to Christianity in the temples of Athens', *DOP* 19: 187–205

FRICKEL, J. (1984) *Hellenistische Erlösung in christlicher Deutung* (Leiden)

FRIEDRICH, P. (1978) *The Meaning of Aphrodite* (Chicago and London)

FRITZ, K. von (1940) *Pythagorean Politics in Southern Italy* (New York)

FULLER, C.J. (1992) *The Camphor Flame. Popular Hinduism and Society in India* (Princeton, NJ)

FURLEY, W.D. (1995) 'Praise and persuasion in Greek hymns', *JHS* 115: 29–46

(1996) *Andokides and the Herms. A Study of Crisis in Fifth-Century Athenian Religion* (*BICS* Supp. 65) (London)

GABBA, E. (1981) 'True history and false history in classical antiquity', *JRS* 71: 50–62

GÀBRICI, E. (1927) 'Il santuario della Malophoros a Selinunte', *Monumenti Antichi* 32: 1–419

GAGER, J.G. (1992) *Curse Tablets and Binding Spells from the Ancient World* (New York and Oxford)

GARLAND, R.S.J. (1984) 'Religious authority in archaic and classical Athens', *BSA* 79: 75–123

(1985) *The Greek Way of Death* (London)

(1990a) *The Greek Way of Life* (London)

(1990b) 'Priests and power in classical Athens', in Beard and North (1990), 75–91

(1992) *Introducing New Gods. The Politics of Athenian Religion* (London)

GARNSEY, P. (1984) 'Religious toleration in classical antiquity', in W.J. Sheils (ed.), *Persecution and Toleration* (*Studies in Church History* 21) (Oxford), 1–27

GARNSEY, P. et al. (eds.) (1983) *Trade in the Ancient Economy* (London)

GEBHARD, E. (1974) 'The form of the orchestra in the early Greek theater', *Hesperia* 43: 428–40

GERNET, L. and A. BOULANGER (1932) *Le génie grec dans la religion* (Paris) (repr. with supp. bibliog. 1970)

GINZBURG, C. (1990) *Ecstasies: Deciphering the Witches' Sabbath* (London)

GIOVANNINI, A. (1990) 'Le Parthenon, le trésor d'Athène et le tribut des alliés', *Historia* 39: 129–48

GÖDECKEN, K.B. (1986) 'Beobachtungen und Funde an der Heiligen Strasse zwischen Milet und Didyma, 1984', *ZPE* 66: 217–53

GOLDEN, M. (1985) '"Donatus" and Athenian phratries', *CQ* N.S. 35: 9–13

(1990) *Children and Childhood in Classical Athens* (Baltimore and London)

(1998) *Sport and Society in Ancient Greece* (Cambridge)

GOLDHILL, S. (1987) 'The Great Dionysia and civic ideology', *JHS* 107: 58–76, revised in J.J. Winkler and F.I. Zeitlin (eds.) (1990), *Nothing to Do with*

*Dionysus? Athenian Drama in its Social Context* (Princeton, NJ), 97–129

GOODMAN, M. (1999) 'Josephus, *Against Apion*', in M. Edwards, M. Goodman, S. Price and C. Rowland (eds.), *Apologetics in the Roman Empire* (Oxford), 45–58

GORDON, R.L. (1972) 'Fear of freedom? Selective continuity in religion during the Hellenistic period', *Didaskalos* 4: 48–60

(1979) 'The real and the imaginary: production and religion in the Greco-Roman world', *Art History* 2: 5–34 (repr. in his *Image and Value in the Graeco-Roman World* (Aldershot, Hampshire, and Brookfield, VA, 1996)

(1981) (ed.) *Myth, Religion and Society: Structuralist Essays* by M. Detienne, L. Gernet, J.-P. Vernant and P. Vidal-Naquet (Cambridge)

GOULD, J. (1980) 'Law, custom and myth: aspects of the social position of women in classical Athens', *JHS* 100: 38–59

(1985) 'On making sense of Greek religion', in Easterling and Muir (1985), 1–33

(1994) 'Herodotus and religion', in S. Hornblower (ed.), *Greek Historiography* (Oxford), 91–106

GRAF, F. (1991) 'Textes orphiques et rituel bacchique. A propos des lamelles de Pélinna', in Borgeaud (1991), 87–102

(1992) 'An oracle against pestilence from a western Anatolian town', *ZPE* 92: 267–79

(1993a) *Greek Mythology* (Baltimore and London)

(1993b) 'Dionysian and Orphic eschatology: new texts and old questions', in T.H. Carpenter and C.A. Faraone (eds.), *Masks of Dionysus* (Ithaca, NY and London), 239–58

(1994) *La magie dans l'antiquité gréco-romaine* (Paris)

(1996) '*Pompai* in Greece: some considerations about space and ritual in the Greek *polis*', in Hägg (1996), 55–65

GRANT, F.C. (1953) *Hellenistic Religions* (Indianapolis)

GREGORY, T.E. (1986) 'The survival of paganism in Christian Greece: a critical essay', *AJPhil* 107: 229–42

GRIFFIN, J. (1980) *Homer on Life and Death* (Oxford)

GRUEN, E.S. (1990) *Studies in Greek Culture and Roman Policy* (Cincinnati Classical Studies N.S. 7) (Leiden)

GUTHRIE, W.K.C. (1950) *The Greeks and their Gods* (London)

HABICHT, Chr. (1969) *Altertümer von Pergamon* 8.3 (Berlin)

(1991) 'Milesische Theoren in Athen', *Chiron* 21: 325–9, repr. in Habicht (1994), 256–60

(1993) 'Attische Fluchtafeln aus der Zeit Alexanders des Grossen', *Illinois Classical Studies* 18: 113–18, repr. in Habicht (1994), 14–18

(1994) *Athen in hellenistischer Zeit* (Munich)

(1997) *Athens from Alexander to Antony* (Cambridge, MA and London)

HÄGG, R. (ed.) (1996) *The Role of Religion in the Early Greek Polis* (Stockholm)

HALL, J.M. (1995) 'How Argive was the 'Argive' Heraion? The political and cultic geography of the Argive plain, 900–400 BC', *AJA* 99: 577–613

HAMILTON, R. (1992) *Choes and Anthesteria. Athenian Iconography and Ritual* (Ann Arbor, MI)

HAMMERSTAEDT, J. (1988) *Die Orakelkritik des Kynikers Oenomaus* (Frankfurt am Main)

HANSEN, M.H. (1987) *The Athenian Assembly in the Age of Demosthenes* (Oxford)
(1995) *The Trial of Sokrates – from the Athenian Point of View* (Historisk-filosofiske Meddelelser 71, Det Kongelige Danske Videnskabernes Selskab) (Copenhagen)

HANSON, V.D. (ed.) (1991) *Hoplites: the Classical Greek Battle Experience* (London and New York)

HARDIE, P.R. (1992) 'Plutarch and the interpretation of myth', *ANRW* 2.33.6: 4743–87

HARDING, P. (1985) *From the End of the Peloponnesian War to the Battle of Ipsus* (Cambridge)

HARL, K.W. (1990) 'Sacrifice and pagan belief in fifth- and sixth-century Byzantium', *Past and Present* 128: 7–27

HARRIS, D. (1990–1) 'Gold and silver on the Athenian Acropolis', *Horos* 8–9: 75–82
(1995) *The Treasures of the Parthenon and Erechtheion* (Oxford)

HARTOG, F. (1988) *The Mirror of Herodotus* (Berkeley) (French original 1980)

HEATH, M. (1988) 'Receiving the *Komos*: the context and performance of epinician', *AJPhil* 109: 180–95

HEDRICK, C.W. (1991) 'Phratry shrines of Attica and Athens', *Hesperia* 60: 241–68

HELLSTRÖM, P. and B. ALROTH (eds.) (1996) *Religion and Power in the Ancient Greek World (Boreas* 24) (Uppsala)

HENDERSON, JEFFREY (1993) 'Problems in Greek literary history: the case of Aristophanes' *Clouds*', in R.M. Rosen and J. Farrell (eds.), *Nomodeiktes. Greek Studies in Honor of Martin Ostwald* (Ann Arbor, MI), 591–601

HENDERSON, JOHN (1994) '*Timeo Danaos*: Amazons in early Greek art and pottery', in S. Goldhill and R. Osborne (eds.), *Art and Text in Ancient Greek Culture* (Cambridge), 85–137

HENRICHS, A. (1972a) 'Die Kritik der stoischen Theologie in *PHerc*. 1428', *GRBS* 13: 67–98
(ed.) (1972b) *Lollianus Phoenicica* (Bonn)
(1978) 'Greek maenadism from Olympias to Messalina', *HSCP* 82: 121–60
(1987) 'Three approaches to Greek mythology', in Bremmer (1987), 242–77
(1990) 'Between country and city: cultic dimensions of Dionysus in Athens and Attica', in M. Griffith and D.J. Mastronarde (eds.), *Cabinet of the Muses. Essays on Classical Comparative Literature in Honour of T.G. Rosenmeyer* (Atlanta, GA), 257–77

HERINGTON, C.J. (1955) *Athena Parthenos and Athena Polias* (Manchester)

HOLLADAY, C.R. (1995) *Fragments from Hellenistic Jewish Authors. III Aristobulus* (SBL Texts and Translations 39) (Atlanta, GA)

HOLLOWAY, R.R. (1992) 'Why korai?', *Oxford Journal of Archaeology* 11: 267–74

HONORÉ, T. (1978) *Tribonian* (London)

HOOKER, G.T.W. (ed.) (1963) *Parthenos and Parthenon (Greece and Rome* Supp. 10) (Oxford)

HOPKINSON, N. (ed.) (1994) *Studies in the* Dionysiaca *of Nonnus* (*PCPhS* Supp. 17) (Cambridge)

HOPPER, R.J. (1971) *The Acropolis* (London)

HORNBLOWER, S. (1992) 'The religious dimension to the Peloponnesian War, or what Thucydides does not tell us', *HSCP* 94: 169–97

HORSLEY, G.H.R. (1992) 'The Mysteries of Artemis Ephesia in Pisidia: a new inscribed relief', *Anatolian Studies* 42: 119–50

HUFFMAN, C.A. (1993) *Philolaus of Croton. Pythagorean and Presocratic* (Cambridge)

HUMPHREYS, S. (1985) 'Lycurgus of Butadae: an Athenian aristocrat', in J.W. Eadie and J. Ober (eds.) (1985), *The Craft of the Ancient Historian. Essays in Honor of Chester G. Starr* (Lanham, MD and London), 199–252

HUSSEY, E. (1972) *The Presocratics* (London)

ISAGER, S. and J.E. SKYDSGAARD (1992) *Ancient Greek Agriculture* (London and New York)

JACKSON, A. (1991) 'Hoplites and the gods: the dedication of captured arms and armour', in Hanson (1991), 228–49

JACOB, C. (1993) 'Paysage et bois sacré: *alsos* dans la *Périégèse de la Grèce* de Pausanias', in de Cazanove and Scheid (1993), 31–44

JACOBY, F. (1949) *Atthis. The Local Chronicles of Ancient Athens* (Oxford)

JACQUEMIN, A. (1991) 'Remarques sur le budget sacrificiel d'une cité: Délos indépendante', in R. Etienne and M.-T. Le Dinahet (eds.), *L'espace sacrificiel dans les civilisations méditerranéennes de l'antiquité* (Paris), 93–8

JAMESON, M.H. (1988a) 'Sacrifice and ritual: Greece', in M. Grant and R. Kitzinger (eds.), *Civilisation of the Ancient Mediterranean. Greece and Rome*, 3 vols. (New York), II. 959–79

(1988b) 'Sacrifice and animal husbandry in classical Greece', in C.R. Whittaker (ed.), *Pastoral Economies in Classical Antiquity* (*PCPhS* Supp. 14) (Cambridge), 87–119

(1990) 'Private space and the Greek city', in Murray and Price (1990), 171–95

(1991) 'Sacrifice before battle', in Hanson (1991), 197–227

JAMESON, M.H., D.R. JORDAN and R.D. KOTANSKY (1993) *A Lex Sacra from Selinous* (*GRBS* Monogr. 11) (Durham, NC)

JENKINS, I. (1994) *The Parthenon Frieze* (London)

JONES, C.P. (1993) 'Greek drama in the Roman empire', in R. Scodel (ed.), *Theater and Society in the Classical World* (Ann Arbor, MI), 39–51

JONES, N.F. (1987) *Public Organisation in Ancient Greece: A Documentary Study* (*Mem. Amer. Philos. Soc.* 176) (Philadelphia, PA)

JORDAN, B. (1989) *Servants of the Gods* (*Hypomnemata* 55) (Göttingen)

JOST, M. (1994) 'The distribution of sanctuaries in civic space in Arkadia', in Alcock and Osborne (1994), 217–30

KAHIL, L. (1983) 'Mythological repertoire of Brauron', in W.G. Moon (ed.), *Ancient Greek Art and Iconography* (Madison, WI and London), 231–44

(1988) 'Le sanctuaire de Brauron et la religion grecque', *Comptes rendus de l'académie d'inscriptions* 1988: 799–813

KALLET-MARX, L. (1989) 'Did tribute fund the Parthenon?', *Classical Antiquity* 8: 252–66

KARIVIERI, A. (1995) 'The Christianisation of an ancient pilgrimage site: a case study of the Athenian Asklepieion', in *Akten des XII. Int. Kong. für christ. Arch. (JbAC* Supp. 20) (Münster), 2. 898–905

KÄSTNER, V. (1994) 'Gigantennamen', *Istanbuler Mitteilungen* 44: 125–34

KEARNS, E. (1985) 'Change and continuity in religious structures after Kleisthenes', in Cartledge and Harvey (1985), 189–207

(1989) *The Heroes of Attica (Bulletin of the Institute of Classical Studies* Supp. 57) (London)

(1992) 'Between god and man: status and function of the heroes and their sanctuaries', in Schachter (1992), 65–107

KERFERD, G.B. (1981) *The Sophistic Movement* (Cambridge)

KING, H. (1983) 'Bound to bleed: Artemis and Greek women', in A. Cameron and A. Kuhrt (eds.), *Images of Women in Antiquity* (London and Canberra), 109–27 (repr. with additions 1993)

KIRK, G.S., J.E. RAVEN and M. SCHOFIELD (1983) *The Presocratic Philosophers* (Cambridge)

KNIGGE, U. (1988) *The Athenian Kerameikos* (Athens and Berlin)

KNOEPFLER, D. (ed.) (1988) *Comptes et inventaires dans la cité grecque* (Neuchâtel)

KOUMANOUDIS, S.T. (1976) 'Thiseos sikos', *Ephimeris Arkhaiologiki* 1976: 194–216

KRAEMER, R.S. (1988) *Maenads, Martyrs, Matrons, Monastics. A Sourcebook on Women's Religions in the Greco-Roman World* (Philadelphia, PA)

KRON, U. (1996) 'Priesthoods, dedications and euergetism. What part did religion play in the political and social status of Greek women?', in Hellström and Alroth (1996), 139–82

KURKE, L. (1991) *The Traffic in Praise. Pindar and the Poetics of Social Economy* (Ithaca and London)

KURTZ, D.C. and J. BOARDMAN (1971) *Greek Burial Customs* (London)

KYRIELEIS, H. (1981) *Führer durch das Heraion von Samos* (Athens)

(1993) 'The Heraion at Samos', in Marinatos and Hägg (1993), 125–53

LAKS, A. and G.W. MOST (eds.) (1997) *Studies on the Derveni Papyrus* (Oxford)

LAMBERT, S.D. (1993) *The Phratries of Attica* (Ann Arbor, MI)

LANE FOX, R. (1986) *Pagans and Christians* (Harmondsworth)

LANGDON, M.K. (1987) 'An Attic decree concerning Oropos', *Hesperia* 56: 47–58

LARDINOIS, A. (1992) 'Greek myths for Athenian rituals: religion and politics in Aeschylus' *Eumenides* and Sophocles' *Oedipus Coloneus*', *GRBS* 33: 309–27

LARSON, J. (1995) *Greek Heroine Cults* (Wisconsin Studies in Classics) (Madison, WI and London)

LATTE, K. (1960) *Römische Religionsgeschichte* (Munich)

LATTIMORE, R. (1942) *Themes in Greek and Latin Epitaphs* (Urbana)

LE BONNIEC, H. (1958) *Le culte de Cérès à Rome des origines à la fin de la République* (Paris)

LEHMANN, K. (1975) *Samothrace: A Guide to the Excavations and the Museum* (4th edn) (Locust Valley, NY)

LESHER, J.H. (1992) *Xenophanes of Colophon (Phoenix* Supp. 30) (Toronto)

LEWIS, D.M. (1955) 'Notes on Attic inscriptions XXIII. Who was Lysistrata?', *BSA*

50: 1–12, repr. in his *Selected Papers in Greek and Near Eastern History* (Cambridge, 1997), 187–95

(1973) 'The Athenian rationes centesimarum', in M.I. Finley (ed.) (1973), *Problèmes de la terre en Grèce ancienne* (Paris), 187–212

(1986) 'Temple inventories in ancient Greece', in M. Vickers (ed.), *Pots and Pans* (Oxford), 71–81

LI DONNICI, L.R. (1995) *The Epidaurian Miracle Inscriptions. Text, Translation and Commentary* (SBL Texts and Translations 36) (Atlanta, GA)

LINDERS, T. (1972) *Studies in the Treasure Records of Artemis Brauronia Found in Athens* (Skrifter Utgivna av Svenska Institutet i Athen, 4th ser., 19) (Stockholm)

(1987) 'Gods, gifts, society', in Linders and Nordquist (1987), 115–22

(1988) 'The purpose of inventories: a close reading of the Delian inventories of the Independence', in Knoepfler (1988), 37–47

LINDERS, T. and B. ALROTH (eds.) (1992) *The Economics of Cult in the Ancient Greek World* (Uppsala)

LINDERS, T. and G. NORDQUIST (eds.) (1987) *Gifts to the Gods* (Uppsala)

LINDNER, R. (1994) *Mythos und Identität. Studien zur Selbstdarstellung kleinasiatischer Städte in der römischen Kaiserzeit* (Stuttgart)

LINFORTH, I.M. (1941) *The Arts of Orpheus* (Berkeley)

LISSARRAGUE, F. (1990) *The Aesthetics of the Greek Banquet: Images of Wine and Ritual* (Princeton) (French original 1987)

(1992) 'Figures of women', in P. Schmitt Pantel (ed.), *A History of Women: From Ancient Goddesses to Christian Saints* (Cambridge, MA and London), 139–229

LLOYD, G.E.R. (1979) *Magic, Reason and Experience. Studies in the Origin and Development of Greek Science* (Cambridge)

(1987) *The Revolutions of Wisdom. Studies in the Claims and Practice of Ancient Greek Science* (Berkeley)

LONG, A.A. (1990) 'Scepticism about gods in Hellenistic philosophy', in M. Griffith and D.J. Mastronarde (eds.), *The Cabinet of the Muses. Essays on Classical and Comparative Literature in Honour of T.G. Rosenmeyer* (Atlanta, GA), 279–91

LONG, A.A. and D.N. SEDLEY (1987) *The Hellenistic Philosophers*, 2 vols. (Cambridge)

LONSDALE, S.H. (1993) *Dance and Ritual Play in Greek Religion* (Baltimore and London)

LORAUX, N. (1992) 'What is a goddess?', in P. Schmitt Pantel (ed.), *A History of Women: From Ancient Goddesses to Christian Saints* (Cambridge, MA), 11–44

(1993) *The Children of Athena* (Princeton, NJ) (French orig. 1984)

LOWE, N.J. (1998) 'Thesmophoria and Haloa: myth, physics and mysteries', in Blundell and Williamson (1998), 149–73

MACDOWELL, D. (1962) *Andokides On the Mysteries* (Oxford)

MACMULLEN, R. (1997) *Christianity and Paganism in the Fourth to Eighth Centuries* (New Haven, NJ and London)

MACMULLEN, R. and E.N. LANE (1982) *Paganism and Christianity 100–425 C.E. A Sourcebook* (Minneapolis)

MAIER, F.G. (1959) *Griechische Mauerbauinschriften* (*Vestigia* 1) (Heidelberg)

MALKIN, I. (1987) *Religion and Colonisation in Ancient Greece* (Leiden)

MANGO, C. (1995) 'The conversion of the Parthenon into a church: the Tübingen Theosophy', *Deltion tis Christianikis Archaiologikis Etaireias* 17: 201–3

MANSFIELD, J.M. (1985) 'The Robe of Athena and the Panathenaic Peplos' (Ph.D. dissertation Berkeley)

MANTIS, A.G. (1990) *Provlimata tis ikonographias ton iereion kai ton iereon stin archaia Elliniki techni* (Athens)

MARINATOS, N. and R. HÄGG (eds.) (1993) *Greek Sanctuaries: New Approaches* (London and New York)

MARKUS, R.A. (1990) *The End of Ancient Christianity* (Cambridge)

MARROU, H.-I. (1966) *The Meaning of History* (Dublin and Baltimore)

MARTIN, L.H. (1987) *Hellenistic Religions. An Introduction* (New York and Oxford)

MARTIN, R. (1974) *L'urbanisme dans la Grèce antique*, 2nd edn (Paris)

MCGINTY, P. (1978) *Interpretation and Dionysos: Method in the Study of a God* (The Hague)

MCKECHNIE, P. (1989) *Outsiders in the Greek Cities in the Fourth Century* BC (London and New York)

MEIGGS, R. (1972) *The Athenian Empire* (Oxford)

MELAS, E. (ed.) (1973) *Temples and Sanctuaries of Ancient Greece* (London)

MERKELBACH, R. (1962) *Roman und Mysterium in der Antike* (Munich and Berlin)

MIKALSON, J.D. (1975) *The Sacred and Civil Calendar of the Athenian Year* (Princeton, NJ)

(1977) 'Religion in the Attic demes', *AJPhil* 98: 424–35

(1983) *Athenian Popular Religion* (Chapel Hill, NC and London)

(1991) *Honor Thy Gods: Popular Religion in Greek Tragedy* (Chapel Hill, NC and London)

(1998) *Religion in Hellenistic Athens* (Berkeley)

MILLAR, F. (1977) *The Emperor in the Roman World (31 BC–AD 337)* (London) [repr. with new Afterword 1992]

MILLS, S. (1997) *Theseus, Tragedy and the Athenian Empire* (Oxford)

MITCHEL, F.W. (1970) *Lykourgan Athens: 338–322* (Cincinnati)

MITCHELL, S. (1987) 'Imperial building in the eastern Roman provinces', *HSCP* 91: 333–65

(1990) 'Festivals, games, and civic life in Roman Asia Minor', *JRS* 80: 183–93

(1993) *Anatolia*, 2 vols. (Oxford)

MONDI, R. (1990) 'Greek mythic thought in the light of the Near East', in Edmunds (1990), 142–98

MONTEPAONE, C. (1990) 'Bendis tracia ad Atene: l'integrazione del 'nuovo' attraverso forme dell'ideologia', *AION* 12: 103–21

MORAND, A.-F. (1997) 'Orphic gods and other gods', in A.B. Lloyd (ed.), *What is a God? Studies in the Nature of Greek Divinity* (London), 169–81

MORETTI, L. (1986) 'Il regolamento degli Iobacchi Ateniesi', *L'association dionysiaque dans les sociétés anciennes* (Coll. de l'Ecole française de Rome 89) (Paris and Rome), 247–59

MORFORD, M.P.O. and R.J. LENARDON (1995) *Classical Mythology*, 5th edn (White Plains, NY and London)

MORGAN, C. (1990) *Athletes and Oracles: The Transformation of Olympia and Delphi in the Eighth Century BC* (Cambridge)

(1993) 'The origins of pan-Hellenism', in Marinatos and Hägg (1993), 18–44

(1996) 'From palace to polis? Religious developments on the Greek mainland during the Bronze Age/Iron Age transition', in Hellström and Alroth (1996), 41–57

(1997) 'The archaeology of sanctuaries in early Iron Age and Archaic *ethne*: a preliminary view', in L.G. Mitchell and P.J. Rhodes (eds.), *The Development of the* Polis *in Archaic Greece* (London and New York), 168–98

MORRIS, I. (1992) *Death-Ritual and Social Structure in Classical Antiquity* (Cambridge)

MORROW, G.R. (1960) *Plato's Cretan City* (Princeton, NJ)

MOTTE, A., V. PIRENNE-DELFORGE and P. WATHELET (eds.) (1992) *Mentor: Guide bibliographique de la religion grecque* (*Kernos* Supp. 2) (Liège)

(1998) *Mentor 2, 1986–1900: Guide bibliographique de la religion grecque* (*Kernos* Supp. 6) (Liège)

MULLER, A. (1996) *Les terres cuites votives du Thesmophorion de l'atelier au sanctuaire* (*Etudes Thasiennes* 17) (Paris)

MURRAY, SISTER C. (1981) *Rebirth and Afterlife. A Study of the Transmutation of Some Pagan Imagery in Early Christian Funerary Art* (*BAR* Int. Ser. 100) (Oxford)

MURRAY, O. (1990) 'The affair of the Mysteries: democracy and the drinking group', in O. Murray (ed.), *Sympotica* (Oxford), 149–61

MURRAY, O. and S. PRICE (eds.) (1990) *The Greek City from Homer to Alexander* (Oxford)

MYLONAS, G.E. (1961) *Eleusis and the Eleusinian Mysteries* (Princeton, NJ and London)

NEILS, J. et al. (1992) *Goddess and Polis. The Panathenaic Festival in Ancient Athens* (Dartmouth College, Hanover, NH and Princeton, NJ)

(1996) (ed.) *Worshipping Athena. Panathenaia and Parthenon* (Madison WI and London)

NEUMANN, G. (1979) *Probleme des griechischen Weihreliefs* (Tübingen)

NILSSON, M.P. (1940) *Greek Popular Religion* (New York; repr. 1961 Philadelphia as *Greek Folk Religion*)

(1955–67) *Geschichte der griechischen Religion* (I 3rd edn, II 2nd edn) (Munich)

NIXON, L.F. (1990) 'Minoan settlements and Greek sanctuaries', in *Pepragmena tou ΣΤ' Diethnous Kritologikou Sinedriou* (Khania), 59–67

(1995) 'The cults of Demeter and Kore', in R. Hawley and B. Levick (eds.), *Women in Antiquity: New Assessments* (London and New York), 75–96

NOCK, A.D. (1928) 'Greek novels and Egyptian religion', *Gnomon* 4: 485–92, repr. in Nock (1972), I.169–75

(1933) *Conversion: the Old and the New in Religion from Alexander the Great to Augustine of Hippo* (Oxford)

(1942) 'Religious attitudes of the ancient Greeks', *Proc. Amer. Philos. Soc.* 85: 472–82, repr. in Nock (1972), II.534–50

(1972) *Essays on Religion and the Ancient World*, ed. Z. Stewart, 2 vols. (Oxford)

OAKLEY, J.H. and R.H. SINOS (1993) *The Wedding in Ancient Athens* (Madison, WI)

OBBINK, D. (1984) '*P. Oxy.* 215 and Epicurean religious *theoria*', *Atti del XVII Congresso Internazionale di Papirologia* (Naples), 2.607–19

(1988) 'The origins of Greek sacrifice: Theophrastos on religion and cultural history', in W.W. Fortenbaugh and R.W. Sharples (eds.), *Theophrastan Studies* (Rutgers Univ. Stud. in Class. Humanities 3) (New Brunswick, NJ and Oxford), 272–95

(1992) '"What all men believe – must be true": common conceptions and *consensio omnium* in Aristotle and Hellenistic philosophy', *Oxford Studies in Ancient Philosophy* 10: 193–231

(1996) *Philodemus On Piety Part I, Critical Text with Commentary* (Oxford)

OGDEN, D. (1997) *The Crooked Kings of Ancient Greece* (London)

OLIVER, J.H. (1940) 'Julia Domna as Athena Polias', in *Athenian Studies Presented to William Scott Ferguson* (*HSCP* Supp. 1), 521–30

(1950) *The Athenian Expounders of the Sacred and Ancestral Law* (Baltimore)

OSBORNE, M.J. (1970) 'Honours for Sthorys (*IG* II² 17)', *BSA* 65: 151–74

(1981–3) *Naturalisation in Athens* (Brussels)

OSBORNE, R.G. (1985) 'The erection and mutilation of the Hermai', *PCPhS* 31: 47–73

(1987) *Classical Landscape with Figures: The Ancient Greek City and its Countryside* (London)

(1990) 'The *demos* and its divisions in classical Athens', in Murray and Price (1990) 265–93

(1993) 'Women and sacrifice in classical Greece', *CQ* 43: 392–405

OSBORNE, R.G. and S. HORNBLOWER (eds.) (1994) *Ritual, Finance, Politics. Democratic Accounts Presented to D.M. Lewis* (Oxford)

OSTER, R.E. (1976) 'The Ephesian Artemis as an opponent of early Christianity', *Jahrbuch für Antike und Christentum* 19: 27–44

PAGELS, E. (1988) *Adam, Eve, and the Serpent* (New York)

PAKKANEN, P. (1996) *Interpreting Early Hellenistic Religion* (Helsinki)

PALAIOKRASSA, L. (1991) *To hiero tis Artemidos Mounichias* (Athens)

PARENTE, F. (1987) 'L'idea di conversione da Nock ad oggi', *Augustinanum* 27: 7–25

PARKE, H.W. (1967) *Greek Oracles* (London)

(1977) *Festivals of the Athenians* (London and New York)

(1985) *The Oracles of Apollo in Asia Minor* (London)

PARKER, R.C.T. (1983) *Miasma* (Oxford)

(1985) 'Greek states and Greek oracles', in Cartledge and Harvey (1985) 298–326

(1986) 'Greek religion', in J. Boardman, J. Griffin and O. Murray (eds.), *The Oxford History of the Classical World* (Oxford and New York), 254–74

(1987a) 'Festivals of the Attic demes', in Linders and Nordquist (1987) 137–47

(1987b) 'Myths of early Athens', in Bremmer (1987) 187–214

(1989) 'Spartan religion', in A. Powell (ed.), *Classical Sparta: Techniques behind her Success* (London), 142–72

(1991) 'The *Hymn to Demeter* and the *Homeric Hymns*', *Greece and Rome* 38: 1–17

(1992) 'The origins of Pronoia: a mystery', in *Apodosis. Essays Presented to Dr. W.W. Cruickshank to mark his Eightieth birthday* (London), 84–94

(1994) 'Athenian religion abroad', in Osborne and Hornblower (1994), 339–46

(1995) 'Early Orphism', in A. Powell (ed.), *The Greek World* (London and New York), 483–510

(1996) *Athenian Religion: A History* (Oxford)

(1997) 'Gods cruel and kind: tragic and civic theology', in Pelling (1997), 143–60

(1998) 'Pleasing thighs: reciprocity in Greek religion', in C. Gill, N. Postlethwaite and R. Seaford (eds.), *Reciprocity in Ancient Greece* (Oxford), 105–25

PASCHOUD, F. (1971–89) *Zosime, Histoire Nouvelle* (Paris)

PAYNE, H. and G. MACKWORTH-YOUNG (1950) *Archaic Marble Sculpture from the Akropolis*, 2nd edn (London)

PEIRCE, S. (1993) 'Death, revelry, and *thysia*', *Classical Antiquity* 12: 219–66

PÉLÉKIDIS, C. (1962) *Histoire de l'éphébie attique* (Paris)

PELLING, C. (ed.) (1997) *Greek Tragedy and the Historian* (Oxford)

PHILLIPS, C.R. (1986) 'The sociology of religious knowledge in the Roman empire to AD 284', *ANRW* 2.16.3: 2677–773

PICKARD-CAMBRIDGE, A.W. (1968) *The Dramatic Festivals of Athens* (2nd edn by J. Gould and D.M. Lewis, corrected 1988) (Oxford)

PIRENNE-DELFORGE, V. (1994) *L'Aphrodite grecque* (*Kernos* Supp. 4) (Athens–Liège)

POLACCO, L. (1990) *Il teatro di Dioniso Eleutereo ad Atene* (Rome)

POOLE, F.J.P. (1986) 'Metaphor and maps: towards comparison in the anthropology of religion', *Journal of the American Academy of Religion* 54: 411–57

PÖTSCHER, W. (1964) *Theophrastos Peri Eusebeias* (Leiden)

PRICE, M.J. and B.L. TRELL (1977) *Coins and their Cities* (London and Detroit)

PRICE, S.R.F. (1984a) *Rituals and Power: the Roman Imperial Cult in Asia Minor* (Cambridge)

(1984b) 'Gods and emperors: the Greek language of the Roman imperial cult', *JHS* 104: 79–95

(1985) 'Delphi and divination', in Easterling and Muir (1985), 128–54

(1986) 'The future of dreams: from Freud to Artemidorus', *Past and Present* 113: 3–37

(1987) 'From noble funeral to divine cult: the consecration of Roman emperors', in D.N. Cannadine and S.R.F. Price (eds.), *Rituals of Royalty: Power and Ceremonial in Traditional Societies* (Cambridge), 56–105

PRÜCKNER, H. (1968) *Die lokrischer Tonreliefs* (Mainz)

PULLEYN, S. (1997) *Prayer in Greek Religion* (Oxford)

RADT, W. (1988) *Pergamon* (Köln)

RASCHKE, W.J. (ed.) (1988) *The Archaeology of the Olympics* (Madison, WI)

RAUBITSCHEK, A.E. and L.H. JEFFERY (1949) *Dedications from the Athenian Akropolis* (Cambridge, MA)

REMUS, H. (1996) 'Voluntary association and networks. Aelius Aristides at the Asclepieion in Pergamon', in J.S. Kloppenborg and S.G. Wilson (eds.), *Voluntary Associations in the Graeco-Roman World* (London and New York), 146–75

RENFREW, C. (1985) *The Archaeology of Cult, the Sanctuary at Phylakopi* (*BSA* Supp. 18) (London)

RENFREW C. and M. WAGSTAFF (eds.) (1982) *An Island Polity: The Archaeology of Exploitation in Melos* (Cambridge)

RHODES, P.J. (1972) *The Athenian Boule* (Oxford) (repr. with corr. and add. 1985) (1991) 'The Athenian code of laws, 410–399 BC', *JHS* 111: 87–100

RICE, D.G. and J.E. STAMBAUGH (1979) *Sources for the Study of Greek Religion* (SBL Sources for Biblical Study 14) (No place)

RIDGWAY, B.S. (1977) *The Archaic Style in Greek Sculpture* (Princeton, NJ) (ed.) (1994) *Greek Sculpture in the Art Museum, Princeton University* (Princeton, NJ)

RIEDWEG, G. (1993) *Jüdisch-hellenistische Imitation eines orphischen Hieros Logos* (Tübingen)

ROBERT, L. (1948) *Hellenica* 6 (Paris) (1960) *Hellenica* 11–12 (Paris) (1966) *Documents de l'Asie Mineure méridionale* (Geneva and Paris) (1973) 'De Cilicie à Messine et à Plymouth avec deux inscriptions grecques errantes', *Journal des Savants* 1973: 161–211, reprinted in his *Opera Minora Selecta* 7: 225–75 (1977) 'Documents d'Asie Mineure', *BCH* 101: 43–132, repr. in his *Documents d'Asie Mineure* (Paris, 1987), 1–90

ROBERTSON, M. (1975) *A History of Greek Art* (Cambridge)

ROGERS, G.M. (1991) *The Sacred Identity of Ephesus* (London and New York)

ROSE, H.J. (1958) *A Handbook of Greek Mythology* (5th edn, repr. 1989) (London)

ROSIVACH, V.J. (1994) *The System of Public Sacrifice in Fourth-Century Athens* (American Classical Studies 34) (Atlanta, GA)

ROUGEMONT, G. (1973) 'La hiéroménie des Pythia et les 'trêves sacrées' d'Eleusis, de Delphes et d'Olympie', *BCH* 97: 75–106

ROUSE, W.H.D. (1902) *Greek Votive Offerings* (Cambridge, repr. Hildesheim and New York 1976)

ROUX, G. (1976) *Delphes* (Paris) (1984) 'Trésors, temples, tholos', in Roux (ed.), *Temples et Sanctuaires* (Paris), 153–71

RUDHARDT, J. (1970) 'Les mythes grecs relatifs à l'instauration du sacrifice; les rôles corrélatifs de Prométhée et de son fils Deucalion', *Museum Helveticum* 27: 1–15, revised in J. Rudhardt (1981), *Du mythe, de la religion grecque et de la compréhension d'autrui* (Rev. eur. des sciences sociales 19) (Geneva), 209–26 (1991) 'Quelques réflexions sur les hymnes orphiques', in Borgeaud (ed.) (1991), 263–88 (1992) 'De l'attitude des grecs à l'égard des religions étrangères', *Revue de l'histoire des religions* 209: 219–38

RUPP, D.W. (1983) 'Reflections on the development of altars in the eighth century BC', in R. Hägg (ed.), *The Greek Renaissance of the Eighth Century BC* (Stockholm), 101–7

RUSSELL, D.A. (1990) 'Aristides and the prose hymn', in Russell (ed.), *Antonine Literature* (Oxford), 199–219

RUSSELL, D.A. and N.G. WILSON (1981) *Menander Rhetor* (Oxford)

RUTHERFORD, R.B. (1989) *The Meditations of Marcus Aurelius: a Study* (Oxford)

SABBATUCCI, D. (1965) *Saggio sul misticismo greco* (Rome)

SACKS, K.S. (1990) *Diodorus Siculus and the First Century* (Princeton, NJ)

STE. CROIX, G.E.M. DE (1972) *The Origins of the Peloponnesian War* (London)

SALE, W. (1975) 'The temple-legends of the arkteia', *Rheinisches Museum* 118: 265–84

SALER, B. (1993) *Conceptualizing Religion: Immanent Anthropologists, Transcendent Natives, and Unbounded Categories (Numen* Book Series 56) (Leiden)

SAUNDERS, T.J. (1991) *Plato's Penal Code* (Oxford)

SCHACHTER, A. (ed.) (1992) *Le sanctuaire grec* (Entretiens Hardt 37) (Geneva)

SCHEID, J. (1995) '*Graeco ritu*: a typically Roman way of honoring the gods', *HSCPh* 97: 15–31

SCHMIDT, F. (ed.) (1987) *The Inconceivable Polytheism: Studies in Religious Historiography* (History and Anthropology 3) (London, Paris, New York)

SCHMIDT, M. (1991) 'Bemerkungen zu Orpheus in Unterwelts- und Thraker-darstellungen', in Borgeaud (1991), 31–50

SCHNEIDER, P. (1987) 'Heilige Strasse von Milet nach Didyma', *Archäologischer Anzeiger* 1987: 101–29

SCHRADER, H. (1939) *Die archaischen Marmorbildwerke der Akropolis* (Frankfurt am Main)

SCHRODER, R.V. (1974) *Ancient Greece from the Air* (London)

SCHÜRER, E. (1973–87) *The History of the Jewish People in the Age of Jesus Christ*, ed. G. Vermes, F. Millar and M. Goodman, 3 vols. (Edinburgh)

SCHWENK, C.J. (1985) *Athens in the Age of Alexander* (Chicago)

SEAFORD, R. (1994) *Reciprocity and Ritual. Homer and Tragedy in the Developing City-State* (Oxford)

SEGAL, A.F. (1981) 'Hellenistic magic: some questions of definition', in R. van den Broek and M.J. Vermaseren (eds.), *Studies in Gnosticism and Hellenistic Religions (EPRO* 91) (Leiden), 349–75

SERWINT, N. (1993) 'The female athletic costume at the Heraia and prenuptial initiation rites', *AJA* 97: 403–22

SHAPIRO, H.A. (1991) 'The iconography of mourning in Athenian art', *AJA* 95: 629–56

SHEAR, T.L. (1982) 'The demolished temple at Eleusis', *Studies in Athenian Architecture, Sculpture and Topography Presented to Homer A. Thompson (Hesperia* Supp. 20) (Princeton, NJ), 128–40

SHERWIN-WHITE, S.M. (1978) *Ancient Cos* (Hypomnemata 51) (Göttingen)

SIEWERT, P. (1977) 'The ephebic oath in fifth-century Athens', *JHS* 97: 102–11

SIMMS, R.R. (1988) 'The cult of the Thracian goddess Bendis in Athens and Attica', *Ancient World* 18: 59–76

SIMON, C.G. (1986) 'The Archaic Votive Offerings and Cults of Ionia' (unpublished Ph.D. dissertation, Berkeley)

SIMON, E. (1983) *Festivals of Attica. An Archaeological Commentary* (Madison, WI)

SIMPSON, M. (1976) *Gods and Heroes of the Greeks. The Library of Apollodorus* (Amherst, MA)

SMITH, R.R.R. (1991) *Hellenistic Sculpture* (London)

SMITH, R.R.R. and C. RATTÉ (1995) 'Archaeological research at Aphrodisias in Caria, 1993', *AJA* 99: 33–58

SNODGRASS, A.M. (1983) 'Heavy freight in Archaic Greece', in Garnsey et al. (1983), 16–26

SORABJI, R. (1993) *Animal Minds and Human Morals: the Origins of the Western Debate* (London)

SOURVINOU-INWOOD, C. (1978) 'Persephone and Aphrodite at Locri: a model for personality definitions in Greek religion', *JHS* 98: 101–21, reprinted in Sourvinou-Inwood (1991), 147–88

(1979) 'The myth of the first temples at Delphi', *CQ* N.S. 29: 231–51, revised in Sourvinou-Inwood (1991), 192–216

(1988a) 'Further aspects of polis religion', *AION* 10: 259–74 (publ. c.1992)

(1988b) *Studies in Girls' Transitions. Aspects of the Arkteia and Age Representation in Attic Iconography* (Athens)

(1990) 'What is polis religion?', in Murray and Price (1990), 295–322

(1991) *'Reading' Greek Culture: Texts and Images, Rituals and Myths* (Oxford)

(1994) 'Something to do with Athens: tragedy and ritual', in Osborne and Hornblower (1994), 269–90

(1997a) 'Reconstructing change: ideology and the Eleusinian mysteries', in M. Golden and P. Toohey (eds.), *Inventing Ancient Culture. Historicism, Periodisation and the Ancient World* (London and New York), 132–64

(1997b) 'Tragedy and religion: constructs and readings', in Pelling (1997), 161–86

SPAWFORTH, A.J. (1992) 'Spartan cults under the Roman empire: some notes', in J.M. Sanders (ed.), *Philolakon. Lakonian Studies in Honour of Hector Catling* (Oxford and Athens), 227–38

SPAWFORTH, A.J. and S. WALKER (1985) 'The world of the Panhellenion I. Athens and Eleusis', *JRS* 75: 78–104

SPIESER, J.-M. (1976) 'La christianisation des sanctuaires païens en Grèce', in U. Jantzen (ed.), *Neue Forschungen in griechischen Heiligtümern* (Tübingen), 309–20

STEAD, C. (1994) *Philosophy in Christian Antiquity* (Cambridge)

STEINBY, E.M. (ed.) (1993–) *Lexikon Topographicum Urbis Romae* (Rome)

STEWART, Z. (1977) 'La religione', in R. Bianchi Bandinelli (ed.), *Storia e civiltà dei greci 8: La società ellenistica: economia, diritto, religione* (Milan), 503–616

SWAIN, S. (1996) *Hellenism and Empire. Language, Classicism, and Power in the Greek World AD 50–250* (Oxford)

TAPLIN, O. (1993) *Comic Angels, and Other Approaches to Greek Drama through Vase-Paintings* (Oxford)

TAYLOR, C.C.W. (ed.) (1997) *Routledge History of Philosophy I. From the Beginning to Plato* (London and New York)

THEMELIS, P.G. (1968) 'Skillous', *Arkhaiologikon Deltion* 23A: 284–92

THOMPSON, H.A. (1936) 'Pnyx and Thesmophorion', *Hesperia* 5: 151–200
(1960) 'Activities in the Athenian Agora: 1959', *Hesperia* 29: 327–68

THOMPSON, H.A. and R.E. WYCHERLEY (1972) *The Agora of Athens* (The Athenian Agora 14) (Princeton, NJ)

TIELEMAN, T. (1996) *Galen and Chrysippus on the Soul. Argument and Refutation in the De Placitis Books II–III* (Philosophia Antiqua 68) (Leiden)

TOBIN, J. (1997) *Herodes Attikos and the City of Athens. Patronage and Conflict under the Antonines* (Amsterdam)

TOD, M.N. (1932) *Sidelights on Greek History* (Oxford)

TODD, S. (1996) 'Lysias against Nikomakhos: the fate of the expert in Athenian law', in L. Foxhall and A.D.E. Lewis (eds.), *Greek Law in its Political Setting* (Oxford), 101–31

TOMLINSON, R.A. (1976) *Greek Sanctuaries* (London)

TOURNIKIOTIS, P. (ed.) (1994) *The Parthenon and its Impact in Modern Times* (Athens)

TRACY, S.V. (1991) 'The Panathenaic festival and games: an epigraphic enquiry', *Nikephoros* 4: 133–53

TRAVLOS, J. (1971) *Pictorial Dictionary of Ancient Athens* (London)
(1988) *Bildlexikon zur Topographie des antiken Attika* (Tübingen)

TRESP, A. (1914) *Die Fragmente der griechischen Kultschriftsteller* (Giessen, repr. New York 1975)

TROMBLEY, F.R. (1985) 'Paganism in the Greek world at the end of antiquity: the case of rural Anatolia and Greece', *HThR* 78: 327–52
(1993) *Hellenic Religion and Christianisation, c. 370–529*, 2 vols. (Leiden)

TUCHELT, K. (1991) *Branchidai-Didyma* (Antike Welt 22, Sondernummer) (Mainz am Rhein)

TYRRELL, W.B. (1984) *Amazons: A Study in Athenian Mythmaking* (Baltimore)

TYRRELL, W.B. and F.S. BROWN (1991) *Athenian Myths and Institutions* (New York and Oxford)

TZACHOU-ALEXANDRI, O. (ed.) (1989) *Mind and Body: Athletic Contests in Ancient Greece* (Athens)

VAES, J. (1984–6) 'Christliche Wiederverwendung antiker Bauten: ein Forschungsbericht', *Ancient Society* 15–17: 305–443

VALLET, G. (1968) 'La cité et son territoire dans les colonies grecques d'Occident', *Atti del settimo convegno di studi sulla Magna Grecia* (Naples), 68–142

VALLET, G., F. VILLARD and P. AUBERSON (1976) *Mégara Hyblaea I* (Paris and Rome)
(1983) *Mégara Hyblaea: Guide des fouilles* (Paris and Rome)

VAN STRATEN, F.T. (1981) 'Gifts for the gods', in Versnel (1981a), 65–151
(1992) 'Votives and votaries in Greek sanctuaries', in Schachter (1992), 247–84
(1995) *Hiera Kala. Images of Animal Sacrifice in Archaic and Classical Greece* (Leiden)

VERNANT, J.-P. (1974) 'Parole et signes muets', in J.-P. Vernant (ed.) (1974), *Divination et rationalité* (Paris), 9–25, translated in Vernant (1991), 303–17
(1980) *Myth and Society in Ancient Greece* (Brighton and Atlantic Highlands, NJ) (French original 1974)
(1982) 'From Oedipus to Periander: lameness, tyranny, incest in legend and history', *Arethusa* 15: 19–38
(1983) *Myth and Thought among the Greeks* (London and Boston) (French original 1965)
(1991) *Mortals and Immortals. Collected Essays*, ed. F. Zeitlin (Princeton, NJ)
VERSNEL, H.S. (ed.) (1981a) *Faith, Hope, and Worship* (Leiden)
(1981b) 'Religious mentality in ancient prayer', in Versnel (1981a), 1–64
(1990a) *Ter Unus. Isis, Dionysos, Hermes. Three Studies in Henotheism* (Leiden)
(1990b) 'What's sauce for the goose is sauce for the gander: myth and ritual, old and new', in Edmunds (1990), 25–90, revised in H.S. Versnel (1993), *Transition and Reversal in Myth and Ritual* (Leiden), 15–88
VEYNE, P. (1988) *Did the Greeks Believe in their Myths?* (Chicago) (French original 1983)
VIDAL-NAQUET, P. (1986) *The Black Hunter: Forms of Thought and Forms of Society in the Greek World* (Baltimore and London) (French original 1981)
VINOGRADOV, J.G. (1991) 'Zur sachlichen und geschichtlichen Deutung der Orphiker-Plättchen von Olbia', in Borgeaud (1991), 77–86
VLASTOS, G. (1952) 'Theology and philosophy in early Greek thought', *Philosophical Quarterly* 2: 97–123, repr. in D.J. Furley and R.E. Allen (eds.), *Studies in Presocratic Philosophy* 1, 92–129 (London); and in his *Studies in Greek Philosophy* 1, ed. D.W. Graham (1995), 3–31
(1991) *Socrates* (Cambridge)
WACHSMUTH, D. (1967) *Pompimos ho Daimon* (Dissertation Berlin)
WALBANK, F.W. (1957) *A Historical Commentary on Polybius I* (Oxford)
(1981) *The Hellenistic World* (London) (2nd edn 1992)
WALBANK, M.B. (1983) 'Leases of sacred property in Attica', *Hesperia* 52: 100–35, 177–231
WALBANK, MARY (1989) 'Pausanias, Octavia and Temple E at Corinth', *BSA* 84: 361–94
WALKER, H.J. (1995) *Theseus and Athens* (New York and Oxford)
WALKER, S. and A. CAMERON (eds.) (1989) *The Greek Renaissance in the Roman Empire* (BICS Supp. 55) (London)
WEBER, M. (1968) *Economy and Society* (Berkeley and London) (German original 1925)
WEISS, P. (1984) 'Lebendiger Mythos. Gründerheroen und städtische Gründungs-traditionen im griechisch-römischen Osten', *Würzburger Jahrbücher* N.S. 10: 179–208
WEST, M.L. (1965) 'The Dictaean hymn to the Kouros', *JHS* 85: 149–59
(1982) 'The Orphics of Olbia', *ZPE* 45: 17–29
(1983) *The Orphic Poems* (Oxford)
(1992) *Ancient Greek Music* (Oxford)

(1995) 'The date of the *Iliad*', *Museum Helveticum* 52: 203–19

WHITBY, M. (1991) 'John of Ephesus and the pagans: pagan survivals in the sixth century', in M. Salamon (ed.), *Paganism in the Later Roman Empire and in Byzantium* (Cracow), 111–31

WHITEHEAD, D. (1986) *The Demes of Attica 508/7– ca. 250 BC. A Political and Social Study* (Princeton, NJ)

WILLIAMS, C.K. (1989) 'A re-evaluation of Temple E and the west end of the forum of Corinth', in Walker and Cameron (1989), 156–62

WILSON, B.R. (1982) *Religion in Sociological Perspective* (Oxford)

WINKLER, J.J. (1980) 'Lollianus and the desperadoes', *JHS* 100: 155–81

WINTER, E. (1996) *Staatliche Baupolitik und Baufürsorge in den römischen Provinzen des kaiserzeitlichen Kleinasien (Asia Minor Studien* 20) (Bonn)

WISSOWA, G. (1912) *Religion und Kultus der Römer* (2nd edn; reprinted 1971) (Munich)

WYCHERLEY, R.E. (1978) *The Stones of Athens* (Princeton)

YUNIS, H. (1988) *A New Creed: Fundamental Religious Beliefs in the Athenian Polis and Euripidean Drama (Hypomnemata* 91) (Göttingen)

ZUNTZ, G. (1971) *Persephone: Three Essays in Religion and Thought in Magna Graecia* (Oxford)

# Index